Digital Games and Language Learning

Advances in Digital Language Learning and Teaching

Series Editors

Michael Thomas, Liverpool John Moores University, UK
Mark Peterson, Kyoto University, Japan
Mark Warschauer, University of California – Irvine, USA

Today's language educators need support to understand how their learners are changing and the ways technology can be used to aid their teaching and learning strategies. The movement towards different modes of language learning – from presence-based to autonomous as well as blended and fully online modes – requires different skill sets such as e-moderation and new ways of designing and developing language learning tasks in the digital age. Theoretical studies that include practical case studies and high-quality empirical studies incorporating critical perspectives are necessary to move the field further. This series is committed to providing such an outlet for high-quality work on digital language learning and teaching. Volumes in the series focus on a number of areas including but not limited to:

- task-based learning and teaching approaches utilizing technology
- language-learner creativity
- e-moderation and teaching languages online
- blended language learning
- designing courses for online and distance language learning
- mobile-assisted language learning
- autonomous language learning, both in and outside of formal educational contexts
- the use of web 2.0/social media technologies
- immersive and virtual language-learning environments
- digital game-based language learning
- language educator professional development with digital technologies
- teaching language skills with technologies

Enquiries about the series can be made by contacting the series editors: Michael Thomas (m.thomas@ljmu.ac.uk), Mark Peterson (tufsmp@yahoo.com) and Mark Warschauer (markw@uci.edu).

Titles in the Series Include:

Digital Games and Language Learning

Theory, Development and Implementation

Edited by
Mark Peterson, Kasumi Yamazaki
and Michael Thomas

BLOOMSBURY ACADEMIC
LONDON • NEW YORK • OXFORD • NEW DELHI • SYDNEY

BLOOMSBURY ACADEMIC
Bloomsbury Publishing Plc
50 Bedford Square, London, WC1B 3DP, UK
1385 Broadway, New York, NY 10018, USA
29 Earlsfort Terrace, Dublin 2, Ireland

BLOOMSBURY, BLOOMSBURY ACADEMIC and the Diana logo
are trademarks of Bloomsbury Publishing Plc

First published in Great Britain 2021
This paperback edition published 2022

Cover design by James Watson
Cover image © Shutterstock

A catalogue record for this book is available from the British Library.

Library of Congress Cataloging-in-Publication Data

Names: Peterson, Mark, 1965-editor. | Yamazaki, Kasumi, editor. |
Thomas, Michael, 1969-editor.
Title: Digital games and language learning: theory, development and
implementation / edited by Mark Peterson, Kasumi Yamazaki and Michael Thomas.
Description: London; New York: Bloomsbury Academic, 2021. |
Series: Advances in digital language learning and teaching |
Includes bibliographical references and index. |
Identifiers: LCCN 2020050407 (print) | LCCN 2020050408 (ebook) |
ISBN 9781350133006 (hardback) | ISBN 9781350133013 (ebook) |
ISBN 9781350133020 (epub)
Subjects: LCSH: Language and languages–Computer-assisted instruction. |
Electronic games in education. | Gamification.
Classification: LCC P53.299.D54 2021 (print) | LCC P53.299 (ebook) |
DDC 418.0078–dc23
LC record available at https://lccn.loc.gov/2020050407
LC ebook record available at https://lccn.loc.gov/2020050408

ISBN: HB: 978-1-3501-3300-6
PB: 978-1-3502-3317-1
ePDF: 978-1-3501-3301-3
eBook: 978-1-3501-3302-0

Series: Advances in Digital Language Learning and Teaching

Typeset by Newgen KnowledgeWorks Pvt. Ltd., Chennai, India

To find out more about our authors and books visit
www.bloomsbury.com and sign up for our newsletters.

Contents

Figures

Tables

Contributors

Alex Bacalja is a lecturer in Language and Literacy and member of the language and literacy research hub in the Melbourne graduate school of education, University of Melbourne. He is currently the Victorian Delegate for the Australian Association for the Teaching of English. His work and publications have focused on digital literacy and the impact of digital technologies on the teaching of English.

Silvia Benini works as research assistant in the School of Languages, Literatures and Cultures at the University College Cork. Areas of research interest include CALL, games-based learning, intercultural communication, language policy and planning. Her latest co-authored publication is 'Applying Digital Learning to Facilitate Student Transitions within Higher Education Mobility Programmes: Implementing the "Digilanguages.ie" Portal' (2019). She is a committee member of the Irish Association for Applied Linguistics (IRAAL) and a member of the Centre for Applied Language Studies (CALS).

Kate Euphemia Clark is an interdisciplinary researcher at the University of Melbourne. Her areas of interest are video games, affect theory and new materialist theory. Kate's recent research focuses on how people experience video games, and how this experience goes on to shape how they experience events off-screen. Kate also teaches game studies, sociology, social theory, gender studies and culture and media studies at the University of Melbourne.

Douglas W. Coleman is professor emeritus in the Department of English, the University of Toledo. His interests in CALL and sim-gaming extend back to the 1980s. He has served as chair of the TESOL CALL Interest Section, has been on the editorial board of Simulation and Gaming (which he has also guest edited) and has been research editor of CAELL Journal. His work on CALL has been published in numerous journals (including System, SAGSET Journal, Simulation & Gaming, CAELL Journal and C.A.L.L.) and as chapters in a number of edited volumes.

Jonathan deHaan is an associate professor in the Faculty of International Relations at the University of Shizuoka. He has been researching and teaching language and literacy with games for twenty years. He is co-editor of the *Ludic Language Pedagogy* journal. He tweets using the #gameterakoya hashtag.

Euan Dempster is a lecturer in the School of Design and Informatics at Abertay University, Scotland. His research interests include using games for learning and assessment, augmented reality and its use via mobile technology and the use of AI techniques to assist in the selection of media for censorship. His most recent publications are 'RPGs to Enhance the Second Language Acquisition of Both Mandarin and English' (2019), 'Innovative Strategies for 3D Visualisation Using Photogrammetry and 3D Scanning for Mobile Phones' (2019) and 'A Review of Age Estimation Research to Evaluate Its Inclusion in Automated Child Pornography Detection' (2020).

Charly Harbord is a lecturer on the Masters of Professional Practice Orientation Programme (MPPOP) at Abertay University, Scotland. Her research interests focus on the effective use of RPGs to enhance second language acquisition with a particular emphasis on Mandarin and English, avatars and perception and Mandarin and dyslexia. Her most recent publication is 'Avatars: The Other Side of Proteus's Mirror' (2019).

Nasser Jabbari is a lecturer in Applied Linguistics and Language Teaching at the University of Essex (UK) department of language and linguistics. He received a PhD (in curriculum and instruction, ESL) from Texas A&M University (United States). His research interests include both 'naturalistic' and 'tutorial' CALL, more specifically, language use and learning in social media and online gaming environments. His current research focuses on the psycholinguistic and sociocultural processes underlying SLA and L2 socialization in multilingual and multicultural contexts of massively multiplayer online (role-playing) games.

Darshana Jayemanne is a lecturer in Art, Media and Computer Games at Abertay University and is the author of *Performativity in Art, Literature and Videogames* (2017). This book's title highlights many of his main research interests that include developing a media studies approach to performance in digital space and time. He was co-investigator on the AHRC-funded *Reality Remix* project. His work has appeared in Games & Culture, the Journal of Broadcasting and Electronic Media, Fibreculture Journal and Westminster Papers in Communication and Culture.

Daniel J. Mills is an associate professor in the Faculty of Economics at Ritsumeikan University. He holds a doctorate degree in education with a focus on instructional technology from the University of Wyoming and a masters in TESOL education from Shenandoah University. Daniel has published several articles related to game-based learning and teaching including a comprehensive survey of digital game acceptance and usage in the Japanese university context. In addition, his research includes work on informal learning, mobile learning, technology acceptance and adoptions and study abroad. Daniel's research has informed his work on several textbook projects that integrate digital technology into the analogue medium.

Mark Peterson (PhD, the University of Edinburgh) is an associate professor at Kyoto University, Japan, where he established and now directs a research lab focusing on computer-assisted language learning (https://petersonlab.weebly. com). Dr Peterson has published widely and is author of *Computer Games and Language Learning* (2013), editor of volume IV of *Digital Language Learning and Teaching: Critical and Primary Sources, New Developments in Computer Assisted Language Learning* (2017) and joint editor of *New Technological Applications for Foreign and Second Language Learning and Teaching* (2020).

Jonathon Reinhardt (PhD, Penn State) is an associate professor of English applied linguistics and second language acquisition and teaching at the University of Arizona. His research explores the informal and formal practices of technology-enhanced language learning and teaching, especially with emergent practices like social media and digital gaming. He has published in numerous edited volumes and journals such as CALICO Journal and Language Learning and Technology. He is the author of *Gameful Second and Foreign Language Teaching and Learning: Theory, Research, and Practice* (2019).

Liss Kerstin Sylvén is a professor of Language Education at the University of Gothenburg. She obtained her PhD in English linguistics, and her research interests include various perspectives of content and language integrated learning (CLIL), computer-assisted language learning (CALL), second language vocabulary acquisition, motivation, individual differences and extramural English. Recently, she has focused on informal and incidental learning of L2 English through extramural exposure among young children (aged 4–12), an area of research that thus far has attracted very little scholarly attention. Sylvén has co-authored a book about extramural English (2016) and edited a volume on CLIL (2019). She has published in various journals, among them CALICO Journal, the International Journal of Bilingual Education and Bilingualism, Journal of Immersion and Content-Based Education, Studies in Second Language Learning and Teaching and ReCALL.

Benjamin Thanyawatpokin is currently an English language lecturer and researcher at Ritsumeikan University in Kyoto, Japan. He received his MEd in English Education from Ritsumeikan in 2015. His research interests include game-based language teaching and game-based language learning. Recently, he has been involved in projects which include extramural language learning through games, twenty-first-century skills and games and language learner identity transformation through games and gamification in the classroom. Projects outside of GBLT and gamification include explorations into plurilingualism in the Japanese language classroom and the investigation of certain types of intervention in conversation activities to enhance communication-focused classrooms.

Dr Michael Thomas is a professor of education at Liverpool John Moores University in the UK. His research interests focus on digital education, social justice and educational policy. He has published widely in the field of digital education and his most recent authored books include *Project-Based Language Learning with Technology: Learner Collaboration in a Language Classroom in Japan* (2017) and *Language Teaching with Video-Based Technologies: Creativity and CALL Teacher Education* (2020). He is the founding series editor of the book series *Digital Education and Learning* and *Advances in Digital Language Learning and Teaching*.

Kasumi Yamazaki is associate professor of Japanese at the University of Toledo, United States. Her research focuses on a wide range of contemporary CALL pedagogy and integration, namely the use of 3D simulation games and virtual realities (VRs). Her recent publications include papers in ReCALL and Foreign Language Annals; she is also a recipient of The Best of JALT (2019) and Outstanding World Language Technology Award (2019). She currently serves as editor-in-chief of Technology in Language Teaching & Learning.

Kazuhiro Yonemoto is an assistant professor at the Institute of Global Affairs Tokyo Medical and Dental University, where he coordinates the Japanese language program. His research interests include educational sociolinguistics, technology implementation in language learning and affective dimensions of second language teaching and learning particularly in the context of Japanese as a second language.

James York is a lecturer at Tokyo Denki University where he conducts research on the pedagogical application of games for language learning. His main project is curricular development using tabletop games as the centrepiece of a task-based language teaching and multiliteracies approach. James is co-editor of Ludic Language Pedagogy, an open-access, open peer-reviewed journal exploring games and play, language and literacies, teaching and pedagogy. James's previous projects include the development and management of an online Japanese learning community which utilized Minecraft as the domain for interactive, experiential learning activities.

Preface

The idea for this volume first emerged from conversations between the editors focusing on the importance of understanding the impact of digital games on contemporary computer-assisted language learning (CALL). As research in this area has greatly expanded in recent years, it was the editors' view that an edited volume that examines aspects of this important phenomenon from a broad perspective was now timely. This conviction was further strengthened by the realization that monographs in this specific area of CALL, though increasing, are limited in both number and scope. Given this context, the editors decided to issue a call for chapters. While not all submissions could be accepted due to length limitations, the editors were delighted by the response and decided to forge ahead with the production of this edited volume.

This volume brings together work from researchers located in various countries and draws attention to significant new work and perspectives on the use of digital games in CALL. Although no single volume can capture the full extent of work in this diverse and rapidly developing area, it is the editors' opinion that this volume offers a wide-ranging perspective on this increasingly influential area of research. In addition, the variety of research themes investigated affords educators, developers and researchers the opportunity to access both the range of work in this area and its potential. Moving forward, it is the editors' earnest hope that this volume will act as a guide and stimulus to successful future classroom projects and research.

Foreword

As even the casual observer would agree, the field of computer-assisted language learning (CALL) has expanded greatly in recent years. In my capacity as editor of *Computer Assisted Language Learning*, I can attest to the dramatic expansion in contemporary CALL research. As technology has advanced, researchers have not been slow to utilize the latest technological innovations in the service of language learning. The field now reflects this phenomenon and is not only dynamic but also highly diverse. Of the many new developments in contemporary CALL research, there can be little doubt that one of the most influential has been the increase in work that investigates the use of both commercial off-the-shelf and serious digital games. Although work in this area has a long history, the emergence of a new generation of digital games coupled to the global expansion in gaming has led to renewed interest in their use. This situation draws attention to the need for publications that enable both practitioners and researchers to stay abreast of the latest developments in this rapidly evolving area.

The collection of papers in this edited volume meets this need by providing access to a wide range of cutting-edge work. Moreover, the chapters supply a perspective on four important aspects that are central to advances in this area. The first of these is theory. As is emphasized in the literature, theory-based work is essential for principled development in CALL. The chapters in this volume draw on theories of second language acquisition to provide a robust rationale for successful development in this area. The second area concerns development. Chapters in this volume provide detailed accounts that shed new light on aspects of the practice of game development for language learning. This work provides educators and developers with a potentially valuable resource on which to draw when conducting their own game development projects. The third area focuses on the application of digital games in learner-based research projects. Contributors to this volume report findings from studies involving learners from different L1 backgrounds and conducted in a variety of contexts. These chapters make an important contribution to our understanding of how language development may be enhanced by the appropriate use of digital games. The final area concerns the future. In an attempt to set an innovative agenda for work in this area going forward, chapters in this volume provide insights into the future use of digital games in CALL in terms of both research and pedagogy. The body of work presented in this volume offers not only a window into state-of-the-art research but also a unique perspective on the nature of language learning with digital games.

Jozef Colpert
Director
The Institute for Language and Communication
The University of Antwerp
Belgium

Acknowledgements

The editors would like to take this opportunity to thank all the authors who contributed to this volume for their outstanding work and the many reviewers who freely contributed their time in order to support this publication.

Digital games and language learning: The state of play

Mark Peterson, Michael Thomas and Kasumi Yamazaki

Introduction

In surveying the landscape of contemporary scholarship on digital language learning it becomes readily apparent that the application of digital games represents an area of growing importance. The editors of this volume have become aware that over the past few years, publication in this area has expanded significantly, a development highlighting the fact that there is renewed interest on the part of researchers in this area of computer-assisted language learning (CALL) research (Reinhardt 2017; Hung et al. 2018; Xu et al. 2019; Peterson et al. 2020). In this context, an edited volume of previously unpublished work that provides a window on state-of-the-art developments in this dynamic field is now timely. In selecting contributions for this volume, the editors had several motivations. As research on the use of digital games and gamification is increasing (Peterson 2017; Reinders 2017; Reinhardt 2018; Dehghanzadeh et al. 2019), one motivation was to provide access to a comprehensive research review that reports on the findings of contemporary work involving digital games conducted from a variety of perspectives and in a range of contexts. Included in the first section of this volume is a review chapter of this nature. A further motivation reflected in the first section of this volume lies in the domain of theory. Acknowledging the importance of theory-led development work in CALL (Huh and Hu 2005) and in particular the linkage between developments in this area and advances in second language acquisition (SLA) research (Chapelle 2009), the editors have included chapters that focus on this area. Included in the first section are chapters that provide theory-informed rationales for the use of particular digital games. These chapters also explore the theoretical issues raised by the application of digital games in second and foreign language education.

Another motivation that influenced the selection of chapters lay in the desire to provide readers with access to recent cutting-edge learner-based research. In the second section of the book, in order to meet the need identified in the literature for studies that focus on language learners game-based or game-related learning and experiences (Cornillie, Thorne and Desmet 2012; Godwin-Jones 2014) the editors have selected chapters that investigate the development and application of digital games in a variety of both formal and informal contexts. Contributions in this section investigate the application in learner-based projects of both commercial off-the-shelf (COTS) games and also serious games designed specifically to facilitate language learning. A final factor that is reflected in the third section was the need to provide access to work that investigates the role of the teacher and the pedagogical aspects of the implementation of digital games in language education. In the editor's view, this approach offers the prospect of yielding potentially valuable insights as it provides the advantage of supplying a holistic and balanced perspective on advances in this wide-ranging and rapidly expanding area.

Overview of this book

The second chapter in this volume examines research relating to the application of gamification and digital games in foreign and second language learning. In order to provide a context for the discussion in the later chapters, this chapter provides an overview of theoretically informed work in this area. In this chapter entitled 'A critical review of research on gamification and second language acquisition', Silvia Benini and Michael Thomas provide a comprehensive research review of work conducted over the period 2014–20. In their review, the above authors show that research is expanding rapidly with an increasing number of publications reported in the literature. The authors show that research is wide-ranging and has involved a variety of game types, methodologies and contexts. In terms of significant findings, the above researchers report on positive findings that indicate that the affordances provided by digital games and the use of gamification may enhance affective factors such as learner motivation. However, they also emphasize that empirical research remains limited and that the use of digital games and game elements is not without challenges.

The remaining chapters in the first section of the book deal with theoretical issues. In the third chapter 'Second language development in the context of massively multiplayer online games: Theoretical perspectives', Nasser Jabbari observes that a significant amount of contemporary research work on the use of this type of digital game in CALL lacks a substantive base in theories of language learning. In order to provide a robust theory-driven basis for future development work in this area, the author draws on relevant theoretical constructs articulated in interactionist and sociocultural SLA research in order to propose a comprehensive and credible rationale for the use of massively multiplayer online role-playing games in L2 teaching and learning. In the next chapter, 'Not all MMOGS are created equal: A design-informed approach to the study of L2 learning in multiplayer online games', Jonathon Reinhardt asserts that many of the claims made in the literature regarding the benefits of engaging learners in multiplayer online role-playing games run the risk of being the result of overgeneralizations. In this chapter, the author draws attention to the differences between individual games within this genre and makes the case for evaluating the affordances for learning provided by online role-playing games from an ecological perspective, taking into account the variables of specific game design, context and player behaviour. Reinhardt argues for a design-informed and ecologically influenced approach to the evaluation of L2 learning in online multiplayer games. In the fifth chapter, 'Human linguistics as a framework for analysing simulation-gaming', Douglas W. Coleman identifies some important issues with the evaluation of language learning with a particular game type, simulation games. The author claims that to date, much research on the use of this game type lacks a rigorous formal framework for analysis and that this situation is hampering development in the field. In this chapter, it is asserted that Human Linguistics provides a basis for rigorous future research and development work in this area.

The chapters in the second section of this book move the focus of investigation to studies that report on game development and application in both institutional and out-of-school contexts. In the sixth chapter, 'Playing with digital game pedagogies', Alex Bacalja and Kate Euphemia Clark report on the use of digital games as texts in two learner-based case studies. The first study involved the use of a digital game in combination with traditional texts as part of a unit of study. The second study explored the use of digital game as a means to facilitate experiential reading. The authors claim based on their findings that both games provided a valuable learning experience for the participants. In the next chapter, 'The use of avatars in digital role-playing games (RPGs) in computer-assisted language learning (CALL)', Charly Harbord, Euan Dempster and Darshana Jayemanne draw on SLA research to provide a rationale for the use of the above game type in language education. The authors identify the most common types of RPG utilized in contemporary research and review the literature in this area. They further report on a preliminary pilot study that investigates undergraduate English as a foreign language (EFL) learners' in-game avatar choice and attitudes. This chapter concludes with a discussion of several areas with potential in future research. In Chapter 8 entitled 'Reinforcing international students' language skills for disaster preparedness: A case study of gamification that utilizes augmented reality technology', Kazuhiro Yonemoto reports on a study conducted in Japan in which gamification was utilized in combination with augmented reality technology in a beginner-level Japanese as a foreign language course. The study involved both campus-based and off-campus learning activities. Data analysis from learner feedback and researcher field notes revealed that use of game- and place-based augmented reality activities improved participants' understanding of target language vocabulary.

The remaining chapters in this section deal with a somewhat under-researched area in the literature on digital gaming in language learning (Sundqvist 2019), namely gaming in informal out-of-school contexts. In Chapter 9, 'The relationship between extramural digital gameplay and twenty-first-century skills in the language classroom', Daniel J. Mills and Benjamin Thanyawatpokin report on the results of a large-scale survey conducted at two universities of Japan that investigated the relationship between participation in out-of-classroom gaming and the development of twenty-first-century skills. Analysis of the participants' responses indicated that there was only a low correlation between extramural gameplay and twenty-first-century skills. However, the data also showed that the majority of learners appear to highly regard digital games as a learning tool. In the final chapter in this section, 'Gaming as a gateway to L2 English learning: A case study of a young L1 Swedish boy', Liss Kerstin Sylven presents the findings of a case study that investigated the effects of participation in out-of-school gaming on the language development of a Swedish adolescent. Analysis of multiple data sources including test scores, interviews and audio recordings collecting during this longitudinal research project revealed that the participants made remarkable progress in developing their L2 proficiency through playing digital games over several years. The author further examines the pedagogical implications of the role of digital gaming in enhancing foreign language proficiency.

The chapters in the third section of this volume examine the current state of game-based language learning and set out an agenda for future research and development work. The chapter by James York and Benjamin Thanyawatpokin entitled 'Issues in the current state of teaching languages with games' provides an examination of the literature on the application of games in language learning and identifies a number of important issues with current work. These authors draw attention to a number of issues relating to terminology and propose new objective-based terms to assist work in this area. In addition, they identify several weaknesses in the current body of research work. Echoing concerns raised in the literature (Peterson 2013) they note that to date, there is an overemphasis on exploratory studies that do not provide a basis for actual classroom application. The authors propose a future research agenda that focuses on empirical work and that emphasizes the investigation of teacher roles in enhancing game-based language learning.

In the final chapter of this volume, 'Is game-based language learning "vaporware"?', Jonathan deHaan critiques the literature on the use of digital games in language learning. The author argues that going forward, in order for sustained and meaningful progress to be made in the field, researchers and practitioners must work together. Moreover, in a call to arms, the author argues that for game-based language learning to become fully normalized (Chambers and Bax 2006) in language classrooms there is a pressing need to refocus work on pedagogy-first game-based language teaching where the teacher plays a central role in facilitating optimal learning outcomes.

Conclusion

In selecting contributions for this volume, the editors were keenly aware that no single publication can incorporate all significant work in this dynamic and rapidly evolving area of research. Nonetheless, it is the editors' hope that the chapters included in this volume reflect both the depth and range of contemporary high-quality scholarship in this increasingly influential field. Looking forward, it is the editors' firm conviction that the work included in this volume will play a valuable role in informing the development of an innovative research agenda on the use of digital games in language education that considers gaming both inside and outside the language classroom.

References

Chambers, A., and S. Bax (2006), 'Making CALL Work: Towards Normalisation', *System* 34 (4): 465–79.

Chapelle, C. (2009), 'The Relationship between Second Language Acquisition Theory and Computer-Assisted Language Learning', *Modern Language Journal* 93 (S1): 741–53.

Cornillie, F., S. L. Thorne and P. Desmet (2012), 'Digital Games for Language Learning: From Hype to Insight?', *ReCALL* 24 (3): 243–56.

Dehghanzadeh, H., H. Fardanesh, J. Hatami, E. Talaee and O. Noroozi (2019), 'Using Gamification to Support Learning English as a Second Language: A Systematic Review', *Computer Assisted Language Learning*, 1–24.

Godwin-Jones, R. (2014), 'Games in Language Learning: Opportunities and Challenges', *Language Learning & Technology* 18 (2): 9–19.

Huh, K., and W.-C. Hu (2005), 'Criteria for Effective CALL Research', in J. L. Egbert and G. M. Petrie (eds), *CALL Research Perspectives*, 9–21, Mahwah, NJ: Lawrence Erlbaum.

Hung, H.-T., J. C. Yang, G.-J. Hwang, H.-C. Chu and C.-C. Wang (2018), 'A Scoping Review of Research on Digital Game-Based Language Learning', *Computers & Education* 126: 89–104.

Jabbari, N., and Z. R. Eslami (2019), 'Second Language Learning in the Context of Massively Multiplayer Online Games: A Scoping Review', *ReCALL* 31 (1): 92–113.

Peterson, M. (2013), *Computer Games and Language Learning*, New York: Palgrave Macmillan.

Peterson, M. (2017), 'Introduction', in M. Peterson (ed.), *Digital Language Learning and Teaching: Critical and Primary Sources, New Developments in CALL*, 1–18, London: Bloomsbury.

Peterson, M., J. White, M. S. Mirzaei and Q. Wang (2020), 'A Review of Research on the Application of Digital Games in Foreign Language Education', in M. Kruk and M. Peterson (eds), *New Technological Applications for Foreign and Second Language Learning and Teaching*, 69–92, Hershey, PA: IGI Global.

Reinders, H. (2017), 'Digital Games and Second Language Learning', in S. May and S. Thorne (eds), *Encyclopedia of Language and Education Vol 9: Language, Education, and Technology*, 1–15, New York: Springer.

Reinhardt, J. (2017), 'Digital Gaming in L2 Teaching and Learning', in C. Chapelle and S. Sauro (eds), *The Handbook of Technology in Second Language Teaching and Learning*, 202–16, Hoboken, NJ: John Wiley & Sons.

Reinhardt, J. (2018), *Gameful Second and Foreign Language Teaching and Learning: Theory, Research, and Practice*, Basingstoke: Palgrave Macmillan.

Sundqvist, P. (2019), 'Commercial-Off-the-Shelf Games in the Digital Wild and L2 Learner Vocabulary', *Language Learning & Technology* 23 (1): 87–113.

Xu, Z., Z. Chen, L. Eutsler, Z. Geng and A. Kogut (2019), 'A Scoping Review of Digital Game-Based Technology on English Language Learning', *Education Technology Research and Development* 67: 1–28.

Part One

Theory and research

2

A critical review of research on gamification and second language acquisition

Silvia Benini and Michael Thomas

Introduction

The use of digital games in education has become increasingly popular over the last decade as a means of fostering learner motivation and engagement (Johnson et al. 2014). Moreover, a growing amount of research has been undertaken on games and game principles in second language learning in particular where they have become an increasingly integral part of the language learning process since the advent of more communicative approaches. This chapter provides a critical review of the research on games during the period 2014–20 to examine the current state of work on gamification, games design and second language learning (L2 learning). To do this it investigates the theoretical perspectives that inform current research in the field; discusses gaming as a motivational tool in L2 Learning; identifies the affordances and challenges of gaming in general and in 3D virtual learning environments (3DVLEs) for L2 learning and teaching in particular; and explores the limitations of existing research.

Background

It is important to identify at the outset that frequently used categories and concepts in the field of game-based learning (GBL) are not always clearly defined or used consistently. Several authors, for example, use the terms gamification and GBL synonymously to describe the same concept (Epper, Derryberry and Jackson 2012; Callaghan et al. 2013). The most frequently occurring terms in the research include game-inspired design, gamification, GBL, serious games and simulations, and it is important at the outset to distinguish between them:

1. Game-inspired design focuses on the use of ideas and dynamics to better support learning and intrinsic motivation (Kiryakova, Angelova and Yordanova 2014).
2. The term 'gamification' was coined initially by Pelling (2011) and is associated with the use of points, levels, leader boards and badges (Hamari, Koivisto and Sarsa 2014; Seaborn and Fels 2015).
3. GBL focuses on the use of digital or non-digital games in the classroom to enhance the learning and teaching experience (Van Eck 2006).
4. Serious games aim to use gaming technologies for educational and training purposes (Kiryakova, Angelova and Yordanova 2014).
5. Simulations focus on user training in a simulated real-world setting but do not always have rules or require competition between participants (Wiggins 2016).

Research suggests that integrating game mechanics into the classroom may increase students' intrinsic motivation to learn as well as their engagement and learning outcomes (Clark et al. 2011; McGonigal 2011; Hanus and Fox 2015). A gamified curriculum offers students the possibility to obtain a visual display of their progress while having the freedom to explore multiple identities and experiences and to fail without the fear of penalty when learning (Klopfer, Osterweil and Salen 2009; Lee and Hamer 2011; Kapp 2012).

Games have been researched across all levels of education but most emphasis has been placed on the primary and secondary education contexts to date (Lim and Ong 2012; Dib and Adamo-Villani 2013; Su and Cheng 2015; Wiggins 2016). In these contexts, as in further and higher education, however, several barriers have been identified, including lack of support for teachers willing to integrate games into the curriculum, the logistics of game-school integration (Klopfer, Osterweil and Salen 2009) and, as Lee and Hammer (2011: 4) pointed out, the challenge of a gamified curriculum that 'might absorb resources, or teach students that they should learn only when provided with external rewards'. It is therefore crucial to understand the foundation of games design in order to effectively integrate games into second language curricula.

Since the end of the last century, second language acquisition has experienced an important shift, moving from a cognitive orientation to a more social one, from closed classroom settings to more open and naturalistic ones and from L2 learning to L2 use (Firth and Wagner 1997; Block 2003; Johnson 2008).

Within computer-assisted language learning (CALL) and second language acquisition (SLA) contexts, gamification has been the subject of extensive research as it potentially offers opportunities for L2 learners and teachers to enhance their language learning/teaching and, at the same time, acquire and foster their digital literacy skills. Gamification offers L2 learners the opportunity to interact among peers as implied by a social game. In addition, motivation may increase in gamified instructional environments where learners' performance is recognized by a reward system (Buckingham 2014). When gaming badges are implemented in SLA, for example, they serve not only as a motivational tool for students who can be involved in more competitive tasks but also as a type of formative assessment (Glover 2013; Flores 2015). In this sense, L2 teachers have the flexibility to plan the language learning experience and related tasks while rethinking their practices in accordance with the similarities they may find in games and learning.

Methodology

In a review of the literature on gamification, Caponetto, Earp and Ott (2014) focused on the period 2011–13, demonstrating how the number of works published in the field grew exponentially from 206 in 2011 to 1,620 in 2013. Koivisto and Hamari (2014) confirmed this trend with their analysis of search hits for gamification which showed a fivefold increase over the same period. Moreover, de Sousa Borges et al. (2014) conducted a systematic mapping process to provide an overview on gamification by analysing 357 papers on the subject. Recently, Ofosu-Ampong (2020) examined gamification literature since 2011, identifying and analysing thirty-two published papers. The review presented here aims to continue these investigations by researching the number of studies on gamification, education and language learning during the period 2014–20.

Searches for the terms *gamification* and *education* were conducted and visualized (see Figure 2.1) and confirmed the trend already suggested by the studies above of a constantly increasing interest in the subject over the last five years. Based on searches involving the following keywords (game design, gamification, games, education, motivation, learning, language learning, language teaching and language education) with the databases Google Scholar, ERIC (Cambridge Scientific Abstracts), JSTOR Education, SAGE Full-Text Collection, SCOPUS and Web of Science, relevant books, chapters and articles were selected.

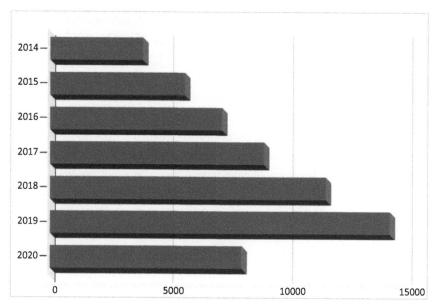

Figure 2.1 Number of scientific works published annually (from 2014 to eight months into 2020).

Table 2.1 Empirical research in books and related chapters

No.	Book	No. of chapters	Item(s)
1	Shernoff et al. (2014)	1	Crisp (2014)
2	Werbach and Hunter (2015)		
3	Kapp (2016)		
4	Benson and Voller (2014)		
5	Chou (2015)		

For this study the works were organized in several tables and analysed accordingly: the distribution of empirical research in books and related chapters (Table 2.1); empirical research in journals (Table 2.2); non-empirical research (Table 2.3); reports and funded projects (Table 2.4); and dissertation studies (Table 2.5).

Arising from the preliminary background analysis of the broader educational research, three main research questions were identified to guide the study:

1. Which aspects of gamification are dominant in the research on L2 learning and teaching?

Table 2.2 Empirical research in journals

No.	Journal title	No. of articles	Item(s)
1	*Computers in Human Behavior*	8	Koivisto and Hamari (2014); Seaborn and Fels (2015); da Rocha Seixas, Gomes and de Melo Filho (2016); Kuo and Chuang (2016); Hamari (2017); Landers and Armstrong (2017); Mekler et al. (2017); Sailer et al. (2017)
2	*Computers & Education*	2	Barzilai and Blau (2014); de-Marcos, Garcia-Lopez and Garcia-Cabot (2016)
3	*Procedia. Social and Behavioral Science*	1	Martí-Parreño, Seguí-Mas and Seguí-Mas (2016)
4	*Journal of e-Learning and Knowledge Society*	1	Galbis-Córdova, Martí-Parreño and Currás-Pérez (2017)
5	*Research in Learning Technology*	2	Barr (2017); Young and Nichols (2017)
6	*Transaction on Learning and Technologies*	1	Ibáñez, Di-Serio and Delgado-Kloos (2014)
7	*Proceedings*	1	Ramirez et al. (2014)
8	*Psychological Bulletin*	1	Cerasoli, Nicklin and Ford (2014)
9	*Language Learning & Technology*	2	Chik (2014); Reinhardt (2014)
10	*Interactive Learning Environments*	1	Hung, Sun and Yu (2015)
11	*IEEE Transactions on Affective Computing*	1	Sabourin and Lester (2014)
12	*Sustainability*	1	Parra-González et al. (2020)

2. In what ways is gamification used as a motivational tool for L2 learning and teaching?
3. What are the affordances and challenges of games in 3DVLEs for L2 learning and teaching?

Table 2.3 Non-empirical research

No.	Category	Item(s)
1	Conceptual discussion	Articles: de Sousa Borges et al. (2014); Caponetto et al. (2014); Hamari (2014); Kiryakova, Angelova and Yordanova (2014); Dicheva et al. (2015); Erenli (2015); Flores (2015); Kim and Lee (2015); Mora et al. (2015); Muntean and Nardini (2015); Ortiz, Chiluiza and Valcke (2016); Majuri, Koivisto and Hamari (2018); Subhash and Cudney (2018); Sykes (2018); Ofosu-Ampong (2020) Book chapters: Reinhardt and Thorne (2016).

Table 2.4 Reports and funded projects

No.	Reports	Funded projects
1	Johnson et al. (2014)	Persico et al. (2017)

Table 2.5 Dissertation studies

No.	Type of items(s)
1 2	Master's dissertation: Arabul Yayla (2015); Jackson (2016); Reeves (2016); Birsen (2017); Nordengen and Brinch (2018) PhD thesis: Martinez (2014); Fis Erumit (2016); Boendermaker (2017); Exton (2017)

Findings and discussion

Gamification was initially coined by Pelling to refer to the application of game-like accelerated user interface design principles to make electronic transactions both enjoyable and fast (Pelling 2011). Later on, the term was applied more widely to situations where game design elements were implemented in non-game settings in order to change user behaviour. Some researchers have referred to the concept of placing a 'game layer' over everything (Priebatsch 2010); however, the majority of researchers seem to agree on the definition of gamification as the use of game elements and mechanics in non-game situations in order to support and motivate users to perform tasks (Deterding et al. 2011; Werbach and Hunter 2012; Johnson et al. 2013; Hamari, Koivisto and Sarsa 2014; Flores 2015; Seaborn and Fels 2015). Because of its extensive use and integration in fields other than the education, as Reinhardt and Thorne (2016) suggest, various scholars and game designers have criticized gamification as a simplification of the game medium created by marketers and big business for the purpose of easy profit. However, many advocates of the term have highlighted in both their theoretical and empirical studies that gamification should not be considered as an easy addition to learning which makes it enjoyable and fun; rather, it should be investigated as a core educational approach that has the potential to improve learning performance (Ibáñez, Di-Serio and Delgado-Kloos 2014; de-Marcos, Garcia-Lopez and Garcia-Cabot 2016; Galbis-Córdova, Martí-Parreño and Currás-Pérez 2017; Ofosu-Ampong 2020; Parra-González et al. 2020); to attract, motivate, engage and retain users (Ibáñez, Di-Serio and Delgado-Kloos 2014; da Rocha Seixas, Gomes and de Melo Filho 2016; Kuo and Chuang 2016; Landers and Armstrong 2017; Mekler et al. 2017); and to improve the user experience of interactive systems in terms of design (Seaborn and Fels 2015). As stated by Reinhardt and Thorne (2016: 423), 'Much of the debate surrounding gamification revolves around terminology and the problematic definition of game, which is sometimes as much in the disposition of the players as in the rules that define it.'

Werbach and Hunter (2015) differentiate between three types of gamification: internal, external and behaviour-change. Internal gamification targets employees, external gamification focuses on customers' engagement, while behaviour-change gamification aims to explore habit formation. Educational gamification systems fall into this third category. Several researchers have suggested applying game mechanics and game elements, core features of gamification, to learning. De-Marcos et al. (2014), for example, have stated that using games in education has several advantages and game design mechanics have been successful in the educational field. Based on previous literature, Kim and Lee (2015) emphasized the cognitive, emotional and social benefits of game-based techniques in education. First, Lee and Hammer (2011), Stott and Neustaedter (2013) and later Dicheva et al. (2015) identified four types of game dynamics which have proven to be successful in an educational context, namely freedom to fail, rapid feedback, progression and storytelling. According to Kapp (2016), games can be extremely useful for providing instant feedback. One example of this is in-class teachers who provide feedback to one student at a time within contexts that are shaped by time constraints. Therefore, integrating the frequent and immediate feedback mechanisms found in game design may prove to be extremely beneficial in terms of establishing a more personalized learning approach.

Muntean (2015) suggested designing rewards that could be obtained when appropriate behaviour is observed in a gamified classroom. Furthermore, teachers usually present information to their students by dividing it into different categories according to difficulty levels. It may be challenging sometimes to accommodate each student's needs and in this sense, as indicated by Kyriakova and Angelova (2014), games may provide difficulty progression on an individual basis, keeping players at a particular level until they have demonstrated that they are able to pass that level and progress to the next one. Armstrong and Landers (2017) indicate that creating a narrative around a specific task may enhance motivation and engagement, while other elements of game design usually applied to gamification, such as leader boards and badges, encourage competition and participation as well as offering a visual representation of progress (Hamari 2017).

Looking at future directions, Sykes (2018) proposed three ideas which new research on gamification should focus on: (1) increased access to community-based games, (2) meaningful incorporation of virtual reality and (3) increased access to commercial games. These suggestions find their roots in a previous study by Sykes et al. (2012) in which she highlighted five relevant features of games for language teaching and learning, each of which parallels best practices in second language teaching and learning:

1. There is a learner-directed goal orientation: tasks and goals set for learning are dynamic, learner-driven and directly related to learning objectives.
2. There are opportunities for interaction with the game, through the game and around the game.
3. Just-in-time and individualized feedback is provided.
4. The relevant use of narrative and context is important: this means the creation of a space in which both of these features can be cultivated to create a meaningful experience.
5. Motivation is central as it is often the result of powerful learning experiences in which the players continually engage.

The positive impact of gaming in the educational sphere, as demonstrated above, has been increasingly investigated since the 1980s; however, this review will focus on the potential value of gamification in relation to several important aspects for SLA: motivation, autonomy and community, game context and feedback.

Gamification as a motivational tool to engage learners

In the educational field, games are considered an important part of the development of knowledge and play a role in the engagement of students.

Gamification techniques offer the possibility of incorporating games into learning situations while promoting the engagement of students. Several key studies (Caponetto, Earp and Ott 2014; de Sousa Borges et al. 2014; Hamari, Koivisto and Sarsa 2014; Reinhardt and Thorne 2016) have emphasized that gamification has become an area of great interest for researchers because it provides a valuable alternative to engage and motivate students during their learning process.

According to the NMC Horizon Report (Johnson et al. 2014: 42), the motivational potential of games stems from the way 'designed games can stimulate large gains in productivity and creativity among learners'. Furthermore, to support this view, Ramirez et al. (2014: 647) argue that 'gamification techniques are a critical set of design tools in an educator's toolbox'. Accordingly, the motivational aspect of games has been discussed widely in the literature and examined through the lens of different theories and approaches. Reinhardt and Thorne (2016: 426), for example, explain the concept of motivation in game design theory 'as emerging from the balance between challenge and reward or accomplishment. Game designers try to keep players engaged by providing challenges and rewards through goal and feedback systems targeted at, or just beyond, a player's level.' This status or level of engagement goes back to flow theory as proposed by Czikszentmihalyi in which a feeling of mastery, complete engagement and intrinsic motivation is at the core of the activity (Shernoff et al. 2014). Moreover, in gamification maintaining 'flow' is a means of motivating behavioural and psychological outcomes (Koivisto and Hamari 2014).

Ryan and Deci (2000) identified two types of motivation, intrinsic and extrinsic, in their self-determination theory (SDT). Intrinsic motivation refers to the pursuit of an activity because it is inherently interesting and enjoyable, while extrinsic motivation refers to doing something because it leads to a separable outcome such as receiving rewards and reducing pressure. SDT has attracted considerable research across a range of different disciplines (Ryan and Deci 2000; Denis and Jouvelot 2005; Standage, Duda and Ntoumanis 2005; Ryan and Deci 2006) and been shown to be a valuable theory to examine motivation in relation to games and gamification (Deterding 2011). Several recent studies have addressed the need to evaluate the impact of gamification on intrinsic and extrinsic motivation as they are some of the most frequently discussed, yet rarely empirically studied, constructs in gamification research (Hamari et al. 2014; Seaborn and Fels 2015; Mekler et al. 2017).

Luma da Rocha Seixas, Gomes and de Melo Filho (2016) discussed the effectiveness of gamification as a motivation and engagement tool among students in the elementary school sector. In this study, students who presented the highest levels of engagement with respect to the indicators were also those who had more badges given by the teacher and, on the contrary, those with lower levels of engagement were those with fewer badges from the teacher. Findings highlighted how the process of building gamification strategies must also be aligned with educational purposes and that both extrinsic and intrinsic motivation promote performance gains as well as increases in the quality of effort that students put into a given task as discussed in Cerasoli, Nicklin and Ford (2014).

Games are typically considered to provide enjoyable, intrinsic motivation, and gamification tries to employ these characteristics in non-game applications. Because learners may lack intrinsic motivation for non-game applications, extrinsic motivation, as seen in the form of rewards or other mechanisms, may be necessary to make them engage in the gamifying process.

The concepts of autonomy and community, together with related concepts such as independent learning, self-direction, cooperation and co-action, are at the core of discussions on learning in general and gamification in particular. The notion of autonomy has a strong link with motivation and was introduced into L2 motivation studies mainly by Deci and Ryan (2000) via SDT. Their work highlights the importance of 'a sense of personal autonomy' in the learning process, which they define as a feeling that learners experience when their behaviour 'is truly chosen by them rather than imposed by some external source' (2000: 70). This concept, as Benson and Voller (2014) indicate, together with the concept of independence, has grown exponentially over the last two decades, becoming mainstreamed as a key concept in educational planning. The authors also offered a definition of a learning community as 'consist[ing] of individuals who come together to accomplish a specific end or goal' (2014: 70). As indicated by Thorne, Fischer and Lu (2012) and Reinhardt and Sykes (2014), when applied to digital gaming and L2 learning, the concepts of autonomy and community are crucial for two specific reasons. First, gamers are often in the position to make independent decisions when playing. Second, the use of communal resources external to the games themselves (such as dedicated blogs or social media pages) is an integral aspect to the overall experience. Gamers do in fact participate in online communities and produce game-related paratexts as a result. Therefore, as Chik (2014: 87) stated in her study, 'when digital gaming is a community-based activity, the autonomous learning involved will inevitably be community-based as well'. Chik's empirical research (2014) further discussed the concepts of autonomy and community within the digital gaming field and second language learning (L2) in East Asia. It recommended that teachers and researchers should provide precise structures and guidance for young L2 learners on how to use digital games to enhance autonomy when learning. As a result, Chik (2014: 97) concluded that 'students can be made aware that they have the ability to turn their preferred leisure activities into learning practices, and learn how to seek help from online communities' to bolster their individual progress.

Game context and feedback provision

According to Reinhardt and Thorne (2016: 426), 'game context can be understood as the context represented by the game narratives around the rules (i.e. the context-in-the-game of abstractions), as well as the cultural and situational context of where, when, and by whom the game is played (i.e. the context-of-the-game)'. Game narratives play an essential role in enhancing cultural competence and improving participation, while enhancing different language skills. Gamers and specifically students use games to learn as they are immersed in a game context and are exposed to flow experiences (Hamari et al. 2014) which may lead to positive learning outcomes (Barzilai and Blau 2014; Sabourin and Lester 2014; Hung, Sun and Yu 2015). As a consequence, Crisp (2014) suggested that as learning and gamified curricula become more common, learner engagement and flow will improve.

Several research studies have shown how gamification has the potential to provide immediate and effective feedback (Flores 2015; Kapp 2016; Reinhardt and Thorne 2016) which is something that L2 instruction, for example, may not been able to provide easily. When it comes to game design, feedback can be offered through points, sounds and messages. As Reinhardt and Thorne (2016: 425) discussed, in game contexts feedback is 'instructional rather than punitive, and is formative rather than summative' as it is provided in a timely fashion thus giving the possibility to the players to understand the action that caused it, and may be personalized, as it takes into account the feedback already provided, while the quality and quantity of the feedback are also adjusted.

Game design and game elements

Sailer et al. (2017) provided specific definitions of the terms involved in gamification, focusing first on the term 'game' itself, moving then to 'element' and finally 'design'. Game design can be described therefore as the action of adjusting all aspects related to games while deciding what a game should be (Schell 2014). Arising from this, Salen and Zimmerman (2004) provided a set of game design principles that should be considered in the designing process:

- Understanding systems and interactivity, as well as player choice, action and outcomes
- Including a study of rule-making and rule-breaking, game experience and representation and social interaction
- Adding and focusing on the connection between the rules of a game and the play that the rules engender, the pleasures games invoke, the meanings they construct, the ideologies they embody and the stories they tell.

Moving on from these principles, researchers have focused on the identification of the different game elements and how they should be incorporated and organized together in order to obtain a successful overall game design (Brathwaite and Schreiber 2009; Reeves 2016). On the one hand, Brathwaite and Schreiber (2009: 112) used the term 'game design atoms' to introduce the basic elements of games, including game states, players, avatars and game bits as well as game mechanics, game dynamics, goals and themes. On the other hand, Reeves (2016) pointed out the ten components that make game design successful include other factors such as self-representations, three-dimensional environments, narrative, feedback, reputation ranks and levels, marketplaces and economies, competition within a rule-based context, teams, communication and finally time pressure.

As Mora et al. (2015) explain, after having organized and integrated game elements into game design fundamentals, what should follow is a standardized structure that brings them together into a framework. However, it is evident that game design is such a flexible process that it does not always need to fall into a precise framework (Kuutti 2013). Having said that, a set of conditions such as interface design pattern, dynamics, design and heuristic principles should be met in the designing process in order to have a positive playing experience. This was confirmed by Detering et al. (2011) who indicated that a global set of components is necessary in game design to reach *gamefulness*, namely game interface design patterns, game design patterns and mechanics, game design principles and heuristics, game models and game design methods.

Game elements

Game elements are core ingredients of gamification as they are the specific components through which the agency of a game can be constructed and/or analysed. There have been several attempts to create comprehensive lists of game elements that can be applied to gamification (Zichermann and Cunningham 2011; Kapp 2012; Robinson and Bellotti 2013; Werbach and Hunter 2015; Sailer et al. 2017). Typical game elements or 'components', as described in some cases, include badges, leader boards, progress bars, performance graphs, quests and avatars. Indeed, Kapp (2012) suggests a list where typical game elements include goals, rules, conflict, competition, cooperation, time, reward structures, feedback, levels, storytelling, curve of interest and aesthetics, whereas other authors like Robinson and Bellotti (2013) provide detailed lists of elements with their functions in various gamification settings. As indicated by Sailer et al. (2017: 30), it is important to understand that 'different authors follow distinct strategies in their attempts to create such lists. One is to create liberal sets of elements found in any game. Another strategy is to provide a constrained set of elements, which are unique to specific games.' Arising from this research, we propose the use of a broad list of game elements for SLA teachers and researchers involved in gamification design (see Table 2.6) with the aim of being as exhaustive as possible.

Werbach and Hunter (2015) took the elements that they consider to be the most important from their own experience of game playing and provided a comprehensive description of the key elements of games organizing them into three distinct categories: dynamics, mechanics and components. Structured as a pyramid, components form the base layer, mechanics the central layer and dynamics the uppermost layer (see Figure 2.2).

As the base of the pyramid, components provide the largest group of game elements. They are the least abstract among the three categories presented and they provide the tools that can be used to integrate gamification into a field of interest (see Table 2.6).

Mechanics refers to the basic processes that guide users to engage with the content of the game while continuing to drive the action forward. Specifically, the mechanics elements include challenges, chance, competition, cooperation, feedback, resource acquisition, reward system, transactions, turns and win states. Table 2.7 provides a list of game mechanics and related definitions based on Werbach and Hunter's work (2015).

Table 2.6 Game components and related definitions according to the literature analysed

Components	Definitions
Avatar	Visual representation of a player or alter ego
Badges	Visual representations of achievements
Boss fights	Particularly hard challenges at the culmination of a level
Collection	Set of items or badges accumulated
Combat	A defined battle, typically short-lived
Content unlocking	Elements available only when players reach objectives
Gifting	The opportunity to share and give items to other players as a reward or as part of a specific team strategy
Leader boards	The ranking of players based on the number of points they have been awarded
Levels	A section or part of the game outlining the number of points a player has. As a player progresses, the levels become increasingly difficult
Points	Numeric accumulation awarded for certain activities
Progress bar	Shows the status of a player
Quests	Specific tasks player have to complete in a game
Social elements	Relationship with other players within the game
Social graphs	Representation of player's social network within a game
Teams	Group of players working together to reach common goals
Virtual goods	Items that can be purchased by performing specific tasks within a game

Finally, dynamics represent the highest conceptual level involving elements in a game. There are five dynamics elements: constraints, emotions, narrative, progression and relationships, and these elements must be considered and managed when developing a gamified system. Dynamics elements constitute the abstract notion of a game and when they are included in the design process, gamification occurs naturally. Table 2.8 provides a list of game dynamics and related definitions based on Werbach and Hunter's work (2015).

Gamification and SLA

Having reviewed the context of gamification, the aim of the final section is to investigate the use of digital gamification for foreign language teaching and

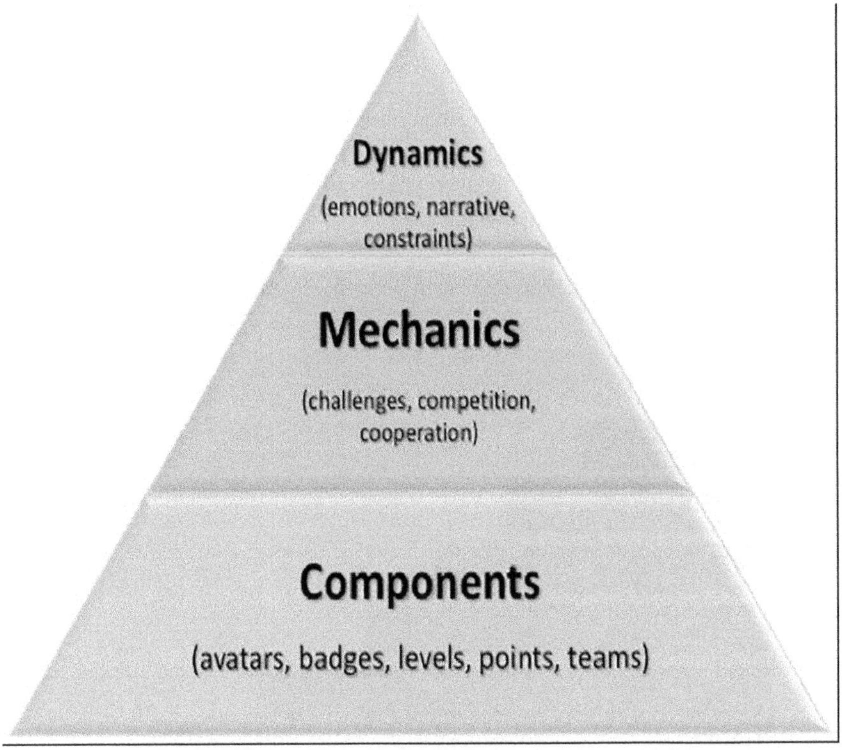

Figure 2.2 Categories of game elements (Werbach and Hunter 2015).

Table 2.7 Game mechanics and related definitions based on Werbach and Hunter (2015)

Mechanics	Definitions
Challenges	Tasks presented that prompt the player to generate a solution
Chance	Element(s) of possibility/randomness in a game
Competition	Intuitive mechanic where one player (or a team) wins or loses
Cooperation	Player(s) who works best together to achieve a specific goal within a game
Feedback	Providing information on how a player is performing
Resource acquisition	Acquiring useful or collectible items as the player progresses
Reward system	System to motivate player to accomplish a quest
Transactions	Trades between users (they can be either direct or through an intermediary)
Turns	Sequential participation of players
Win states	Objectives that make one player the winner (note that it is also possible to have 'draw' and 'loss' states)

Table 2.8 Game dynamics and related definitions based on Werbach and Hunter (2015)

Dynamics	Definitions
Constraints	Limitations or trade-offs that need to be considered when designing a game
Emotions	Feelings that drive the interaction and engagement with a game
Narrative	Storyline characterizing a game
Progression	Growth and development of a player navigating a game
Relationships	Social interactions that occur when games are played

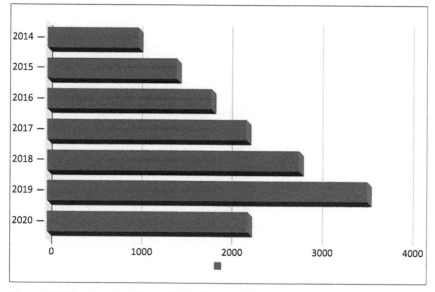

Figure 2.3 Number of articles published by year (from 2014 to eight months into 2020).

learning in 3DVLEs. A detailed table is provided in Appendix 1 indicating a summary of the studies analysed on gamification and SLA in terms of, among other variables, the subject of the articles, the methodology employed, the number of participants and the target language. As Figure 2.3 indicates, the highest number of studies were published in 2018 but it is noteworthy that the number of research papers has increased from 2014 onwards as has the number specifically addressing digital gamification in 3DVLEs. Given current trends, it is anticipated that the number of studies will increase.

A total of thirty-six publications were identified as falling within the scope of our research and analysed accordingly. A list of several keywords – gamification, Second Life, 3DVLEs and/or language learning and second language

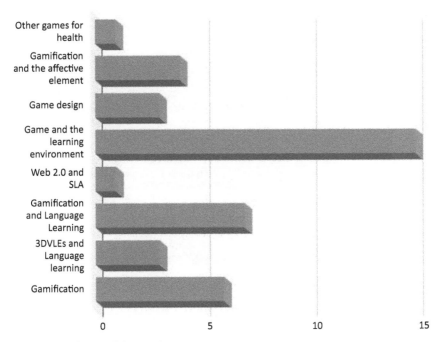

Figure 2.4 Theme of the articles.

acquisition – were used to identify research in the following databases: Ebsco, Google Scholar and Proquest. Figure 2.4 presents the distribution of the selected publications according to the themes they focused on.

According to Figure 2.4, the dominant theme was games and the learning environment (n = 15) followed by gamification in general (n = 6) and gamification and language learning in particular (n = 7). An important theme at the core of some of the research analysed was the role of gamification and game elements in evoking a sense of emotional engagement in the player (n = 4). Figure 2.5 shows the distribution of the data collections methods used in the reviewed studies.

Examining the research more carefully it can be seen that it mainly consisted of quantitative studies (n = 14); qualitative studies and meta-analysis had the same number (n = 11). It is evident that most of the quantitative research included semi-experimental studies (n = 8), qualitative research included case studies (n = 9) and the meta-analysis included literature reviews (n = 8).

The distributions of the data collection tools used in the examined studies show that questionnaires (n = 15) were the highest together with interviews and focus group discussions (n = 6). Alternative tools such as concept maps,

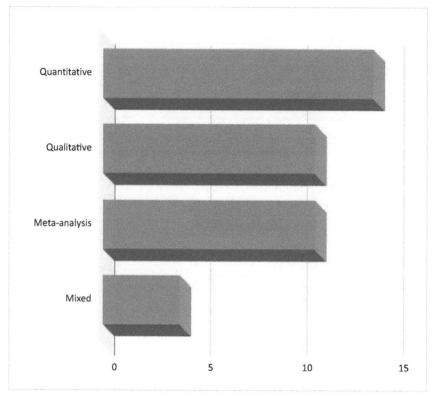

Figure 2.5 Data collection methods of the articles.

portfolios and performance tests (n = 6) were also quite popular. No data collection tool was specified in twelve of the studies presented.

The distributions of the reviewed studies according to the sample showed that the majority of studies were conducted at the undergraduate level. Figure 2.6 presents the distributions of the reviewed studies according to the number of participants and indicates that sample sizes smaller than one hundred and larger than thirty were the preferred option (28 per cent, n = 11), and this may have been related to the use of parametric tests during data analysis.

Finally, Figure 2.7 presents the distribution of the reviewed studies according to data analysis methods. This figure shows that no data analysis was performed in eleven of the reviewed studies. In the other studies, quantitative analysis techniques were much more intensively employed (n = 34). Among the descriptive statistics used, frequency and representations of central tendency (mean, mode, median) (n = 9) were the most frequently used.

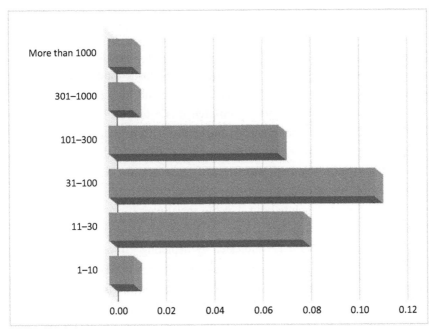

Figure 2.6 Number of participants.

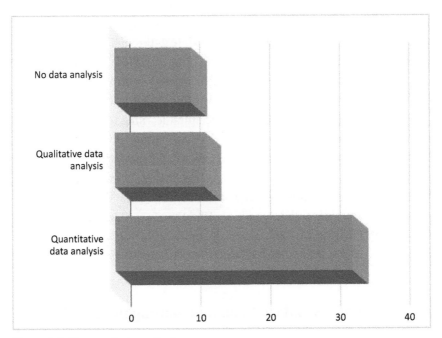

Figure 2.7 Data analysis method.

3DVLEs and language learning

According to Krashen (2014) language learning requires learners to be exposed to rich, comprehensible, varied and compelling linguistic input. Learners need to exploit the foreign language in social, authentic and meaningful contexts to negotiate meaning and to produce comprehensible output. Moreover, as Ellis (2005) has argued, while grammatical competence is important, intercultural and pragmatic competences need to be employed in the learning of the target language.

Research suggests that both the nature of games and the elements that make games fun are intrinsically motivating (Adams et al. 2012). A constructivist approach to GBL has pointed out that the social play continuum (Broadhead 2006) concurs with Vygotsky's zone of proximal development (ZPD), as Liu, Yuen and Rao (2015: 11) indicate, 'by depicting a progression of social development through play', thus providing a framework in which games can be used to develop social competence and social status. Furthermore, according to Galbis-Córdova, Martí-Parreño and Currás-Pérez (2017), research also provides evidence that GBL improves competencies such as critical thinking and decision-making, problem-solving, conflict resolution and communication skills.

In her review of digital games and language learning, Sykes (2018) concluded that studies have examined both game-enhanced learning (e.g. through the use of commercial, off-the-shelf games) and GBL (e.g. through the use of digital games built explicitly for the teaching and learning of world languages) and have shown that digital games support learning in a variety of areas. Benefits include the creation of a learning community (Bryant 2006; Reinhardt and Zander 2011; Peterson 2013), the opportunity for intercultural learning (e.g. Thorne 2008), access to a diversity and complexity of written and spoken discourse (e.g. Liang 2012; Thorne, Fischer and Lu 2012), access to authentic texts (Squire 2008; Reinhardt 2013), evidence of authentic socio-literacy practice (Steinkuehler 2007; Thorne, Black and Sykes 2009) and affordances for the sociocognitive processes of learning and language socialization (e.g. Piirainen-Marsh and Tainio 2009; Zheng et al. 2009), especially of lexis (Purushotma 2005; Neville 2010; Sundqvist and Sylvén 2012; Hitosugi, Schmidt and Hayashi 2014).

Affordances and challenges of gaming in 3DVLEs

In the game design arena, Lazzaro (2005) identified four keys to unlocking players' emotions: (1) providing opportunities for challenge, strategy and problem-solving (hard fun); (2) introducing elements that foster mystery, intrigue and curiosity (easy fun); (3) leading players to excitement or relief moods (altered states); and (4) promoting competition and teamwork (people fun). On the other hand, LeBlanc (2000) organized the types of player pleasure into eight categories: sensation, fantasy, narrative, challenge, fellowship, discovery, expression and submission as cited by Schell (2014). Successful game use, according to LeBlanc (2000), found ways to balance combinations of these categories effectively.

In this respect, Van Eck (2006: 4) asserts that 'games embody well-established principles and models of learning. For instance, games are effective partly because the learning takes place within a meaningful (to the game) context'. This is called situated cognition where the learner takes the environment in which the learning takes place into account. Researchers have also pointed out that play is a primary form of socialization and a learning mechanism common to all human cultures. Games provide modelling and play strategies in learning and thus help the learners through the use of a constant cycle of hypothesis formulation, testing and revision.

On the other hand, to facilitate foreign language learning, 3DVLEs bring new opportunities to the field, as Warburton (2009: 421) indicates, in that virtual worlds (VWs) enable:

1. exposure to authentic content and culture, which could facilitate also the exposure to authentic language;
2. the use of visualization, contextualization and simulation to facilitate comprehensible and compelling input;
3. opportunities for extended and rich interactions between individuals and communities, as well as humans and objects which could help learners use the language for negotiation of meaning;
4. immersion in a 3D environment using an augmented sense of virtual presence that could enable learners to experience the language in its authentic and natural environment;
5. content production and the creation and ownership of objects in the learning environment that could help learners with the personalization of the communication and autonomy in learning the target language.

When these affordances are integrated into games, games in 3DVLEs may become an invaluable tool for language learning. However, the use of games in 3DVLEs for learning languages does not come without drawbacks. Van Eck (2006: 22) posits that the digital game-based learning (DGBL) approach is likely to be viewed as nothing more than a fad until educators can 'point to persuasive examples that show games are being used effectively in education and that educators and parents view them as they now view textbooks and other instructional media'.

It is clear, then, that there are several challenges associated with games and 3DVLEs before they can be viewed as in any sense 'normalized'. Warburton (2009) and Warburton and Perez-Garcia (2010) report on a survey of newsgroups, blog posts and recent research literature and identified eight broad challenges: (1) technical, (2) identity, (3) culture, (4) collaboration, (5) time, (6) economic, (7) standards and (8) scaffolding persistence and social discovery. *Technical issues* are either computer-related like bandwidth, hardware and firewalls, or server issues such as down time and lag, or use-related issues like navigation, creating objects and manipulating one's avatar. *Identity issues* describe how freedom to play with identity and manage reputation can become a cause for concern, and accountability for actions becomes displaced. *Culture issues* involve sets of codes, norms and etiquette for joining communities. *Collaboration issues* relate to the need to build trust and authenticity while cooperating through co-construction and because minimal social network schemes may operate within the VLEs. *Time constraints* could occur by validating, running and teaching activities. Checking object permissions, intellectual property rights and accessibility also requires a lot of time. *Economic issues* involve costs. Even though basic user accounts to access VWs like Second Life are typically free, anything else costs money such as buying land to build, creating teaching spaces or uploading images and textures. *Standardization* is a problem related to the lack of interoperability between various virtual platforms. *Scaffolding persistence* and *social discovery issues* such as when an avatar remains trapped at the centre of its own community and in-world profiles associated with each avatar provide a limited mechanism for the social discovery of other people, unlike other social networking services.

It is clear that 3D virtual worlds have gained in popularity in recent years. The use of 3DVLEs has also increased variation in online and distance education. Playing with educational content scaffolds learners to construct knowledge, enables better retention of knowledge, creates the necessary social environment for learning, and helps in the application of that knowledge in novel situations. Thus, using educational games that are designed in 3DVLEs with learners in various levels and educational contexts is also gaining prominence.

Designing games for such 3D VWs is potentially extending the possible uses of these virtual environments as well. Through educational games or game-like applications VWs could be exploited much more effectively by learners and educators. Games or game-like applications that were created in 3D environments could enable learners to immerse themselves in individual or collaborative play (Thomas et al. 2018; Thomas, Schneider and Can 2019). The contexts in which 3D games could be used vary according to the need and interest of the learners. For instance, vocabulary games or game-like scenarios involving role plays with avatars could be used for foreign language learning. Rankin, Gold and Gooch (2006: 33) support the idea that 'game play experiences foster learning in the VW as players accomplish game tasks'. Other educational games in mathematics and science have also been designed and used in 3D VWs using foreign languages as the medium of instruction to take advantage of these affordances, and that is an area for future research.

Conclusion

This review has found that empirical research is still limited when it comes to analysing the effectiveness of gamification in educational and SLA settings and practices. Many empirical gamification studies focus in fact on the usefulness of specific game elements in particular learning contexts (Dicheva et al. 2015); however, the scope of the elements being explored is still limited (e.g. points, badges or levels and leader boards), as well as the relation to specific theories (e.g. SDT). Further research is needed to address the most and least effective game elements and their implementation in relation to specific contexts since, as Seaborn and Fels (2015: 29) argue, 'gamification in action is defined by applying a limited number of game elements to an interactive system, future research should aim to isolate the most promising and least promising game elements in particular contexts for particular types of end-users'.

In addition, research analysing students' attitudes towards gamification in online learning environments is still limited. As Ortiz, Chiluiza and Valcke (2016) pointed out, there is a lack of validated psychometric measurements that have been designed in accordance with rigorous research methodologies. In relation to game design, further research should be conducted to understand how gamification design elements and methods function and how they interact with individual dispositions, situational circumstances and the features of particular target activities, as indicated also by Hamari et al. (2014). In relation to this point, empirical research studies are needed to inform both theories and practices.

Appendix 1 Summary of the studies analysed on gamification and SLA

No.	Publication	Subject of the article	Empirical study	Non-empirical study	Methodology	Participants/sample	Target language(s)
1	Lan et al. (2015)	Games and learning environments	Empirical		Quantitative	n = 36 (undergraduate students)	Mandarin Chinese
2	Young et al. (2012)	Games and learning environments		Non-empirical	Literature review	>300 articles analysed	N/a
3	Udjaja, and Sari (2017)	Games and learning environments	Empirical		Qualitative	n = 16 (lectures, undergraduate students and college students)	Indonesian as first language + English as FL
4	Wang and Vásquez (2012)	Web 2.0 and SLA		Non-empirical	Literature review	Eighty-five articles analysed	N/a
5	Sykes (2018)	Gamification and language learning		Non-empirical	Literature review	Not specified	N/a
6	Si (2015)	3DVLEs and SLA	Empirical		Quantitative	n = 20 primary education students (6–8 years old)	Mandarin Chinese
7	da Rocha Seixas, Gomes and de Melo Filho (2016)	Gamification	Empirical		Quantitative + qualitative	n = 61 primary education students (8 years old)	N/a
8	Seaborn and Fels (2015)	Gamification		Non-empirical	Literature review	n = 60 articles analysed (over n = 769 search results)	N/a

No.	Publication	Subject of the article	Empirical study	Non-empirical study	Methodology	Participants/sample	Target language(s)
9	Homer, Hew and Tan (2018)	Gamification and SLA	Empirical		Quantitative	n = 120 primary education students (age range 6–11)	Chinese as first language) + English as FL
10	Rieber (1996)	Games and learning environments		Non-empirical	Literature review	Not specified	N/a
10	Rawendy et al. (2017)	Gamification and language learning	Empirical		Quantitative	n = 30 primary education students (age range 6–12)	Chinese
11	Martí-Parreño, Segui-Mas and Segui-Mas (2016)	Gamification and learning	Empirical		Quantitative (snowball sampling)	n = 98 teachers serving in higher education	N/a
12	Pasfield-Neofitou, Huang and Grant (2015)	3DVLEs and language learning	Empirical		Qualitative (two case studies)	Case study 1: n = 14 higher education students (age range 18–45) Case study 2: n = 11 higher education students (age range 18–25)	Chinese
13	Mekler et al. (2017)	Gamification and learning	Empirical		Quantitative	Between one hundred and three hundred participants (age range 17–68)	N/a
14	de-Marcos, Garcia-Lopez and Garcia-Cabot (2016)	Games and learning environments	Empirical		Quantitative (quasi-experimental research)	n = 379 undergraduate students	N/a

(Continued)

Appendix 1 *Continued*

No.	Publication	Subject of the article	Empirical study	Non-empirical study	Methodology	Participants/ sample	Target language(s)
15	Lu and Kharrazi (2018)	Games for health		Non-empirical	Literature review	n = 1743 health games analysed	N/a
16	Landers and Armstrong (2017)	Games and learning environments	Empirical		Quantitative (quasi-experimental research)	n = 262 undergraduate students	N/a
17	Kuo and Chuang (2016)	Gamification	Empirical		Quantitative + qualitative	n = 31–100 faculty members + internet visitors	N/a
18	Kuhn and Stevens (2017)	Game design	Empirical		Qualitative (case study)	Not specified (language teachers)	N/a
19	Ku, Huang and Hus (2015)	Games and learning environments	Empirical		Quantitative (quasi-experimental research)	n = 31–100 students (10–11 years old)	Chinese
20	Koivisto and Hamari (2014)	Gamification	Empirical		Quantitative (survey)	n = 195 responses gathered through a discussion forum	N/a

No.	Publication	Subject of the article	Empirical study	Non-empirical study	Methodology	Participants/ sample	Target language(s)
21	Kayımbaşıoğlu, Oktekin, and Hacı (2016)	Games design and learning environments	Empirical		Quantitative (pre-experimental -games developed + analysis of usage-)	n = 60 preschool students (5 years old)	N/a
22	Jee et al. (2014)	3DVLEs and language learning	Empirical		Qualitative (case study)	n = 34 higher education institute	English
23	Jackson (2016)	Games and learning environments		Non-empirical	Literature review	Not specified	N/a
24	İliç and Arıkan (2016)	Gamification and language learning	Empirical		Qualitative (case study)	n = 24 undergraduate students	English
25	Ibáñez, Di-Serio and Delgado-Kloos (2014)	Games and learning environments	Empirical		Quantitative + qualitative	n = 22 undergraduate students	(C-programming language)
26	Hanson-Smith (2016)	Games and learning		Non-empirical	Literature review	Not specified	N/a
27	Gafni, Achituv and Rahmani (2017)	Games and learning environments	Empirical		Quantitative (quasi-experimental research)	n = 107 secondary education students	English and French as foreign languages

(Continued)

Appendix 1 *Continued*

No.	Publication	Subject of the article	Empirical study	Non-empirical study	Methodology	Participants/ sample	Target language(s)
28	de Freitas (2018)	Games and learning environments		Non-empirical	Literature review (grounded theory)	Not specified	N/a
29	Flores (2015)	Gamification and language learning		Non-empirical	Literature review	Not specified	N/a
30	Dickey (2015)	Games and learning environments	Empirical		Qualitative	K-12 educators	N/a
31	Galbis-Córdova, Martí-Parreño and Currás-Pérez (2017)	Gamification and learning	Empirical		Quantitative	n = 128 undergraduate students	N/a
32	Amoia et al. (2012)	Game design	Empirical		Quantitative	Not specified	French
33	Uusi-Mäkelä (2015)	Gamification and language learning	Empirical		Quantitative + qualitative (case study)	n = 19 secondary education students	English
34	Slovak et al. (2018)	Games and learning environments	Empirical		Qualitative (case study)	Students 8–13 years old (number not specified)	N/a
35	Majuri, Koivisto and Hamari (2018)	Gamification		Non-empirical	Literature review	Not specified	N/a
36	Subhash and Cudney (2018)	Gamification and learning		Non-empirical	Literature review	Higher education context	N/a

Looking at future directions in gamification and SLA, it has been proposed that new research should focus on the implications of the increased access to community-based games, the use of virtual reality and the potential of commercial games (Sykes 2018). These suggestions are in line with the features of games used for language teaching and learning that this review has highlighted, specifically the importance of interaction, engagement and motivation; the central role of context and narrative; the potential of individualized feedback; and the requirement for a learner-driven, dynamic approach.

References

Adams, D. M., R. E. Mayer, A. MacNamara, A. Koenig and R. Wainess (2012), 'Narrative Games for Learning: Testing the Discovery and Narrative Hypotheses', *Journal of Educational Psychology* 104 (1): 235–49.

Amoia, M., T. Brétaudière, A. Denis, C. Gardent and L. Perez-Beltrachini (2012), 'A Serious Game for Second Language Acquisition in a Virtual Environment', *Journal on Systemics, Cybernetics and Informatics* 10 (1): 24–34.

Arabul Yayla, H. (2015), 'A Prototype Suggestion Including a Game Based Environment to Support the Language Education of Children with Down Syndrome', unpublished master's thesis, Istanbul: Bahcesehir University.

Barr, M. (2017), 'Press Start: The Value of an Online Student-Led, Peer-Reviewed Game Studies Journal', *Research in Learning Technology*, 25.

Barzilai, S., and I. Blau (2014), 'Scaffolding Game-Based Learning: Impact on Learning Achievements, Perceived Learning, and Game Experiences', *Computers & Education* 70: 65–79.

Benson, P., and P. Voller (2014), *Autonomy and Independence in Language Learning*, London: Routledge.

Birsen, P. (2017), 'Effect of Gamified Game-Based Learning on L2 Vocabulary Retention by Young Learners', unpublished master's thesis, Bahcesehir: University of Istanbul.

Block, D. (2003), *The Social Turn in Second Language Acquisition*, Washington, DC: Georgetown University Press.

Boendermaker, W. J. (2017), 'Serious Gamification: Motivating Adolescents to Do Cognitive Training', unpublished PhD thesis, Amsterdam: University of Amsterdam.

Brathwaite, B., and I. Schreiber (2009), *Challenges for Game Designers*, New York: Nelson Education.

Broadhead, P. (2006), 'Developing an Understanding of Young Children's Learning through Play: The Place of Observation, Interaction and Reflection', *British Educational Research Journal* 32 (2): 191–207.

Bryant, J., and J. Davies (2006), 'Selective Exposure to Video Games', in S. Vorderer and J. Bryant (eds), *Playing Video Games: Motives, Responses and Consequences*, 181–94, Mahwah, NJ: Erlbaum.

Buckingham, J. (2014), 'Open Digital Badges for the Uninitiated', *Electronic Journal for English as a Second Language* 18 (1): 1–11.

Callaghan, M. J., K. McCusker, J. L. Losada, J. Harkin and S. Wilson (2013), 'Using Game-Based Learning in Virtual Worlds to Teach Electronic and Electrical Engineering', *IEEE Transactions on Industrial Informatics* 9 (1): 575–84.

Caponetto, I., J. Earp and M. Ott (2014), 'Gamification and Education: A Literature Review', in *European Conference on Games Based Learning*. Academic Conferences International Limited 1: 50–7.

Cerasoli, C. P., J. M. Nicklin and M.T. Ford (2014), 'Intrinsic Motivation and Extrinsic Incentives Jointly Predict Performance: A 40-Year Meta-analysis', *Psychological Bulletin* 140 (4): 980.

Chik, A. (2014), 'Digital Gaming and Language Learning: Autonomy and Community', *Language Learning & Technology* 18 (2): 85–100.

Chou, Y. K. (2015), *Actionable Gamification: Beyond Points, Badges, and Leaderboards*, London: Octalysis Group.

Clark, D. B., B. C. Nelson, H. Y. Chang, M. Martinez-Garza, K. Slack and C. M. D'Angelo (2011), 'Exploring Newtonian Mechanics in a Conceptually-Integrated Digital Game: Comparison of Learning and Affective Outcomes for Students in Taiwan and the United States', *Computers & Education* 57 (3): 2178–95.

Crisp, G. T. (2014), 'Assessment in Next generation Learning Spaces', in K. Fraser (ed.), *The Future of Learning and Teaching in Next Generation Learning Spaces*, 85–100, London: Emerald Group.

da Rocha Seixas, L., A. S. Gomes and I. J. de Melo Filho (2016), 'Effectiveness of Gamification in the Engagement of Students', *Computers in Human Behavior* 58: 48–63.

de Freitas, S. (2018), 'Are Games Effective Learning Tools? A Review of educational Games', *Educational Technology & Society* 21 (2): 74–84.

de-Marcos, L., A. Domínguez, J. Saenz-de-Navarrete and C. Pagés (2014), 'An Empirical Study Comparing Gamification and Social Networking on E-Learning', *Computers & Education* 75: 82–91.

de-Marcos, L., E. Garcia-Lopez and A. Garcia-Cabot (2016), 'On the Effectiveness of Game-Like and Social Approaches in Learning: Comparing Educational Gaming, Gamification & Social Networking', *Computers & Education* 95: 99–113.

de Sousa Borges, S., V. H. Durelli, H. M. Reis and S. Isotani (2014, March), 'A Systematic Mapping on Gamification Applied to Education', in *Proceedings of the 29th Annual ACM Symposium on Applied Computing*, 216–22, London: ACM.

Denis, G., and P. Jouvelot (2005), 'Motivation-Driven Educational Game Design: Applying Best Practices to Music Education', in *Proceedings of the 2005 ACM SIGCHI*

International Conference on Advances in Computer Entertainment Technology, 462–5, London: ACM.

Deterding, S. (2011), 'Situated Motivational Affordances of Game Elements: A Conceptual Model', *Gamification: Using Game Design Elements in Non-Gaming Contexts, a Workshop at CHI*, 3–6.

Deterding, S., D. Dixon, R. Khaled and L. Nacke (2011), 'From Game Design Elements to Gamefulness: Defining Gamification', in *Proceedings of the 15th International Academic MindTrek Conference: Envisioning Future Media Environments*, 9–15, London: ACM.

Dib, H., and N. Adamo-Villani (2013), 'Serious Sustainability Challenge Game to Promote Teaching and Learning of Building Sustainability', *Journal of Computing in Civil Engineering* 28 (5): A4014007.

Dicheva, D., C. Dichev, C. Agre and G. Angelova (2015), 'Gamification in Education: A Systematic Mapping Study', *Journal of Educational Technology & Society* 18 (3): 75.

Dickey, M. D. (2015), 'K-12 Teachers Encounter Digital Games: A Qualitative Investigation of Teachers' Perceptions of the Potential of Digital Games for K-12 Education', *Interactive Learning Environments* 23 (4): 485–95.

Ellis, R. (2005), 'Principles of Instructed Language Learning', *System* 33 (2): 209–24.

Epper, R. M., A. Derryberry and S. Jackson (2012), 'Game-Based Learning: Developing an Institutional Strategy', *Research Bulletin Louisville, CO: EDUCAUSE Center for Applied Research*.

Erenli, K. (2015), 'Gamification and Law', in T. Reiners and L. C. Wood (eds), *Gamification in Education and Business*, 535–52, Cham: Springer.

Exton, G. (2017), 'Gamification as a Motivational Tool for Software Systems, as Illustrated in a Second-Language Learning Environment', unpublished PhD thesis, Limerick: University of Limerick.

Firth, A., and J. Wagner (1997), 'On Discourse, Communication, and (Some) Fundamental Concepts in SLA Research', *Modern Language Journal* 81 (3): 285–300.

Fis Erumit, S. (2016), *Using Gamification Approaches in Education: A Design Based Research*, unpublished doctoral dissertation, Erzurum: Ataturk University.

Flores, J. F. F. (2015), 'Using Gamification to Enhance Second Language Learning', *Digital Education Review* 27: 32–54.

Gafni, R., D. B. Achituv and G. Rahmani (2017), 'Learning Foreign Languages Using Mobile Applications', *Journal of Information Technology Education: Research* 16: 301–17.

Galbis-Córdova, A., J. Martí-Parreño and R. Currás-Pérez (2017), 'Higher Education Students' Attitude towards the Use of Gamification for Competencies Development', *Journal of e-Learning and Knowledge Society* 13 (1): 129–46.

Glover, I. (2013), 'Play as You Learn: Gamification as a Technique for Motivating Learners', in J. Herrington, A. Couros and V. Irvine (eds), *Proceedings of World Conference on Educational Multimedia, Hypermedia and Telecommunications*, 1999–2008, Chesapeake, VA: AACE.

Hamari, J. (2017), 'Do Badges Increase User Activity? A Field Experiment on the Effects of Gamification', *Computers in Human Behaviour* 71: 469–78.

Hamari, J., J. Koivisto and H. Sarsa (2014), 'Does Gamification Work? A Literature Review of Empirical Studies on Gamification', in *System Sciences (HICSS), 2014 47th Hawaii International Conference*, 3025–34, London: IEEE.

Hanson-Smith, E. (2016), 'Games, Gaming and Gamification: Some Aspects of Motivation', *TESOL Journal* 7 (1): 227–32.

Hanus, M. D., and J. Fox (2015), 'Assessing the Effects of Gamification in the Classroom: A Longitudinal Study on Intrinsic Motivation, Social Comparison, Satisfaction, Effort, and Academic Performance', *Computers & Education* 80: 152–61.

Hitosugi, C. I., M. Schmidt and K. Hayashi (2014), 'Digital Game-Based Learning (DGBL) in the L2 Classroom: The Impact of the UN's Off-the-Shelf Videogame, Food Force, on Learner Affect and Vocabulary Retention', *CALICO Journal* 31 (1): 19–39.

Homer, R., K. F. Hew and C. Y. Tan (2018), 'Comparing Digital Badges-and-Points with Classroom Token Systems: Effects on Elementary School ESL Students' Classroom Behavior and English Learning', *Journal of Educational Technology & Society* 21 (1): 137–51.

Hung, C.-Y. J., C.-Y. Sun and P. T. Yu (2015), 'The Benefits of a Challenge: Student Motivation and Flow Experience in Tablet-PC-Game-Based Learning', *Interactive Learning Environments* 23 (2): 172–90.

Ibáñez, M. B., A. Di-Serio and C. Delgado-Kloos (2014), 'Gamification for Engaging Computer Science Students in Learning Activities: A Case Study', *IEEE Transactions on Learning Technologies* 7 (3): 291–301.

İliç, U., and D. Y. Arıkan (2016), 'Second Life Ortamında Yabancı Dil Öğrenimine Yönelik Öğrenci Görüşlerinin İncelenmesi', *Turkish Journal of Qualitative Inquiry* 7 (4): 364–95

Jackson, M. (2016), 'Gamification in Education: A Literature Review'. Retrieved from Abacus.universidadeuropea.es (accessed 1 December 2019).

Jee, H. K., S. Lim, S. Youn and J. Lee (2014), 'An Augmented Reality-Based Authoring Tool for E-Learning Applications', *Multimedia Tools and Applications* 68 (2): 225–35.

Johnson, K. (2008), *An Introduction to Foreign Language Learning and Teaching*, London: Pearson Education.

Johnson, L., S. Adams Becker, M. Cummins, V. Estrada, A. Freeman and H. Ludgate (2013), *NMC Horizon Report: 2013 Higher Education Edition*, Austin, TX: New Media Consortium.

Johnson, L., S. Adams Becker, V. Estrada and A. Freeman (2014), *NMC Horizon Report: 2014 Higher Education Edition*, Austin, TX: New Media Consortium.

Kapp, K. (2012), 'Gaming Elements for Effective Learning', *Training Industry Quarterly* 31-3.

Kapp, K. M. (2016), 'Gamification Designs for Instruction', in K. M. Kapp (ed.), *Instructional-Design Theories and Models, Volume IV*, 367–400, London: Routledge.

Kayımbaşıoğlu, D., B. Oktekin and H. Hacı (2016), 'Integration of Gamification Technology in Education', *Procedia Computer Science* 102: 668–76.

Kim, J. T., and W. H. Lee (2015), 'Dynamical Model for Gamification of Learning (DMGL)', *Multimedia Tools and Applications* 74 (19): 8483–93.

Kiryakova, G., N. Angelova and N. Yordanova (2014), 'Gamification in Education', in *Proceedings of 9th International Balkan Education and Science Conference*, Edirne: Trakya University.

Klopfer, E., S. Osterweil and K. Salen (2009), *Moving Learning Games Forward*, Cambridge, MA: Education Arcade.

Koivisto, J., and J. Hamari (2014), 'Demographic Differences in Perceived Benefits from Gamification', *Computers in Human Behavior* 35: 179–88.

Krashen, S. (2014), 'Does Duolingo "Trump" University-Level Language Learning', *International Journal of Foreign Language Teaching* 9 (1): 13–15.

Ku, D. T., Y. H. Huang and S. C. Hus (2015), 'The Effects of GBL and Learning Styles on Chinese Idiom by Using TUI Device', *Journal of Computer Assisted Learning* 31 (6): 505–15.

Kuhn, J., and V. Stevens (2017), 'Participatory Culture as Professional Development: Preparing Teachers to use Minecraft in the Classroom', *TESOL Journal* 8 (4): 753–67.

Kuo, M. S., and T. Y. Chuang (2016), 'How Gamification Motivates Visits and Engagement for Online Academic Dissemination: An Empirical Study', *Computers in Human Behavior* 55: 16–27.

Kuutti, J. (2013), 'Designing Gamification. Marketing', unpublished master's thesis, Oulu: University of Oulu.

Lan, Y. J., S. Y. Fang, J. Legault and P. Li (2015), 'Second Language Acquisition of Mandarin Chinese Vocabulary: Context of Learning Effects', *Educational Technology Research and Development* 63 (5): 671–90.

Landers, R. N., and M. B. Armstrong (2017), 'Enhancing Instructional Outcomes with Gamification: An Empirical Test of the Technology-Enhanced Training Effectiveness Model', *Computers in Human Behavior* 71: 499–507.

Lazzaro, N. (2005), 'Why We Play Games: Four Keys to More Emotion without Story', *Design* 18: 1–8.

LeBlanc, M. (2000), 'Formal Design Tools – Emergent Complexity & Emergent Narrative', in *Proceedings of the Game Developer's Conference*, San Jose, CA.

Lee, J., and J. Hammer (2011), 'Gamification in Education: What, How, Why Bother?', *Academic Exchange Quarterly* 15 (2): 146.

Liang, M. Y. (2012), 'Foreign Ludicity in Online Role-Playing Games', *Computer Assisted Language Learning* 25 (5): 455–73.

Lim, K. Y., and M. Y. Ong (2012), 'The Rise of Li'Ttledot: A Study of Citizenship Education through Game-Based Learning', *Australasian Journal of Educational Technology* 28 (8): 1420–32.

Liu, S., M. Yuen and N. Rao (2015), 'Outcomes for Young Children's Social Status from Playing Group Games: Experiences from a Primary School in Hong Kong', *Journal of Psychologists and Counsellors in Schools* 25 (2): 217–44.

Lu, A. S., and H. Kharrazi (2018), 'A State-of-the-Art Systematic Content Analysis of Games for Health', *Games for Health Journal* 7 (1): 1–15.

Majuri, J., J. Koivisto and J. Hamari (2018), 'Gamification of Education and Learning: A Review of Empirical Literature', in *Proceedings of the 2nd International GamiFIN Conference, GamiFIN 2018*, CEUR-WS.

Martinez, S. G. (2014), *Using Commercial Games to Support Teaching in Higher Education*, unpublished doctoral dissertation, Montreal: Concordia University.

Martí-Parreño, J., D. Seguí-Mas and E. Seguí-Mas (2016), 'Teachers' Attitude towards and Actual Use of Gamification', *ProcediaSocial and Behavioral Sciences* 228: 682–8.

McGonigal, J. (2011), *Reality Is Broken: Why Games Make Us Better and How They Can Change the World*, London: Penguin.

Mekler, E. D., F. Brühlmann, A. N. Tuch and K. Opwis (2017), 'Towards Understanding the Effects of Individual Gamification Elements on Intrinsic Motivation and Performance', *Computers in Human Behavior* 71: 525–34.

Mora, A., D. Riera, C. Gonzalez and J. Arnedo-Moreno (2015), 'A Literature Review of Gamification Design Frameworks', in *2015 7th International Conference on Games and Virtual Worlds for Serious Applications (VS-Games)*, IEEE, 1–8.

Muntean, C., and F. M. Nardini (2015), 'Gamification in Information Retrieval: State of the Art, Challenges and Opportunities', in *Proceedings of the 6th Italian Information Retrieval Workshop* (IIR 2015).

Neville, D. O. (2010), 'Structuring Narrative in 3D Digital Game-Based Learning Environments to Support Second Language Acquisition', *Foreign Language Annals* 43 (3): 446–69.

Nordengen, J., and S. Brinch (2018), 'Using Game Elements to Increase Students' Motivation for Providing Peer Assistance', master's thesis, Agder: University of Agder.

Ofosu-Ampong, K. (2020), 'The Shift to Gamification in Education: A Review on Dominant Issues', *Journal of Educational Technology Systems* 49 (1): 113–37.

Ortiz, M., K. Chiluiza and M. Valcke (2016), 'Gamification in Higher Education and STEM: A Systematic Review of Literature', in *Proceedings of Edulearn2016: The 8th Annual International Conference on Education and New Learning Technologies*, 6548–58.

Parra-González, M. E., J. López Belmonte, A. Segura-Robles and A. Fuentes Cabrera (2020), 'Active and Emerging Methodologies for Ubiquitous Education: Potentials of Flipped Learning and Gamification', *Sustainability* 12 (2): 602.

Pasfield-Neofitou, S., H. Huang and S. Grant (2015), 'Lost in Second Life: Virtual Embodiment and Language Learning via Multimodal Communication', *Educational Technology Research and Development* 63 (5): 709–26.

Pelling, N. (2011), 'The (Short) Prehistory of Gamification', *Funding Startups (& Other Impossibilities)*, Haettu.

Persico, D., C. Bailey, T. Buijtenweg, F. Dagnino, J. Earp, M. Haggis, F. Manganello, M. Passarelli, C. Perrotta and F. Pozzi (2017), 'Systematic Review and Methodological Framework', Gaming Horizons Deliverable D2.1. Retrieved from https://www.gaminghorizons.eu/deliverables/ (accessed 1 November 2019).

Peterson, M. (2013), *Digital Games in Language Learning and Teaching*, London: Palgrave Macmillan.

Piirainen-Marsh, A., and L. Tainio (2009), 'Other-Repetition as a Resource for Participation in the Activity of Playing a Video Game', *Modern Language Journal* 93 (2): 153–69.

Priebatsch, S. (2010), 'Seth Priebatsch: The Game Layer on Top of the World'. Retrieved from Ted Talks. Retrieved from https://www.ted.com/talks/seth_priebatsch_the_game_layer_on_top_of_the_world.

Purushotma, R. (2005), 'Commentary: You're Not Studying, You're Just …', *Language Learning & Technology* 9 (1): 80–96.

Ramirez, D., S. Seyler, K. Squire and M. Berland (2014), 'I'm a Loser, Baby: Gamer Identity & Failure', in *Proceedings of DiGRA 014*.

Rankin, Y. A., R. Gold and B. Gooch (2006, September), '3D Role-Playing Games as Language Learning Tools', *Eurographics (Education Papers)*, 33–8.

Rawendy, D., Y. Ying, Y. Arifin and K. Rosalin (2017), 'Design and Development Game Chinese Language Learning with Gamification and Using Mnemonic Method', *Procedia Computer Science* 116: 61–7.

Reeves, J. S. (2016), *Experience Points: Learning, Product Literacy and Game Design*, Tempe: Arizona State University.

Reinhardt, J. (2013), 'Digital Game-Mediated Foreign Language Teaching and Learning: Myths, Realities and Opportunities', in M. Derivry-Plard, P. Faure and C. Brudermann (eds), *Apprendre les langues à l'université au 21ème siècle*, 161–78, Paris: Riveneuve.

Reinhardt, J., and J. Sykes (2014), 'Special Issue Commentary: Digital Game and Play Activity in L2 Teaching and Learning', *Language Learning & Technology* 18 (2): 2–8.

Reinhardt, J., and S. Thorne (2016), 'Metaphors for Digital Games and Language Learning', in *The Routledge Handbook of Language Learning and Technology*, 415–30. London: Routledge.

Reinhardt, J., and V. Zander (2011), 'Social Networking in an Intensive English Program Classroom: A Language Socialization Perspective', *CALICO Journal* 28 (2): 1–19.

Rieber, L. P. (1996), 'Seriously Considering Play: Designing Interactive Learning Environments Based on the Blending of Microworlds, Simulations, and Games', *Educational Technology Research and Development* 44 (2): 43–58.

Robinson, D., and V. Bellotti (2013, April), 'A Preliminary Taxonomy of Gamification Elements for Varying Anticipated Commitment', in *Proceedings CHI 2013 Workshop on Designing Gamification: Creating Gameful and Playful Experiences*, Paris: ACM.

Ryan, R. M., and E. L. Deci (2000), 'Self-Determination Theory and the Facilitation of Intrinsic Motivation, Social Development, and Well-Being', *American Psychologist* 55 (1): 68.

Ryan, R. M., and E. L. Deci (2006), 'Self-Regulation and the Problem of Human Autonomy: Does Psychology Need Choice, Self-Determination, and Will?', *Journal of Personality* 74 (6): 1557–86.

Sabourin, J. L., and J. C. Lester (2014), 'Affect and Engagement in Game-Based-Learning Environments', *IEEE Transactions on Affective Computing* 5 (1): 45–56.

Sailer, M., J. U. Hense, S. K. Mayr and H. Mandl (2017), 'How Gamification Motivates: An Experimental Study of the Effects of Specific Game Design Elements on Psychological Need Satisfaction', *Computers in Human Behavior* 69: 371–80.

Salen, K., and E. Zimmerman (2004), *Rules of Play: Game Design Fundamentals*. Cambridge: MIT Press.

Schell, J. (2014), *The Art of Game Design: A book of Lenses*. Burlington, MA: Morgan Kaufmann.

Seaborn, K., and D. I. Fels (2015), 'Gamification in Theory and Action: A Survey', *International Journal of Human-Computer Studies* 74: 14–31.

Shernoff, D. J., M. Csikszentmihalyi, B. Schneider and E. S. Shernoff (2014), 'Student Engagement in High School Classrooms from the Perspective of Flow Theory', in *Applications of Flow in Human Development and Education*, 475–94, Netherlands: Springer.

Si, M. (2015), 'A Virtual Space for Children to Meet and Practice Chinese', *International Journal of Artificial Intelligence in Education* 25 (2): 271–90.

Slovak, P., K. Salen, S. Ta and G. Fitzpatrick (2018, April), 'Mediating Conflicts in Minecraft: Empowering Learning in Online Multiplayer Games', in *Proceedings of the 2018 CHI Conference on Human Factors in Computing Systems*, 1–13.

Squire, K. (2008), 'Video-Game Literacy: A Literacy of Expertise', in J. Coiro, C. Lankshear, M. Knobel and D. Leu (eds), *Handbook of Research on New Literacies*, 635–69, Mahwah, NJ: Lawrence Erlbaum.

Standage, M., J. L. Duda and N. Ntoumanis (2005), 'A Test of Self-Determination Theory in School Physical Education', *British Journal of Educational Psychology* 75 (3): 411–33.

Steinkuehler, C. (2007), 'Massively Multiplayer Online Gaming as a Constellation of Literacy Practices', *E-Learning and Digital Media* 4 (3): 297–318.

Stott, A., and C. Neustaedter (2013), 'Analysis of Gamification in Education', Technical Report 2013-0422-01, Connections Lab, Simon Fraser University, Surrey, BC, Canada.

Su, C. H., and C. H. Cheng (2015), 'A Mobile Gamification Learning System for Improving the Learning Motivation and Achievements', *Journal of Computer Assisted Learning* 31 (3): 268–86.

Subhash, S., and E. A. Cudney (2018), 'Gamified Learning in Higher Education: A systematic Review of the Literature', *Computers in Human Behavior* 87: 192–206.

Sundqvist, P., and L. K. Sylvén (2012), 'World of VocCraft: Computer Games and Swedish Learners' L2 English Vocabulary', in *Digital Games in Language Learning and Teaching*, 189–208, London: Palgrave.

Sykes, J. E., J. Reinhardt, J. E. Liskin-Gasparro and M. Lacorte (2012), *Language at Play: Digital Games in Second and Foreign Language Teaching and Learning*, London: Pearson.

Thomas, M., S. Benini, C. Schneider, C. Rainbow, T. Can, I. Simsek, S. Biber, H. Philp, N. Zwart, B. Turchetta, F. Benedetti, P. Garista and L. Cinganotto (2018), 'Digital Game-Based Language Learning in 3D Immersive Environments: The GUINEVERE Project', in *Proceedings Innovation in Language Learning*, Edition 11, Florence: Filodiritto.

Thomas, M., C. Schneider and T. Can (2019), 'Classification of Games to Be Used in Virtual Learning Environments – Some Reflections Based on the EU Funded GUINEVERE Project', in *Proceedings of Innovation in Language Learning*, Edition 12, Florence: Filodiritto.

Thorne, S. L. (2008), 'Transcultural Communication in Open Internet Environments and Massively Multiplayer Online Games', in S. S. Magan (ed.), *Mediating Discourse Online*, 305–27, Amsterdam: John Benjamins.

Thorne, S. L., R. W. Black and J. M. Sykes (2009), 'Second Language Use, Socialization, and Learning in Internet Interest Communities and Online Gaming', *Modern Language Journal*, 93: 802–21.

Thorne, S. L., I. Fischer and X. Lu (2012), 'The Semiotic Ecology and Linguistic Complexity of an Online Game World', *ReCALL* 24 (3): 279–301.

Udjaja, Y., and A. C. Sari (2017), 'A Gamification Interactive Typing for Primary School Visually Impaired Children', *Indonesia. Procedia Computer Science* 116: 638–44.

Uusi-Mäkelä, M. (2015), 'Learning English in Minecraft: A Case Study on Language Competences and Classroom Practices', master's thesis.

Van Eck, R. (2006), 'Digital Game-Based Learning: It's Not Just the Digital Natives Who Are Restless', *Educause* 41 (2): 16–30.

Wang, S., and C. Vásquez (2012), 'Web 2.0 and Second Language Learning: What Does the Research Tell Us?', *CALICO Journal* 29 (3): 412–30.

Warburton, S. (2009), 'Second Life in Higher Education: Assessing the Potential for and the Barriers to Deploying Virtual Worlds in Learning and Teaching', *British Journal of Educational Technology* 40 (3): 414–26.

Warburton, S., and M. Pérez-García (2010), *3D Design and Collaboration in Massively Multi-User Virtual Environments (MUVEs) Cases on Collaboration in Virtual Learning Environments: Processes and Interactions*, 27–41, Hershey: IGI Global.

Werbach, K., and D. Hunter (2012), *For the Win: How Game Thinking Can Revolutionize Your Business*, Philadelphia, PA: Wharton Digital Press.

Werbach, K., and D. Hunter (2015), *The Gamification Toolkit: Dynamics, Mechanics, and Components for the Win*, Philadelphia, PA: Wharton Digital Press.

Wiggins, B. E. (2016), 'An Overview and Study on the Use of Games, Simulations, and Gamification in Higher Education', *International Journal of Game-Based Learning (IJGBL)* 6 (1): 18–29.

Young, M. F., S. Slota, A. B. Cutter, G. Jalette, G. Mullin, B. Lai and M. Yukhymenko (2012), 'Our Princess Is in Another Castle: A Review of Trends in Serious Gaming for Education', *Review of Educational Research* 82 (1): 61–89.

Young, S., and H. Nichols (2017), 'A Reflexive Evaluation of Technology-Enhanced Learning', *Research in Learning Technology* 25: 1–13.

Zheng, D., M. F. Young, R. A. Brewer and M. Wagner (2009), 'Attitude and Self-Efficacy Change: English Language Learning in Virtual Worlds', *CALICO Journal* 27 (1): 205–31.

Zichermann, G., and C. Cunningham (2011), *Gamification by Design: Implementing Game Mechanics in Web and Mobile Apps*, Sebastopol, CA: O'Reilly Media.

3

Second language development in the context of massively multiplayer online games: Theoretical perspectives

Nasser Jabbari

Introduction

The potential of massively multiplayer online games (MMOGs) for second language (L2) learning has widely been investigated. However, the research in this area lacks rigor in terms of the variety and precision of theoretical frameworks (from second language acquisition (SLA) or related fields like psychology, sociology and anthropology) that can lead the design of the research projects, frame their research questions and be drawn upon to interpret data (Jabbari and Eslami 2019). Researching L2 learning in the context of MMOGs is untenable unless L2 development is conceptualized as the outcome of the interplay between two macro-systems, that is, the learner and the game, each comprising interrelated and interdependent micro-systems or components. Godwin-Jones (2014: 12) highlighted, 'Particularly helpful would be studies that seek to identify what particular user behaviors, game elements, and game resources seem to be the most promising for language learning.' Accordingly, the main question would be: What learner and game-related variables interact to determine L2 development through MMOG play? To answer this question, researchers need to draw on different theories to explain, predict or formulate some propositions about the optimal conditions (e.g. cognitive, social and affective) that MMOGs can afford for L2 development to take place.

Much of the research that examined one or more aspect(s) of L2 development in the contexts of video games including MMOGs lacks a sound theoretical grounding (Jabbari and Eslami 2019) or is not based on theories of learning (Ke 2009; Wu et al. 2012; Whitton 2014). For example, Wu and colleagues (2012) found that only 91 of 567 (16 per cent) game-assisted learning research studies based their investigations in learning theory. Similarly, Jabbari and Eslami (2019) found that ten of thirty-one (32 per cent) studies did not even refer to a single theoretical or conceptual framework. As they reported, among those studies with some theoretical frameworks, Vygotsky's (1978) sociocultural theory (SCT) was the most frequently cited theory but without its principles and constructs determining the research questions, hypotheses or methodologies. There are several theories – originated in different disciplines (e.g., education, sociology, psychology, and anthropology) – that can be woven together to provide a comprehensive foundation upon which different aspects (e.g. cognitive, social and affective) of L2 development in the context of MMOGs can be characterized. A theoretical orientation frames the boundaries of a research study and provides a lens through which the phenomenon under investigation can be explained by first defining the key constructs at play and then establishing the relationships among them. In other words, theory in research determines the most paramount elements of a research study including the research question, the research paradigm (i.e. qualitative or quantitative), the methods or techniques for collecting and analysing data and the lens through which to interpret findings (Reinhardt 2019). Neuman (2003: 65) highlighted the role of theory in research, stating,

> Theory frames how we look at and think about a topic. It gives us concepts, provides basic assumptions, directs us to the important questions, and suggests ways for us to make sense of data. Theory enables us to connect a single study to the immense base of knowledge to which other researchers contribute. To use an analogy, theory helps a researcher see the forest instead of just a single tree.

SLA researchers need well-founded theoretical assumptions to underlie the hypotheses they formulate and the research methodologies they adopt to inquire about particular aspects of L2 learning and socialization through the medium of MMOGs. Therefore, providing a detailed outline and discussion of some relevant theories may enhance the quality of research in this area. This chapter is a small contribution to achieve this goal. To do so, it first describes the context of MMOGs, which has been theorized and investigated by SLA scholars as a potentially ideal setting for L2 development (e.g. Peterson 2010a, 2010b; Bytheway 2014; Reinders and Wattana 2015). Then, a brief overview of Egbert, Chao and Hanson-Smith's (1999) conditions for optimal language learning environment is presented to provide a basis for the examination of similar conditions in the context of MMOGs. The rest of the chapter discusses some of these conditions in the context of MMOGs by drawing on the underlying constructs of SCT (Vygotsky 1978) as the main theoretical framework. These discussions are expanded by providing relevant links between the key constructs in SCT and some related theoretical constructs underlying Long's (1981) Interaction Hypothesis and Lave and Wenger's (1991) Situated Learning Model. This chapter seeks to help researchers construct more theory-driven research questions and design their research studies accordingly. It also aims at providing language educators with insights into some relevant theoretical and conceptual frameworks that rationalize the incorporation of MMOG-mediated activities in L2 teaching and learning practices.

The context of MMOGs

Before learning about relevant theories that can inform this area of research, it is necessary to know the context in which L2 development is theorized and discussed. The focus of this paper is theorizing L2 development in the context of commercially designed off-the-shelf (COTS) MMOGs, which are not designed for educational purposes. Like any other forms of online social media (Kaplan and Haenlein 2010), COTS MMOGs are designed to serve entertainment purposes. These games are played by thousands of players located in different parts of the world. The game players can interact, cooperate and compete to finally level up their characters in the game world. These games, which contain elements of fantasy and science fiction, provide dynamic virtual worlds in highly visually appealing 3D environments. Before entering the game world, players choose the realm (e.g. player versus environment, player versus player) they want to play in, choose and customize their in-game characters (known as avatars) by choosing their race, class, gender and appearance. The gameplay is mostly about gaining rewards and achieving higher levels in the game through completion of various types of quests (or missions), which are assigned by the characters controlled by the game known as non-playing characters (NPCs). Quests involve one or more interrelated activities such as attacking certain enemies or structures, slaying monsters, gathering resources, finding and delivering items. Players have the discretion to complete quests independently; however, as the game progresses, quests grow more challenging warranting collaboration and coordination among players. Players face quite formidable challenges in dungeons (for instance). A typical dungeon (made available around level 15) allows a group of five players to enter. Some dungeons (made available around level 60), however, require more players (e.g. ten, twenty-five or forty) to collaborate in a 'raid' to complete quests. Therefore, players have to form persistent groups (technically known as guilds) to complete quests and accomplish in-game targets. The medium of communication in MMOGs is primarily synchronous text-based chat. For example, in World of Warcraft, the game provides players with different chat channels technically referred to as 'say', 'yell' and 'whisper'. Each chat channel provides gamers with various levels of privacy in communication. For instance, trade and general chat channels are the most public channels that allow all online members in a gamer's faction to read the message and respond back. Two other examples of chat channels are 'guild' and 'party' that are available only for the members of the online guild and questing party, respectively. 'Whispers' or 'tells', on the other hand, are the most private messages that can be shared only between two gamers. In addition to text chat channels, participants can communicate via third-party voice communication software (e.g. TeamSpeak) or simply use Skype whenever required.

L2 development in the context of MMOGs

Second language development in the context of commercially developed or 'vernacular' (Reinhardt and Sykes 2012) MMOGs can be conceptualized as a natural phenomenon (or process) that takes place as L2 is used in an authentically contextualized communication setting (Peterson 2012a; Thorne and Fischer 2012) – the setting in which the learner gets involved in meaningful interactions not only with other gamers but also with the game's environment that features multiple meaning-making media (e.g. sounds and voices, shapes and images, movements and actions, texts, colours and objects). In such a semiotically rich (Thorne and Fischer 2012) and linguistically complex (Thorne, Fischer and Lu 2012) communication environment, the learner undertakes various meaningful, goal-oriented tasks with different *utility condition* (Loschky and Bley-Vroman 1993) – that is 'the degrees of likelihood that a particular structure will be used by learners as they perform a task' (Chapelle 2001: 46). Accordingly, being involved in performing coherently interrelated tasks to, say, complete quests, the learner is exposed to a level of target language that is sometimes beyond his or her linguistic capacity (Thorne, Fischer and Lu 2012). By drawing on his/her cognitive capacities and the clues featured by the game's multimodal environment, the L2 learner attempts to develop links between form and meaning (in the target language). In such conditions, L2 is utilized – as a powerful medium – for a genuine purpose that is co-construction and communication of meaning in an effective and efficient manner. Second language L2 form, which 'can refer to lexical (both phonological and orthographic), grammatical, and pragmalinguistic features' (Ellis 2016: 408–9), is thus focused on whenever it plays a critical role in the gamers' meaning-making endeavours during the gameplay. For example, L2 form is focused on when it triggers a communication breakdown particularly during critical moments in which failure in communication can jeopardize the gamers' (and their teams') status in the game world. On such occasions, L2 learners and other gamers get actively involved in collaborative meaning-making activities to finally bridge the communication gap.

In such communicative contexts, L2 learners can also be considered as autonomous agents (Przybylski, Ryan and Rigby 2009) as they can decide about the class, the role, the gender and the outfits of their virtual characters. They can roam around freely and explore the game world independently. Entirely of their own volition, they can choose to collaborate with other game players in a team or proceed with very little, if any, interaction with other game players. They have the luxury of finding their motives in playing the game (e.g. exploration, socialization, achievement, dissociation) and develop their unique playing styles accordingly (Fuster et al. 2014). Adopting different combinations of the alternatives mentioned determines the quality and the quantity of the target language the learner is exposed to and produces in the game environment. Furthermore, SLA scholars who have focused on this area of research are dealing with a social environment wherein participants' (or gamers') common interests, goals, aspirations, motives to play the game or even common worldviews have united them in small or large 'communities of practice' (Wenger 1998).

Conditions for optimal language learning environments

Spolsky's (1989) general theory of conditions for language acquisition encompasses four macro variables presented in an equation (see Figure 3.1). According to Spolsky, 'abilities' refer to the learner's physiological, biological, intellectual and cognitive skills; and 'opportunity' implies the characteristics of the learning environment (e.g. quality and quantity of exposure to the language in that environment).

The learner's:		
	K*p*	Knowledge in the present
	A	Abilities
	M	Motivation/affect
+	O	Opportunity
	K*f*	Knowledge and skills in the future

Figure 3.1 Spolsky's (1989) theory of conditions for language acquisition (cited in Egbert, Chao and Hanson-Smith 1999: 2).

Spolsky's equation represents the fact that an optimal interplay among cognitive, social and affective variables in a learning environment with well-designed features can provide opportunities for language development. The microanalysis of these variables can lead to a plethora of other significant factors that can play crucial roles in this equation. For example, a learner's current knowledge about a community's social and cultural norms can significantly determine the extent of the learner's later achievements in second language development; or, a learner's 'abilities' to acquire a new language can be affected – either positively or negatively – by other variables such as the learner's current levels of L1 proficiency and the level of divergence (or convergence) of the morphosyntactic and phonological systems of L1 and L2, which can in turn define his/her 'ability' to learn a new language. Similarly, more related variables come into play when the affordances of an environment for providing L2 learning opportunities are taken into scholarly consideration. To name a few, these variables include the amount of L2 exposure, the mode of L2 (i.e. written, spoken or both) and the medium/channel (e.g. face-to-face or computer-mediated) through which a learner is exposed to L2. All these micro-variables can influence the dynamic of the equation proposed by Spolsky. Inspired by Spolsky's theory of conditions for language acquisition, Egbert, Chao and Hanson-Smith (1999: 4) proposed a general model of optimal environmental conditions including: (1) learners have opportunities to interact and negotiate, (2) learners interact in the target language with an authentic audience, (3) learners are involved in authentic tasks, (4) learners are exposed to and encouraged to produce varied and creative language, (5) learners have enough time and feedback, (6) leaners are guided to attend mindfully to the learning process, (7) learners work in an atmosphere with an ideal stress/anxiety level, and (8) learner autonomy is supported. Egbert, Chao and Hanson-Smith (1999) believed that the co-occurrence of these conditions with different degrees and configurations can – contingent upon the learning context – potentially enhance the opportunities for L2 development.

Sociocultural perspective on L2 development in the context of MMOGs

The consideration of commercially developed MMOGs as promising venues for L2 development is well grounded in theories of human development (Cornillie, Thorne and Desmet 2012) such as Vygotsky's (1978) social constructivism or SCT. SCT has established itself as 'a vigorous player' (Mitchell, Myles and Marsden 2013) in the area of SLA research. It is also one of the most commonly referenced theoretical frameworks in the study of second language development in the context of MMOGs (Jabbari and Eslami 2019).

In SCT, learning is viewed as primarily social then individual or first inter- then intra-mental referred to by Vygotsky (1981) as *inner speech*. Therefore, according to this theoretical perspective, interactions with individuals and cultural artefacts – in one's physical, social and cultural environment – play a fundamental role in one's cognitive development. In SCT, 'learning is viewed primarily as a social product yielded by the processes of conversation, discussion, and negotiation' (Woo and Reeves 2007: 18). According to Lantolf, Thorne and Poehner (2015: 207), 'SCT argues that while human neurobiology is a necessary condition for *higher mental processes*, the most important forms of human cognitive activity develop through interaction within social and material environments' (emphasis in original). These interactions are mediated by higher-level symbolic (e.g. language and literacy) and material artefacts/ tools (e.g. computers), which 'serve as a buffer between the person and the environment and act to mediate the relationship between the individual and the social-material world' (Lantolf, Thorne and Poehner 2015: 208). From the sociocultural perspective, the phenomenon of L2 development in the context of MMOGs can be explained by drawing on the key concepts of *interaction, mediation, zone of proximal development* and *regulation*.

According to the concept of regulation, which is 'an important form of mediation' (Lantolf, Thorne and Poehner 2015: 209), the locus of control of human activity shifts – in sequentially developed steps – from object- and other-regulation to self-regulation (Lantolf, Thorne and Poehner 2015). Accordingly, one's development in mastering skills is conceptualized as improving one's independence of object- and other-regulation and gradually moving towards self-regulation. In other words, one's proficiency in the use of mediational resources develops as one advances through developmentally sequenced steps starting from an utter reliance (or dependence) on external mediational means (i.e. object- and other-regulation) and moving towards gaining more control over one's capacity (i.e. self-regulation) to think and act independently in a social setting (Lantolf, Thorne and Poehner 2015). These principles also apply to the development of L2 skills through active participation in the context of MMOGs. In such contexts, L2 as a higher-level symbolic artefact is accompanied – and mostly supported – by a multitude of material artefacts in the game's virtual environment to mediate L2 gamers' higher-order cognitive activities.

The stage of *object-regulation* in the process of meaning construction applies when virtual artefacts in the game environment (e.g. non-player characters' actions, maps and the game's various audio and visual elements) and out of this environment (e.g. game-related wikis and fan pages) afford cognition/activity. At this stage of development, L2 gamers rely primarily on the game's multimodal meditational resources (e.g. images, symbols, colours, movements, (inter)actions and sound effects) to construct meaning. Inspired by the concept of 'object-regulation' as the primary stage of development in one's learning process, L2 researchers can, for instance, investigate the quality and the quantity of learner-game interactions to explore the extent to which L2 learners (at different levels of L2 proficiency) rely on the game's non-verbal meditational tools to construct meaning and the extent to which their reliance on the game-mediated tools can contribute to the development of their proficiency (e.g. complexity, accuracy and fluency) and/or communicative skills in the target language.

As Lantolf, Thorne and Poehner (2015: 209) put it, the state of *other-regulation* 'describes mediation by people and can include explicit or implicit feedback on grammatical form, corrective comments on writing assignments, or guidance from an expert or teacher'. This stage of regulation can be explained by drawing on Jerome Bruner's theory of scaffolding introduced as a part of social constructivist theory. Bruner believed that at the preliminary stages of learning a new concept or acquiring a new skill, children need supports or *scaffolding* from their parents or other competent adults. These supports diminish gradually as children grow more independent in thinking and acting by drawing on internalized knowledge and skills. Bruner's theory of scaffolding was inspired by Vygotsky's concept of the zone of proximal development, which is

> the distance between the actual developmental level as determined by independent problem solving and the level of potential development as determined through problem solving under adult guidance or in collaboration with more capable peers. (Vygotsky 1978: 86)

At the stage of *other-regulation*, L2 gamers (or L2 users in the game context) rely more on proficient speakers of the target language and/or experienced L2 gamers' assistance to communicate, explore, make meaning and act within the game's social and cultural setting. The dialogic interactions between a novice and an expert at this stage of L2 development can provide sufficient scaffolding for an L2 user to make progress and reach the stage of *self-regulation* via benefiting from more proficient L2 users' feedback on his/her use of the target language in an authentically contextualized setting. At this stage of development, individuals 'have internalized external forms of mediation for the execution or completion of a task' (Lantolf, Thorne and Poehner 2015: 209). As in any other social setting (real or virtual), in which semiotically mediated social interactions take place at different levels of complexity, communicating within the world of MMOGs can arguably provide opportunities for L2 users to experience the processes of L2 development through gaining more competencies to think and act independently as they grow more proficient in using mediational resources available in the game environment.

Revisiting the concept of Bruner's scaffolding theory, Beed, Hawkins and Roller (1991) and Wood and Wood (1996) underlined the most essential features of scaffolding that facilitate the internalization of new knowledge and skills by the learner. These features include collaborative interaction between a novice and an expert, adjustable level of support and guidance provided by taking the learner's zone of proximal development into account and temporal support and guidance that dwindle away to nothing depending on the learner's progress towards self-reliance or independence. Researchers (e.g. Lee 2008; Peterson 2010a, 2012b) have widely acknowledged that all three essential features of scaffolding exist when L2 learners join in-game communities and play the game with more proficient L2 users (either native or non-native speakers) and/or more senior members. By drawing on the concept of scaffolding and zone of proximal development, SLA scholars can further investigate how and to what extent collaborative and supportive interactions between an L2 learner and more proficient L2 users can help the learner internalize and develop syntactic, semantic and pragmatic aspects of the target language in the context of MMOGs.

Within the framework of SCT, learning results primarily from social interactions 'in cultural, linguistic, and historically formed settings such as family life, peer group interaction, and institutional contexts like schooling, organized social activities, and workplaces' (Lantolf, Thorne and Poehner 2015: 207). With such emphasis on an individual's participation in and interaction with one's social setting, the construct of *intersubjectivity* also becomes central when SCT guides research. Intersubjectivity refers to the state of shared meaning (e.g. of social and cultural phenomena) that is achieved collaboratively and drawn upon by two or more interactants as a common conceptual ground for subjective interpretation of reality (Jenks 2012). To co-construct meaning and achieve intersubjectivity throughout their interactions, individuals get involved in an array of different activities such as turn-taking, negotiation of meaning, self- and other-corrections and giving and receiving feedback. Based on SCT, these activities allow the interactants' cognitively and socially scaffolded development (Lantolf and Thorne 2006). According to Jenks (2012), studying intersubjectivity can take two different research trajectories: to study how interactants resolve troubles or communication breakdown in dialogues and how they maintain intersubjectivity when there is no apparent communication problem in interactions. Aligned with these domains of inquiry is the study of the opportunities for L2 development from the interactionist perspective on SLA (Pica 1994; Gass 1997).

Interactionist perspective on SLA

Interaction in the target language has widely been identified as playing a crucial role in language learning. Peterson (2010a) outlined two different but overlapping accounts drawn from the interactionist perspective on second language development: sociocultural and psycholinguistic. The sociocultural account looks into the developmental processes an L2 learner undergoes to move from a total reliance on objects and others towards self-reliance in using L2 to co-construct meaning. The psycholinguistic account highlights the roles that negotiations of meaning and negotiations of form play in promoting opportunities for L2 development. In line with this account of the interactionist perspective are Egbert, Chao and Hanson-Smith's (1999) four optimal environmental conditions for L2 learning. They include the conditions in which learners 'have opportunities to interact and negotiate meaning', 'are exposed to and encouraged to produce varied and creative language', 'have enough time and feedback' and 'are guided to attend mindfully to the learning process' (Egbert, Chao and Hanson-Smith 1999: 4).

Many scholars who have adopted this theoretical perspective to examine the phenomenon of SLA have underlined the significance of negotiations of meaning and form as well as interactional modifications in second language development (e.g. Long 1983, 1985; Long and Porter 1985; Porter 1986; Pica et al. 1989). From this theoretical lens, 'negotiation for meaning, and especially negotiation work that triggers interactional adjustments by the NS or more competent interlocutor, facilitates acquisition because it connects input, internal learner capacities, particularly selective attention, and output in productive ways' (Long 1996: 451–2). Long's Interaction Hypothesis incorporates many notions underlying other theories, for example, Krashen's (1985) Input Hypothesis, Swain's (1985) Pushed Output Hypothesis and Schmidt's (1990) Noticing Hypothesis. Long's Interaction Hypothesis lists the occurrence of three most important conditions claimed to be facilitative in the process of L2 development. They include comprehension of L2 input, production of modified output (prompted by either form-focused negotiation work or corrective feedback) and attention to L2 form (or noticing the gap in one's interlanguage).

According to Krashen's Input Hypothesis, the necessary condition for the language 'acquisition' process to operate is being exposed to rich comprehensible L2 input provided by either other L2 users or the context in which conversational exchanges take place. According to Krashen, this comprehensible input needs to be slightly, that is, i + 1, beyond the learner's current L2 linguistic competence. Krashen distinguished between unconscious 'acquisition' and conscious 'learning' processes and claimed that successful SLA is largely the outcome of unconscious processes. Krashen's 'unconscious acquisition' corresponds to the concepts of 'incidental learning' and 'socialisation or tacit learning' suggested by Schugurensky (2007 cited in Sockett 2014). According to Shugurensky, a learner gets involved in 'incidental learning' when s/he does not have the intention to learn but is aware that learning is taking place. During 'socialisation or tacit learning' neither a learner's deliberate intention nor his or her awareness is involved. In other words, 'socialisation or tacit learning is an almost natural assimilation of values, attitudes, behaviour, skills and knowledge which occurs in everyday life' (Sockett 2014: 10). Long's interaction hypothesis underlines the significance of comprehensible input in the process of L2 development. Contrary to Krashen, Long believes in the impact of the input that is made comprehensible through interactional modifications during negotiations of meaning (when communication problems arise) (Ellis 1994). As Scarcella and Higa (1981) maintained, this adjusted input is 'optimal' and more impactful in the process of SLA as it develops from negotiation work that involves the learner's noticing the gap in his or her interlanguage.

According to Swain's (1985) output hypothesis, being pushed – beyond one's repertoire of linguistic knowledge – to produce comprehensible output is crucial in the process of L2 development. Swain (1995) emphasized the role of attention to and awareness of output. In this regard, Swain and Lapkin contended,

In producing the L2, a learner will on occasion become aware of (i.e., notice) a linguistic problem (brought to his/her attention either by external feedback (e.g., clarification requests or internal feedback). Noticing a problem 'pushes' the learner to modify his/her output. In doing so, the learner may sometimes be forced into a more syntactic processing mode than might occur in comprehension. (1995: 373)

Another related notion to Long's interactionist perspective to SLA is Schmidt's (1990) Noticing Hypothesis. According to this hypothesis, learning is impossible without attention and 'awareness'; that is, for input to become intake for learning, it needs to be noticed first by the learner. Unlike Krashen, who believes in the superiority of unconscious acquisition process over conscious processes of learning, many researchers (e.g. Gass 1988; Robinson 1995) agree that a learner needs to consciously attend to and 'notice' linguistic form (i.e. grammar, syntax, pronunciation, etc.) for acquisition.

The optimal conditions for L2 development from the interactionist perspective have been widely investigated by SLA scholars in computer-mediated communication (CMC) settings (e.g. van der Zwaard and Bannink 2014, 2016; Kim 2017; Chen and Chiang 2018; Yanguas and Bergin 2018). This line of research, however, has not been pursued rigorously in the context of MMOGs that are considered as highly interactive social settings. MMOG research framed by the principles underlying the interactionist perspective on SLA can raise a variety of solid research questions such as: What types of tasks within the game context can promote more interactions as opportunities for L2 development? How frequently do L2 learners face communication breakdown (i.e. cases of discourse incomprehension) in their interactions (with other L2 learners and more proficient L2 users) during the gameplay? What are the most prominent sources or triggers (e.g. syntactic, semantic, pragmatic) of discourse incomprehension? How often do the interactants get involved in negotiations and, in turn, reconstruction of meaning? What communication strategies (single and multimodal) do the participants in negotiations apply to bridge the communication gaps? To what extent are these negotiations successful? How far do L2 learners notice (and reflect upon) the gaps in their interlanguage when the source(s) of incomprehension are identified and collaboratively negotiated? How different are the patterns of negotiations across different levels of L2 proficiency?

The second domain of research that Jenks (2012) suggested is to study how interactants maintain intersubjectivity when there is no apparent communication problem. Aligned with this domain of research are the studies that conduct micro-interactional analyses to scrutinize the architecture of jointly produced discourse that yields it intelligible, comprehensible and easy to follow. Mori and Hayashi (2006), for example, studied how first and second language speakers coordinated vocal and non-vocal (i.e. gestures) resources to achieve and maintain intersubjectivity. They found that the L2 speakers' practice of 'embodied completion' 'not only facilitates comprehension but also triggers an incidental opportunity for the L2 speaker to learn more advanced linguistic forms' (Mori and Hayashi 2006: 196). Inspired by this research trajectory, SLA researchers can investigate how and to what extent L2 speakers coordinate talk and gesture – as a communication strategy – to produce a hybrid discourse that can help them establish shared linguistic and non-linguistic resources to achieve and maintain intersubjectivity. In the context of MMOGs, in particular, SLA research can raise and address interesting questions such as: How do L2 learners and more proficient L2 users co-construct intersubjectivity throughout their embodied (i.e. avatar-mediated) interactions using text and/or voice-based chat channels? What linguistic and non-linguistic (e.g. signs, symbols, colours, shapes, sounds, motions and actions, gestures and postures) semiotic tools are available for the interactants in the game context to co-construct meaning and achieve intersubjectivity? How and under what communication circumstances do the interactants fuse linguistic and non-linguistic resources to engender hybrid moves to achieve, maintain or restore intersubjectivity? Or, how and to what extent do these avatar-embodied (inter)actions help L2 learners develop their communication strategies in the target language? This line of process-oriented (Chapelle 2001) research seeks to reveal the extent to which MMOGs can afford the conditions that are hypothesized – from the interactionist perspective – as facilitative of the processes underlying SLA.

Lave and Wenger's Situated Learning Model

Sociocultural perspectives on SLA also view language learning as a process that is affected significantly by the social and cultural variables of the context in which learning takes place. As such, closely related to the core constructs of SCT are the concepts that shape Lave and Wenger's situated learning model (Lave and Wenger 1991). Learning in this model is viewed as a situated activity and is characterized as a process termed by Lave and Wenger as *legitimate peripheral participation*. Mastery of knowledge and skill happens as individuals participate in the sociocultural practices of a community as peripheral members and gradually advance toward becoming core members of the community. In

Lave and Wenger's situated learning model, there are two primary constructs, *situated learning* and *communities of practice*, which will be elaborated and linked to the dynamics of interaction and communication in the context of MMOGs.

Lave and Wenger's situated learning model posits that learning takes place in its non-educational form as an individual is involved in performing meaningful tasks that are authentically situated in social and cultural contexts. From this perspective, learning is experienced, and meaning is co-constructed, as an individual is involved in jointly sharing and developing practices within a community of practice (Lave and Wenger 1991). Lave and Wenger's situated learning model is aligned with two of Egbert, Chao and Hanson-Smith's (1999: 4) conditions for optimal language learning environments: 'Learners interact in the target language with an authentic audience', and 'learners are involved in authentic tasks'. The notion of situated learning is also reflected in some of Gee's (2003) learning principles in video games, for example, *situated meaning principle* and *text principle*. According to the situated meaning principle, 'the meanings of signs (words, actions, objects, artifacts, symbols, texts, etc.) are situated in embodied experience. Meanings are not general or decontextualized. Whatever generality meanings come to have is discovered bottom up via embodied experiences' (Gee 2003: 108). According to the text principle, 'texts are not understood purely verbally ... but are understood in terms of embodied experiences. Learners move back and forth between texts and embodied experiences' (Gee 2003: 108).

In order to achieve higher-level goals in MMOGs, L2 learners (like any other gamers) have to collaborate with other players (represented in games by embodied avatars) – in small or large teams – to undertake goal-oriented and meaningful tasks using the medium of language that is authentically contextualized. In such contexts, L2 is utilized as a prominent medium – in its text or voice forms – to co-construct, negotiate and communicate meaning in an authentic setting as in any other everyday life communication setting (Thorne and Fischer 2012). According to Lave and Wenger's (1991) situated learning theory, learning takes place within communities of practice characterized by joint enterprise, mutual engagement and shared repertoire of communal resources (Wenger 1998). In other words, learning – as a socially and culturally situated phenomenon – takes place informally as an individual gets progressively involved in interactions with more experienced (or senior) members in a community of practice. Eckert and McConnell-Ginet (1992: 464) defined a community of practice as 'an aggregate of people who come together around mutual engagement in an endeavor. Ways of doing things, ways of talking, beliefs, values, power relations – in short, practices emerge in the course of this mutual endeavor.'

The same learning conditions prevail within the communities of practice formed and evolved in (e.g. guilds) and out (e.g. community forum sites and game-external websites) of MMOGs environments. These communities are composed of like-minded game players who bond together, sometimes for years, to share and build on each other's knowledge and experience, to collaborate and accomplish in-game goals, to create and develop their virtual identities and contribute to their communities as committed virtual citizens. In the case of social media in its general sense and MMOGs in particular, joint enterprise or shared domain of interests implies that MMOG online communities are organized on the basis of common interests and shared goals. All users who are identified by their communities seek to communicate their thoughts and share their knowledge with other members of their group. More clearly, online communities develop around goals, interests, concepts and values that matter to each and every one of their members. As another essential characteristic of every community, mutual engagement suggests that MMOG players are constantly engaged in meaningful collaborations to accomplish a set of collective goals. Gamers share and discuss ideas in game-related forums. They invite people to join their networks and participate in a multitude of different activities and social events. These meaningful mutual engagements involve shared meaning-making efforts that are constantly contributing to a user's socio-pragmatic awareness (Blattner and Fiori 2011) and sociocultural learning (McBride 2009). The shared repertoire of communal resources is developed by communities over a period of collaboration and participation. In the case of MMOG online communities, shared repertoire of communal resources refers to a vast repertoire of resources that are constantly shared and developed within communities of gamers. These resources include a wide range of communal assets such as a system of trust and commitment, a set of accumulated technical knowledge and skills, a repertoire of well-discussed ideas and sensibilities as well as cultural and social artefacts (Thorne, Black and Sykes 2009).

Related to the notion of community of practice is the concept of *affinity group*, defined as 'a group that is bonded primarily through shared endeavors, goals, and practices and not shared race, gender, nation, ethnicity, or culture' (Gee 2003: 197). The close examination of online gaming affinity spaces (Gee 2003, 2007), which emerge and evolve within the socially dynamic and interactive world of MMOGs, can provide rich insights for SLA scholars who seek to find out how and to what extent the social structure, cultural characteristics and psychological dynamics of such environments contribute to their affordances as potential venues for practicing and developing L2 skills. For example, Mitchell, Myles and Marsden (2013: 270) contended that 'the social structure of communities [of practice] and the power relations obtaining within them define the learning possibilities available to members'. By drawing on this claim, many research questions can be formulated with regard to the context of MMOGs. To name a few, the questions include the following: What characterizes an optimum social structure of a community of practice that can help to create an environment with ample L2 learning opportunities? What is the dynamic (social, cultural and psychological) of power relations – particularly between novice and expert MMOG players – that creates a favourable condition for L2 development? How are novice members of a community of practice received as legitimate peripheral participants? How do the newcomers gradually inculcate the social and cultural norms of the community and become core members? How significant is the role of L2 – as a prominent semiotic medium of communication – in exploring, negotiating and instilling the community's norms and values? Plenty of other research questions can be raised by SLA researchers who seek to explore the social, cultural and psychological dynamics of MMOG communities and find out how such dynamics can contribute to the affordances of these communities for providing a promising environment for L2 learning and socialization.

Conclusion

MMOGs have recently attracted the attention of SLA scholars, who seek to explore the potential of these virtual social settings for second language learning and pedagogy. Although research in this area is still in an embryonic stage of development, SLA scholars have come up with some promising findings regarding the affordances of these online social contexts for L2 learning and L2 socialization. Reviews, however, suggest that research in this area needs to improve in terms of the theoretical framework(s) underlying its design and hypotheses. This chapter seeks to underscore the significance and implications of theory in constructing solid research questions. This chapter sought to set an example of how the underlying constructs of some relevant theoretical frameworks can inform SLA researchers who are interested in studying MMOGs as potential venues for L2 development. To this end, it focused on SCT and its key underlying constructs to provide some insights into SLA research in the context of MMOGs. SCT is taken up as the point of reference as it is the most prevalently adopted (or at least referred to) in the current literature on MMOG-enhanced L2 learning and pedagogy. The key concepts in SCT are then linked to some other relevant theoretical constructs that originated from the interactionist perspective to SLA. As implied in this chapter, the processes underlying SLA in the context of MMOGs can be theorized and explained by drawing on various related theoretical constructs that come from different theoretical sources. In other words, to capture a wider range of perspectives (e.g. sociocultural, sociolinguistic and psycholinguistic) on SLA in the context of MMOGs, researchers have to draw on a broader range of theoretical frameworks from different primary sources such as linguistics, sociology, psychology and anthropology. It is hoped that research in this area evolves to become more rigorous through being designed and conducted based on an ensemble of relevant theoretical frameworks.

References

Beed, P. L., E. M. Hawkins and C. M. Roller (1991), 'Moving Learners toward Independence: The Power of Scaffolded Instruction', *The Reading Teacher* 44 (9): 648–55.

Blattner, G., and M. Fiori (2011), 'Virtual Social Network Communities: An Investigation of Language Learners' Development of Sociopragmatic Awareness and Multiliteracy Skills', *CALICO Journal* 29 (1): 24–43.

Bytheway, J. (2014), 'In-Game Culture Affects Learners' Use of Vocabulary Learning Strategies in Massively Multiplayer Online Role-Playing Games', *International Journal of Computer-Assisted Language Learning and Teaching* 4 (4): 1–13.

Chapelle, C. A. (2001), *Computer Applications in Second Language Acquisition: Foundations for Teaching, Testing, and Research*, Cambridge: Cambridge University Press.

Chen, J., and C. Chiang (2018), 'The Interplay of Tasks, Strategies and Negotiations in Second Life', *Computer Assisted Language Learning* 31 (8): 960–86.

Cornillie, F., S. L. Thorne and P. Desmet (2012), 'ReCALL Special Issue: Digital Games for Language Learning: Challenges and Opportunities: Editorial Digital Games for Language Learning: From Hype to Insight?', *ReCALL* 24 (3): 243–56.

Eckert, P., and S. McConnell-Ginet (1992), 'Think Practically and Look Locally: Language and Gender as Community-Based Practice', *Annual Review of Anthropology* 21 (1): 461–90.

Egbert, J., C.-C. Chao and E. Hanson-Smith (1999), 'Computer-Enhanced Language Learning Environments: An Overview', in J. Egbert and E. Hanson-Smith (eds), *CALL Environments: Research, Practice, and Critical Issues*, 1–13, Alexandria: Teachers of English to Speakers of Other Languages.

Ellis, R. (1994), *The Study of Second Language Acquisition*, Oxford: Oxford University Press.

Ellis, R. (2016), 'Focus on Form: A Critical Review', *Language Teaching Research* 20 (3): 405–28.

Fuster, H., A. Chamarro, X. Carbonell and R. J. Vallerand (2014), 'Relationship between Passion and Motivation for Gaming in Players of Massively Multiplayer Online Role-Playing Games', *Cyberpsychology, Behavior, and Social Networking* 17 (5): 292–7.

Gass, S. M. (1988), 'Integrating Research Areas: A Framework for Second Language Studies', *Applied Linguistics* 9 (2): 198–217.

Gass, S. M. (1997), *Input, Interaction, and the Second Language Learner*, Mahwah, NJ: Erlbaum.

Gee, J. P. (2003), *What Video Games Have to Teach Us about Learning and Literacy*, New York: Palgrave Macmillan.

Gee, J. P. (2007), *Good Video Games and Good Learning: Collected Essays on Video Games, Learning and Literacy*, New York: Peter Lang.

Godwin-Jones, R. (2014), 'Emerging Technologies Games in Language Learning: Opportunities and Challenges', *Language Learning & Technology* 18 (2): 9–19.

Jabbari, N., and Z. R. Eslami (2019), 'Second Language Learning in the Context of Massively Multiplayer Online Games: A Scoping Review', *ReCALL* 31 (1): 92–113.

Jenks, C. (2012), 'Analysis of Dialogue', in C. Chapelle (ed.), *The Encyclopedia of Applied Linguistics*, 64–9, Oxford: Blackwell.

Kaplan, A. M., and M. Haenlein (2010), 'Users of the World, Unite! The Challenges and Opportunities of Social Media', *Business Horizons* 53 (1): 59–68.

Ke, F. (2009), 'A Qualitative Meta-Analysis of Computer Games as Learning Tools', in R. E. Ferdig (ed.), *Handbook of Research on Effective Electronic Gaming in Education*, 1–32, Hershey, PA: IGI Global.

Kim, N.-Y. (2017), 'Effects of Types of Voice-Based Chat on EFL Students' Negotiation of Meaning According to Proficiency Levels', *English Teaching* 72 (1): 159–81.

Krashen, S. D. (1985), *The Input Hypothesis: Issues and Implications*, London: Longman.

Lantolf, J. P., and S. L. Thorne (2006), *Sociocultural Theory and the Genesis of Second Language Development*, Oxford: Oxford University Press.

Lantolf, J. P., S. L. Thorne and M. E. Poehner (2015), 'Sociocultural Theory and Second Language Development', in B. van Patten and J. Williams (eds), *Theories in Second Language Acquisition*, 207–26, New York: Routledge.

Lave, J., and E. Wenger (1991), *Situated Learning: Legitimate Peripheral Participation*, Cambridge: Cambridge University Press.

Lee, L. (2008), 'Focus-on-Form through Collaborative Scaffolding in Expert-to-Novice Online Interaction', *Language Learning & Technology* 12 (3): 53–72.

Long, M. H. (1981), 'Input, Interaction, and Second Language Acquisition', *Annals of the New York Academy of Sciences* 379 (1): 259–78.

Long, M. H. (1983), 'Linguistic and Conversational Adjustments to Non-Native Speakers', *Studies in Second Language Acquisition* 5 (2): 177–93.

Long, M. H. (1985), 'Input and Second Language Acquisition Theory', in S. M. Gass and C. G. Madden (eds), *Input in Second Language Acquisition*, 377–93, Rowley, MA: Newbury House.

Long, M. H. (1996), 'The Role of the Linguistic Environment in Second Language Acquisition', in W. C. Ritchie and T. K. Bhatia (eds), *Handbook of Second Language Acquisition*, 413–68, New York: Academic Press.

Long, M. H., and P. A. Porter. (1985), 'Group Work, Interlanguage Talk, and Second Language Acquisition', *TESOL Quarterly* 19 (2): 207–25.

Loschky, L., and R. Bley-Vroman (1993), 'Grammar and Task-Based Methodology', in G. Crookes and S. M. Gass (eds), *Tasks and Language Learning: Integrating Theory and Practice*, 123–67, Clevedon: Multilingual Matters.

McBride, K. (2009), 'Social-Networking Sites in Foreign Language Classes: Opportunities for Re-creation', in L. Lomicka and G. Lord (eds), *The Next Generation: Social Networking and Online Collaboration in Foreign Language Learning*, 35–58, San Marco, TX: Calico Press.

Mitchell, R., F. Myles and E. Marsden (2013), *Second Language Learning Theories*, London: Routledge.

Mori, J., and M. Hayashi (2006), 'The Achievement of Intersubjectivity through Embodied Completions: A Study of Interactions between First and Second Language Speakers', *Applied Linguistics* 27 (2): 195–219.

Neuman, L. W. (2003), *Social Research Methods: Qualitative and Quantitative Approaches*, Boston, MA: Allyn and Bacon.

Peterson, M. (2010a), 'Massively Multiplayer Online Role-Playing Games as Arenas for Second Language Learning', *Computer Assisted Language Learning* 23 (5): 429–39.

Peterson, M. (2010b), 'Digital Gaming and Second Language Development: Japanese Learners' Interactions in a MMORPG', *Digital Culture & Education* 3 (1): 56–73.

Peterson, M. (2012a), 'EFL Learner Collaborative Interaction in Second Life', *ReCALL* 24 (1): 20–39.

Peterson, M. (2012b), 'Learner Interaction in a Massively Multiplayer Online Role Playing Game (MMORPG): A Sociocultural Discourse Analysis', *ReCALL* 24 (3): 361–80.

Pica, T. (1994), 'Research on Negotiation: What Does It Reveal about Second-Language Learning Conditions, Processes, and Outcomes?', *Language Learning* 44 (3): 493–527.

Pica, T, L. Holliday, N. Lewis and L. Morgenthaler (1989), 'Comprehensible Output as an Outcome of Linguistic Demands on the Learner', *Studies in Second Language Acquisition* 11 (1): 63–90.

Porter, P. (1986), 'How Learners Talk to Each Other: Input and Interaction in Task-Centered Discussions', in R. R. Day (ed.), *Talking to Learn: Conversation in Second Language Acquisition*, 200–22, Rowley, MA: Newbury House.

Przybylski, A. K., R. M. Ryan and C. S. Rigby (2009), 'The Motivating Role of Violence in Video Games', *Personality and Social Psychology Bulletin* 35 (2): 243–59.

Reinders, H., and S. Wattana (2015), 'The Effects of Digital Game Play on Second Language Interaction', *International Journal of Computer-Assisted Language Learning and Teaching* 5 (1): 1–21.

Reinhardt, J. (2019), *Gameful Second and Foreign Language Teaching and Learning: Theory, Research, and Practice*, Switzerland: Springer Nature.

Reinhardt, J., and J. M. Sykes (2012), 'Conceptualizing Digital Game-Mediated L2 Learning and Pedagogy: Game-Enhanced and Game-Based Research and Practice', in H. Reinders (ed.), *Digital Games in Language Learning and Teaching*, 32–49, Basingstoke: Palgrave Macmillan.

Robinson, P. (1995), 'Attention, Memory and the "Noticing" Hypothesis', *Language Learning* 45 (2): 285–331.

Scarcella, R. C., and C. Higa (1981), 'Input, Negotiation and Age Differences in Second Language Acquisition', *Language Learning* 31 (2): 409–34.

Schmidt, R. W. (1990), 'The Role of Consciousness in Second Language Learning', *Applied Linguistics* 11 (2): 129–58.

Schugurensky, D. (2007), 'Vingt mille lieues sous les mers: Les quatre défis de l'apprentissage informel', *Revue Française de Pédagogie* 3 (160): 13–27.

Sockett, G. (2014), *The Online Informal Learning of English*, Basingstoke: Palgrave Macmillan.

Spolsky, B. (1989), *Conditions for Second Language Learning: Introduction to a General Theory*, Oxford: Oxford University Press.

Swain, M. (1985), 'Communicative Competence: Some Roles of Comprehensible Input and Comprehensible Output in its Development', in S. M. Gass and C. G. Madden (eds), *Input in Second Language Acquisition*, 235–53, Rowley, MA: Newbury House.

Swain, M. (1995), 'Three Functions of Output in Second Language Learning', in M. Swain, G. Cook and B. Seidlhoffer (eds), *Principle and Practice in Applied Linguistics: Studies in Honor of H. G. Widdowson*, 125–44, Oxford: Oxford University Press.

Swain, M., and S. Lapkin (1995), 'Problems in Output and the Cognitive Processes They Generate: A Step towards Second Language Learning', *Applied linguistics* 16 (3): 371–91.

Thorne, S. L., and I. Fischer (2012), 'Online Gaming as Sociable Media', *Alsic. Apprentissage des Langues et Systèmes d'Information et de Communication* 15 (1): 1–25.

Thorne, S. L., I. Fischer and X. Lu (2012), 'The Semiotic Ecology and Linguistic Complexity of an Online Game World', *ReCALL* 24 (3): 279–301.

Thorne, S. L., R. W. Black and J. M. Sykes (2009), 'Second Language Use, Socialization, and Learning in Internet Interest Communities and Online Gaming', *Modern Language Journal* 93 (1): 802–21.

van der Zwaard, R., and A. Bannink (2014), 'Video Call or Chat? Negotiation of Meaning and Issues of Face in Telecollaboration', *System* 44: 137–48.

van der Zwaard, R., and A. Bannink.(2016), 'Nonoccurrence of Negotiation of Meaning in Task-Based Synchronous Computer-Mediated Communication', *Modern Language Journal* 100 (3): 625–40.

Vygotsky, L. S. (1978), *Mind in Society: The Development of Higher Psychological Processes*, Cambridge, MA: Harvard University Press.

Vygotsky, L. S. (1981), 'The Instrumental Method in Psychology', in J. V. Wertsch (ed.), *The Concept of Activity in Soviet Psychology*, 134–43, Armonk, NY: M. E. Sharpe.

Wenger, E. (1998), *Communities of Practice: Learning, Meaning, and Identity*, New York: Cambridge University Press.

Whitton, N. (2014), *Digital Games and Learning: Research and Theory*, London: Routledge.

Woo, Y., and T. C. Reeves (2007). 'Meaningful Interaction in Web-Based Learning: A Social Constructivist Interpretation', *Internet and Higher Education* 10 (1): 15–25.

Wood, D, and H. Wood (1996), 'Vygotsky, Tutoring and Learning', *Oxford Review of Education* 22 (1): 5–16.

Wu, W.-H., W.-B. Chiou, H.-Y. Kao, C.-Hsing A. Hu and S.-H. Huang (2012), 'Re-exploring Game-Assisted Learning Research: The Perspective of Learning Theoretical Bases', *Computers & Education* 59 (4): 1153–61.

Yanguas, I., and T. Bergin (2018), 'Focus on Form in Task-Based L2 Oral Computer-Mediated Communication', *Language Learning & Technology* 22 (3): 65–81.

4

Not all MMOGs are created equal: A design-informed approach to the study of L2 learning in multiplayer online games

Jonathon Reinhardt

Introduction

Vernacular multiplayer online digital games – commercial games not intentionally designed for L2 learning – have come to the forefront of computer-assisted language learning (CALL) research recently because of their attested affordances for L2 learning (Thorne 2008; Sykes and Reinhardt 2012; Peterson 2013; Reinhardt and Thorne 2016; Reinhardt 2019). Having been well researched (see Lai, Ni and Zhao 2012; Peterson 2016), the most well known of these types of games, massively multiplayer online role-playing games (MMORPGs) like *World of Warcraft* (WoW), have been associated with L2 learning affordances, mostly due to the opportunities for meaningful, socio-collaborative linguistic interaction that gameplay offers. These assertions, however, need to be qualified with a caveat, because they may be overgeneralized to mean that all massively multiplayer online games (MMOGs) offer the same opportunities, and that MMOGs are the best game genre for language learning, which is problematic for a few reasons (e.g. Zhao 2016).

Many L2TL (second and foreign language teaching and learning) professionals – educators, administrators and researchers alike – may not have adequate knowledge about how games are designed, in particular, how game mechanics, titles and genres differ and relate to one another (Hunicke, Leblanc and Zubec 2004), in order to understand the assertions critically. Especially when they have little situated experience playing games themselves, they may take the claim at face value. The danger of this claim, however, is that it does not explain exactly what it is about MMOGs that makes them effective, and therefore what might be replicated in educational games or the design of gameful L2 learning environments, including what has been termed 'gamified' environments (Reinhardt and Thorne 2016). Nor can one infer from the general claim that the L2 learning affordances found in some MMOGs can also be found in other, non-MMOGs and in gameful learning activity in general (Reinhardt 2019). Finally, a general claim cannot accommodate the appearance of new multiplayer online games that incorporate new mechanics, for example, open-world, survival and team cooperative designs as of late.

From an ecological perspective (van Lier 2004), affordances for gameful L2 learning (Reinhardt 2019) are contingent on a number of variables aligning that relate to player behaviour, the context of play and the design of the game. While a title usually shares some common mechanics with other titles in its genre, a single game title is designed as a unique combination of mechanics, and each time it is played, different mechanics interact with player action to result in different dynamics, which may include engagement, social interaction, language use and language learning. Therefore, generalizing the implications from the study of L2 gameplay with one title to other titles, even if they are in the same genre, may be risky. A better approach is to focus on the features of the game that can be directly associated with player behaviours, that is, the mechanics themselves.

With this understanding, the purpose of this chapter is to clarify understandings and advocate for a design-informed, ecologically sensitive approach to the analysis of L2 learning in multiplayer online games. This approach considers not only the ecological context and player actions in gameplay but also the designed elements within games that can be associated with L2 learning as directly as possible. First, I cover the history of MMOGs and how the new field of digital game-based language learning (DGBLL) rediscovered them as their popularity grew alongside the social turn in second language acquisition (SLA). Then, I detail the issue at hand and argue that research should take a design-informed approach in addition to describing and evaluating the player experience. I then explain the details of such an approach and its main advantage, that it allows for the alignment of design features and the L2 learning affordances in a given L2 gaming ecology. After then detailing three traditional MMOG design types – role play, adventure/progression and narrative mechanics – I present three more that have emerged recently: survival, open-world and team cooperation. All are presented in terms of how they may be associated with affordances of L2 learning. The conclusion then offers implications for research and practice.

A problem and a potential solution

To situate the issue at hand, it is useful to understand the history of MMOGs and why they became a key focus of DGBLL research. This account frames the issue, that because not all MMOGs are designed and played equally, a design-informed approach to DGBLL that considers how specific mechanics align with learning and gameplay dynamics is merited, because dynamics in turn can be aligned with L2 learning affordances.

MMOGs, the social turn and the rediscovery of DGBLL

Since their appearance in the 1970s, digital games have been recognized for their potential for second and foreign language (L2) learning. Early CALL scholars (Jones 1982; Taylor 1990) understood them as self-contained simulations that could be manipulated through design so that play outcomes would match learning objectives (Jones 1991). Some saw games as authentic media similar to a novel or a movie, for which supplemental materials could be designed and adapted to meet objectives (Meskill 1990; Jordan 1992), and the narrative features of adventure games in particular were recognized for their potential for language learning. There was even discussion of 'game' as a guiding metaphor for CALL development along the lines of tutor and tool (Phillips 1987), but it was rejected because gaming was seen as limited in appeal and dependent on the subjective disposition of the player (Hubbard 1991; see Reinhardt 2019 for additional discussion of gameful dispositions).

From the mid-1990s to the mid-2000s, the communicative potential of networked configurations for L2 learning became more widely recognized (Kern 1995), and the 'social turn' in SLA (Firth and Wagner 1997) began challenging the dominance of cognitive and interactionist paradigms. In particular, new interpretations of sociocultural/cultural-historical theory (Vygotsky 1978; Lantolf and Thorne 2006), which had become more accessible after the fall of the Soviet Union, offered new theoretical frameworks for apprehending the socio-collaborative nature of language development. Inspired by the social turn, other applied linguists (Gee 2003) argued that digital gameplay could be understood as a social literacy practice, recognizing that considerable virtual communities of play and practice (Lave and Wenger 1991) had grown up around many new games. Enabled by Web 2.0, these communities engaged in a wide range of shared discourse practices like discussion boards focused on gameplay strategies, video walk-throughs, gameplay reviews and fan fiction.

While the use of digital games for L2 teaching and learning had never disappeared entirely during this period (e.g. Coleman 2002), the growth of MMOGs renewed scholarly attention toward DGBLL. Because of developments in technology and increased accessibility to broader internet bandwidth by larger markets, MMOGs were becoming more widespread and commercially viable. These games allowed physically separated players to play in real time through client-server architecture, and massive numbers of people, whether friends or strangers, could potentially play the same game together at the same time. Up until then multiplayer modes were more typical of console games, and multiplayer online features could not be core to a game title, since consistent connections and bandwidth broad enough for sustained real-time player–player interactions could not be guaranteed.

Scholars of DGBLL (e.g. Thorne and Black 2007; Lai, Ni and Zhao 2012; Peterson 2016) began to recognize that MMOGs in particular offered heretofore unrecognized affordances for L2 learning because players in them engaged in social collaboration, an SLA concept which now had theoretical weight thanks to the social turn. For example, role differentiation in MMOGs, which allowed players to develop unique skills that complemented others' skills (Sykes, Reinhardt and Thorne 2010), seemed to align with the notion of peer scaffolding, a core concept in sociocultural learning theory. At the same time, MMOG-based learning was also reconcilable with a cognitive perspective on SLA. Peterson (2016), for example, noted that avatar development provided anonymity which lowered affective barriers to learning, that negotiation for meaning occurred in game chat and that the narratives of MMORPGs provided rich sources of input and opportunities for output. Finally, an ecological perspective, which argues that L2 learning is complex, dynamic and multinodal in nature, was also seen in MMO gameplay (e.g. Zheng et al. 2009; Scholz 2016; Zheng and Newgarden 2017). In short, implications were made that MMOGs were ideal L2 learning environments, but sometimes without important design-informed caveats.

Over the past fifteen years DGBLL research has looked at many different aspects of language learning in a variety of MMOG titles, including WoW (e.g. Thorne 2008; Zheng et al. 2009; Rama et al. 2012), *EverQuest 2* (Rankin, Gold and Gooch 2006), *Nori School* (Suh, Kim and Kim 2010), *Wonderland* (Peterson 2012) and *Ragnarok Online* (Reinders and Wattana 2014). Research has focused on showing how MMO gameplay increases learner motivation (Rankin, Gold and Gooch 2006), how MMOG player–player interactions demonstrate learning

(Peterson 2012), how MMOGs may serve as contexts for socialization (Thorne 2008), how MMOG L2 learning environments compare favourably with non-MMOG environments (Suh, Kim and Kim 2010) and how previous MMOG experience may impact outcomes (Rama et al. 2012). To these ends, research has explored how the games are played, analysing gameplay discourse and surveying learners' opinions, usually taking the perspective of the player.

The issue: Not all MMOGs are designed equally

From a game designer's perspective, not all MMOGs are designed equally because they are not meant to be played equally. MMO gameplay is understood not as a single independent variable, but as a bundle or construct of interrelated ones, and while a single MMOG title may share some features with other titles, its particular combination of rules and narratives makes it unique; moreover, gameplay is meant to lead to different outcomes each time the game is played so that designers expect and even encourage play style variation. This may mean in one session there is more or less language use than in another; Zhao (2016), for example, found that players of the MMOG Guild Wars 2, when left to their own devices, took advantage of the design that allowed quest narratives to be bypassed and quests to be done without any interaction with other players. To appeal to broader audiences, most commercially popular MMOG titles today are playable in very different ways, both as theme parks where players journey through different lands and experience every ride once and as playgrounds where players complete activities in whatever combination and order they like; the former gameplay style is made possible by narrative and progression storyline designs, while the latter is typical of 'sandbox' games (see discussion below). Finally, the design of each new version of a game title in a MMOG series like WoW is usually different from its predecessor. For example, sometimes a new title is 'nerfed', that is, made more easily playable by solo players, in an attempt to gain new players and appeal to different play styles.

Growing broadband accessibility has also led to new MMOG design types that stretch the definition of the genre to the point of unrecognizability; the only true common qualities anymore are that MMOGs are online and massively multiplayer, meaning they run persistently on remote servers and multiple players can join through clients and play at the same time, in teams and groups into the hundreds. Besides traditional role play and progressive narrative elements, many new popular multiplayer online games also incorporate open-world, survival and team cooperative elements; for example, *Overwatch* is a first-person shooter team-based multiplayer game, *Fortnite: Battle Royale* is a team-based battle royale with survival and open-world elements and *Defense of the Ancients 2* is a multiplayer online battle arena (MOBA) or action real-time strategy. Each game title is unique because its combination of designed features is unique. Different affordances for social interaction and learning emerge in different ways for different combinations of players.

A design-informed approach

There is a need to qualify the assertion that multiplayer online gameplay promotes L2 learning not only by considering how player experience differs according to context of play but also by shifting research from examination of genres, which are dynamic and difficult to define, to game design mechanics and features. Research needs to more closely examine how multiplayer online game designs specifically impact outcomes – not to the exclusion of player perspectives, but in addition to them. In other words, research needs to approach the issue from the perspective of the designer while still considering the entire gameplay ecology and the perspective of the player (and instructor). A design-informed approach is useful because it can adapt to the evolving designs of new, increasingly popular hybridized multiplayer titles, since it focuses on the relationship between title-agnostic design features and learning/play outcomes, not just on the particular combination of mechanics unique to a single title. In this way, the approach precludes the overgeneralization of findings from a single title to an entire genre, or to all digital games. Already some DGBLL research has taken this game design-informed approach, although it hasn't focused on MMOGs in particular. For example, Cornillie (2017) has examined L2 feedback provision in game designs using an experimental approach, finding that learner-players prefer specific types of feedback. DeHaan, Reed and Kuwada (2010) examined the relationship between learning and player role in action games, finding better outcomes for watchers who did not have to learn rules and thus had arguably lighter cognitive loads than the players. Because these studies have isolated particular variables in their research designs, they have been able to make clearer associations between game design and learning outcomes.

To clarify, the approach is grounded in the concepts of game design mechanics and gameplay dynamics. From a game design perspective, a mechanic is a feature designed into a game operationalized by a game rule that affords and constrains a given type of gameplay behaviour. Mechanics can be thought of as delimiting what is required or optional in a game, like destroying monsters, collecting resources or taking turns. Gameplay dynamics emerge out of the interaction of player behaviour with mechanics, and can be thought of actions that are possible; they can be directly observable, like avatar movement, or indirectly inferable, like engagement and fun. Learning and languaging – that is, meaningful, goal-oriented language use – are dynamics that may emerge from player interaction with a combination of designed mechanics, and with other variables in the context of play, including the behaviour of other players.

Hunicke, Leblanc and Zubek (2004) argue that game designers see a game as a combination of mechanics that afford gameplay dynamics, experienced by the player as aesthetics, which provide a coherent, thematized and relatable experience or feel to the game. The player initially experiences the game via its aesthetics, and gameplay dynamics emerge through interaction with various mechanics and combinations thereof (see Figure 4.1). By interacting with the game at the aesthetic level, the player learns the rules and develops gameplay strategies, often learning and negotiating them with other players. Aesthetic features function as a thematic 'shell' or 'skin' for a particular set of game mechanics, and they can be exchanged out with others; in this way, experienced gamers who are familiar with the mechanics typical of a particular genre are able to transfer their skills to another with different aesthetics. From this perspective a genre is a player-friendly term to refer to a game that typically features certain mechanics, regardless of aesthetic shell. For example, titles in the simulation-management genre may include activities like running an airport, building a city

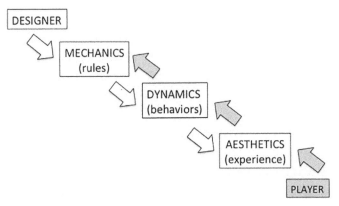

Figure 4.1 A design-informed approach to understanding gameplay (adapted from Hunicke, Leblanc and Zubec 2004).

or managing a restaurant. Mechanics may include game space expansion, budget management or idling (i.e. waiting in real time for a game resource to mature). Seen through game aesthetics, a player understands idling in a restaurant game as waiting for a dish to cook properly, but from a design perspective, it is a means to get the player to return to the game at a later time.

An ecological perspective on gameful L2 learning affordances

A framework commensurable with a design-informed approach for the analysis of L2 multiplayer online gameplay can be found in an ecological perspective that considers the role of affordances (e.g. van Lier 2004; Blin 2016). An affordance (Gibson 1979) is a potential for learning that must be perceived and acted upon under the right conditions in order to be realized. From this perspective, unless the conditions are such that a potential action is both perceived and acted upon, the dynamics of gameful L2 learning will not emerge. Ecological conditions are contingent upon contextual variables (i.e. where, when, with whom and for what reason the game is played), player variables (i.e. the various gaming and L2 proficiencies of the player in relationship to the game) and the availability of gameplay resources in the design of the game itself. In L2 gameplay, this means a player-learner must perceive (1) that they need to know what something means and how to respond or take action accordingly, (2) that they can utilize or interact with an ecological resource to do so (e.g. by clicking on something, deducing meaning from context, interacting with other players, checking a resource, etc.), (3) that they have access to that resource and (4) that they can act on it and reckon with the consequences. From the designer's perspective, whether or not a resource is available is relatively straightforward, because of the constraints of computational logic. Some designed mechanics and features are primary or core, while some are secondary; primary mechanics underlie the basic rules of the game and dictate, for example, movement, turn-taking and what is required or forbidden. Secondary mechanics also dictate rules, but they are not part of all gameplay experiences, or they may be active only in certain stages of gameplay; they may also be optional, unlike core mechanics. To scaffold players into mastery of a game, resources are made available gradually in the tutorial and early levels of a game. In some game designs, resource availability is also contingent on the choices of the player as they make their way through the game, choosing different pathways and/or customizing their avatar and abilities.

Resources in multiplayer games may be distributed among players unevenly and randomly, which then necessitates interaction among them.

An ecological, design-informed approach allows the designed mechanics typical of MMOGs to be aligned with L2 learning affordances. Based on a survey of research, I (Reinhardt 2019, see also Reinhardt and Thorne in press) developed a list of eight common affordances for L2 learning associated with game types (aka genres), including contextualized language use, time, shelter, goal orientation and feedback, languaging, identity investment, location independence and autonomy. Six of those affordances in particular can be associated with the mechanics typically associated with multiplayer online game types (see Table 4.1).

In sum, a design-informed approach is sensitive to the unique features of a given title, at the same time that in theory, it can be used as a framework for analysis of gameplay that is applicable to any game. The approach is ecological and recognizes mechanics as rules, placed in the game by the designers. Dynamics are emergent qualities like engagement or learning that arise out of interaction with the combination of designed mechanics unique to a particular title, but also in interaction with other ecological factors, which can include other players. They are indexed by player behaviours, which are measurable. At the same time, aesthetic qualities, also designed purposefully, contribute to dynamics, and they provide a 'shell' of narrative elements that provide the game title's 'feel', as well as operationalize the rules so that the game can be learned and played meaningfully.

Multiplayer online game types

Traditional multiplayer online game types, which have their roots in analogue tabletop role-playing games like Dungeons and Dragons, have various combinations of role play, progression/adventure and narrative mechanics at their core, which separately and in combination can be associated with different L2 learning affordances, as described in Table 4.1.

Role play

Role play mechanics include avatar customization, the ability to play through the first-person perspective of the avatar and the differentiation of roles among

Table 4.1 Affordances for L2 learning and associated mechanics, principles and game types (adapted from Reinhardt 2019)

Affordance for	Associated mechanics	Commensurable L2 learning and teaching principles	Multiplayer online game types
Contextualized language use	Multimodal form-meaning-use association, interactivity	Semantically related vocabulary learning; contextualized learning; narrative-based learning; narrativization	Narrative, adventure/ progression, open world
Time manipulation	Repeatability, time acceleration, deceleration, and freezing, multiple lives	Time for comprehension, processing and production; working memory capacity; agency, reflection, awareness; comprehensible input; pushed output; development of accuracy, fluency and complexity	Survival, adventure/ progression, open world
Scaffolded shelter	Tutorial zones, levels, anonymity	Scaffolding; zone of proximal development; socio-affective learning principles; affective filter; willingness to communicate	Role play, adventure/ progression
Goal-orienting and feedback	In-game tasks, quests, levels, targeted feedback mechanisms	Task-based learning, meaningful feedback, scaffolding	Adventure/ progression, open world
Languaging, interaction and social collaboration	Cooperation and competition, unequal resource distribution, role differentiation, role complementarity	Languaging; socio-collaborative learning; task-based learning design, negotiation for meaning	Role play, multiplayer, team cooperative
Identity investment	Avatars, anonymity, affinity spaces and practices outside game	Identity investment, work and play; gender, age, sexual orientation; religious, ethnicity and community affiliation; participation in communities of practice and affinity groups	Role play, narrative, open world

players. The ability to customize one's avatar invites identity investment and play; many games allow so many different ways to customize avatars through experience, unique game items that customize appearance and different 'builds' or talent configurations that no two players have the same exact avatars. At the same time, customization allows a player to develop unique skill sets that are meant to complement the sets developed by other players, which then allows for balanced multiplayer coordination in small group or team play. This jigsaw-like complementarity of team roles, based on what is called the 'MMO holy trinity' of tank-healer-damage dealer (warrior-priest-mage in WoW), can promote coordinated strategizing and associated collaborative co-action and languaging.

Adventure/progression

Adventure or progression mechanics underlie games designed as journeys with a beginning and an end. The designs usually resemble a maze or rhizome, with branching, divergent pathways, sometimes with points of reconvergence. Gameplay entails making decisions at points of divergence and progressing through pathways by means of quests and different storylines, which have various impacts on ultimate outcomes. At these points, linguistic comprehension may be pivotal, as a player's fate may depend on it. Because decision-making promotes agency, progression designs may invite risk-taking and the development of autonomy, especially when they are combined with role play and narrative mechanics, which engage player identities. Progression designs allow for the gradual introduction of game rules in tutorial levels. In many RPGs, players progress through levels throughout the game, and at a particular level, players are only given challenges they have a good chance of meeting. In effect, this scaffolds players and provides shelter for mastery learning.

Narrative

All games, not only MMORPGs, include at least some aesthetic, narrative-like elements that complement and contextualize the abstract nature of the game mechanics or rules. Narratives in most games are often language-based, and storytelling or the unfolding of the narratives involves language use. Participating successfully in the narratives therefore requires some comprehension, especially in progression designs where the player's choices influence the development of the story. In many designs, language use is contextualized because it is both represented multimodally and because it is part of a coherent narrative. Such designs afford association of linguistic form, meaning and use, especially for items the player can manipulate or interact with.

Narratives fit well with adventure designs, especially those based on journeys, like the hero's journey (Campbell 1949), with points of increasing tension, crises and resolutions. MMORPGs are often set in fantasy worlds, and the player enters the world as various narratives are unfolding. Quests and other in-game activities may be presented as narratives for which the player's (avatar's) actions are central; this invites the creation of personal narratives (Calleja 2007). Narrativization dynamics emerge as a player experiences various designed narratives through the eyes of their avatar, contextualized in the aesthetics of the gameplay experience; in this way, player identity is engaged. The fictional world or universe of the game that exists in the background as it is played is called its lore; a coherent, well-developed lore can add to a sense of immersion and contribute to aesthetic engagement with the game.

Much of the lexico-grammar of many MMORPGs is complex and sophisticated (Thorne, Fischer and Lu 2012), but since some of it is unique to the fantasy universe of the MMORPG, it may seem impractical to learn it as its usefulness outside of the game is questionable. However, an argument can be made that the unique names and terms are not a detriment but rather a means of creating an immersive and engaging storytelling environment, and that collectively they create a coherent context at the discourse level. If a player is discursively engaged, they are more likely to authenticate the entire experience, even if the language is inauthentic as measured by real-world practical application. In reality, successful uptake by a learner depends not as much on the denotational or transactional meaning of what is being talked about, but that it's being talked about in a coherent way that is meaningful to the uptaker, thus contributing to the development of discourse competence. Belief that learning tasks must be real-world in order to be authenticated has led to game tasks like ordering a cappuccino at a sidewalk cafe, which for some may seem pragmatically useful, but for learner-players may seem gameless and boring. If the cappuccino might contain arsenic because the player is acting as a spy, ordering it becomes meaningful not because of its transactional meaning but because of its role in the aesthetic experience.

New MMOG types

Traditional MMORPGs utilize mechanics typical of role play, adventure and narrative game types that combine in complex ways and lead to the dynamics of engagement and language learning. New MMOG designs, enabled by new sophisticated technologies that allow more players to play and interact more intricately in the same space, have expanded on these traditional mechanics and borrowed from other genres. New rules and parameters appearing in new MMOGs include survival, open-world and team cooperation mechanics. Like traditional mechanics, they may offer affordances for L2 use and learning, although little research has been published on them as of yet.

Survival

Survival mechanics are designed features found increasingly in multiplayer online games that force players to make decisions under time pressure, often while negotiating with teammates, often because something is about to kill their character. Games like *Fortnite: Battle Royale* assign players into small teams that must battle other teams for dominance in an ever-shrinking game space. To the extent that language is necessary to coordinate cooperative actions within a team, linguistic production is pushed, and comprehension may be a matter of life or death. Team coordination and leadership dynamics may emerge as various tactical roles are assigned and taken. The game *Don't Starve Together* combines survival with open-world, role play and team cooperation mechanics, as a team of players must coordinate actions to survive together in an inhospitable landscape, some fighting off predators, some building shelters, some gathering fuel to cook and stay warm and others gathering and cooking food. If too many team members go hungry, they start to go mad and fear overcomes them. Successful communication and social collaboration become necessary for survival.

Incorporating survival mechanics, an L2 learning focused-game might give players different roles and resources and have them communicate under time pressure to survive together (one such game, *Astronautes FLS/Space Team ESL*, already exists and is played through Bluetooth on smartphones). Some time pressure, especially if it is adjusted to the individual capacities of a learner, might promote the development of fluency; whether reward needs to be positive or negative might also be a matter of individual preference. In any case, the mechanisms by which time pressure and other factors 'push' output and afford the dynamics of fluency and social collaboration, in isolation and in conjunction with other factors, remain underexplored. While time provision, rather than time pressure, is often recognized as a positive affordance for L2 learning in CALL and games, the affordances of its opposite – communicate successfully or pay the gameful price – may be going unrecognized.

Open world

If the progressive narrative mechanics of a traditional adventure game can be likened to a maze, journey or haunted house at a carnival, open-world designs can be thought of as a playground, fair or sandbox, where players can do any set of activities in any order, and progressive narratives in the world are not necessarily dependent on one another for overall coherence. From a design-informed perspective, open world means that all or most secondary game mechanics are optional. In open-world games, players create their own personal narratives using the resources and activities provided as prompts or inspiration. While traditional MMORPGs like WoW are not fully open world if played as intended, open-world mechanics are increasingly incorporated into new multiplayer online games along with role play, action-adventure and multiplayer mechanics.

The L2 learning affordances of open-world designs have to do with player agency and choice in finding personalized meaning in a game. While not technically an MMO, the learning affordances of Minecraft have been identified (Smolcec and Smolcec 2014) as focused on collaboration, creativity and participation in player communities. When enough narrative elements are also incorporated, open-world designs may afford 'story-mapping' (Neville 2015), or learning through identity investment. While a progression narrative tells a story to a player by having them experience it, open-world designs provide the player the resources with which they construct their own personal narratives, sometimes in collaboration with other players. To the extent that language use is involved in creating these personalized narratives, open-world mechanics may afford the dynamics of language learning.

Team cooperation

Team cooperation mechanics have grown out of multiplayer role play designs, where players customize their avatars to complement the skills of other players in reciprocally beneficial ways. Inspired by tabletop RPGs and cooperative board games, online multiplayer games – again because broadband has made it more possible – are incorporating increasingly complex designs that rely on nuanced role differentiation. In MOBA games, two teams try to take out the other team's bases, each team member taking on different roles and commanding a small battalion. In the popular game *Overwatch*, players choose to play one of twenty-one heroes, each of which is either a tank, healer or damage dealer class, but with unique abilities compared to others of their class. Random team groupings then challenge players to compensate or balance their performances in relationships to their teammates'.

More role differentiation allows for dozens, if not hundreds, of combinations and configurations that match individuals, pairs, small groups, teams and battalions with and against each other. Game designs distribute goals and resources unevenly among individual players so that an individual might have a personal goal that is aligned or conflicts with that of their group, or an individual might have access to fewer resources of one type, but more of another, compared to another player. Recombine and multiply these variables, and possibilities for outcomes are exponentially diversified. Subsequently, the language needed to lead and participate in such configurations successfully involves not only linguistic but also socio-interactional, pragmatic and intercultural competences. Social collaboration under such conditions necessitates both cooperation and conflict, as well as avoidance, competition and accommodation (Thomas and Kilmann 1997). The various linguistic functions and registers these entail are underexplored.

Research on the design of team cooperation games and the language use they afford might inform the design of game-informed learning activities that go beyond simple jigsaw and basic information gap designs and teach more than just how to negotiate for informational meaning. They might teach how variation in language style and register is associated to status and role in a particular group with a shared focus or purpose – that is, how to negotiate for interpersonal or socially purposeful meaning. What game designers know that L2 learning task designers may not is that when information gaps serve a purpose, that is, when they are contextualized in stories or activities that engage the player's (or learner's) identity, and when cooperation (or lack of it) with the interlocutor serves an ultimate purpose, the exchange is imbued with lasting meaning.

Conclusion

Both the traditional and new mechanics found in the latest multiplayer online games, in isolation and in combination, have yet to be fully explored in DGBLL research. The extent to which they align with the L2 learning affordances identified in Table 4.1 has yet to be fully established, as does the certain existence of other dynamics and learning affordances. The point of undertaking designed-informed research, however, is not to implicate that all vernacular multiplayer online games have immediate application for formal L2 pedagogy. Practically speaking, most will probably need some sort of pedagogical mediation (Shintaku 2016), and many might not be appropriate at all for game-enhanced pedagogy, especially those that do not involve language use or comprehension to play successfully. The point is rather to identify what exactly it is in the designs of vernacular games that leads to learning, within a particular ecology of gameplay. This knowledge, then, might inform the design of materials used to supplement gameplay, the design of educational games specifically for L2 learning and the design of gameful L2 learning in general.

When the mechanic or specific combination thereof is identified, its relationship with learning outcomes can be better understood. It might be manipulated as the independent variable in experimental approaches; for example, a within-subjects study might compare learning and motivation in a game where players play with more or less customized avatars, using identity investment theory to interpret results. A qualitative case study might follow the experiences of an L2 gamer who prefers to play healer roles when she plays in one language, but a damage dealer in another, also depending on with whom she is playing, using discourse analytic techniques and positioning theory to interpret gameplay transcripts. A mixed methods study might record the interactions of a class playing *Astronautes FLS* and examine how time pressure pushed players to produce certain L2 French constructions, and survey them afterwards regarding their experiences and opinions of the game to provide support for their findings. In all cases, the research should acknowledge that various elements in the ecology of gameplay cannot all be controlled for, and thus validity and statistical significance may not necessarily be possible. Still, by focusing on one or a set of interrelated design features and mechanics, a study can better pinpoint what exactly it is about a particular combination of a game, its players and its context of play that promotes L2 learning.

In a world where game-based learning has come to represent the future of education, the first question asked of DGBLL researchers is often which game is best for L2 learning. The real answer, that it depends on the game's design, implies that a designer's perspective is necessary to understand the phenomenon further, and so many dig further until they recognize a seemingly more definitive answer, 'MMOGs'. Until a certain threshold of game design literacy has been reached by those who make decisions about supporting the development and implementation of DGBLL, researchers and practitioners will need to take care to qualify results and educate whenever possible that game genres should not be taken at face value. They are designed, complex experiences that can be broken down into analysable components and operationalizable constructs like mechanics and dynamics, and unless we understand them as such, we miss a key component of how they function as learning environments.

References

Blin, F. (2016), 'Towards an "Ecological" CALL Theory: Theoretical Perspectives and Their Instantiation in CALL Research and Practice', in F. Farr and L. Murray (eds), *Routledge Handbook of Language Learning and Technology*, 39–54, London: Routledge.

Calleja, G. (2007), 'Digital Game Involvement: A Conceptual Model', *Games and Culture* 2 (3): 236–60.

Campbell, J. (1949), *The Hero with a Thousand Faces*, New York: Pantheon.

Coleman, D. (2002), 'On Foot in SIM City: Using SIM Copter as the Basis for an ESL Writing Assignment', *Simulation and Gaming* 33: 217–30.

Cornillie, F. (2017), 'Educationally Designed Game Environments and Feedback', in S. Thorne (ed.), *The Encyclopedia of Language and Education (Edited by S. May): Vol. 9: Language, Education and Technology*, 361–74, Berlin: Springer.

deHaan, J., W. Reed and K. Kuwada (2010), 'The Effect of Interactivity with a Music Video Game on Second Language Vocabulary Recall', *Language Learning and Technology* 14 (2): 74–94.

Firth, A., and J. Wagner (1997), 'On Discourse, Communication, and (Some) Fundamental Concepts in SLA Research', *Modern Language Journal* 81: 285–300.

Gee, J. (2003), *What Video Games Have to Teach Us about Learning and Literacy*, New York: Palgrave Macmillan.

Gibson, J. (1979), *The Ecological Approach to Visual Perception*, New York: Psychology Press.

Hubbard, P. (1991), 'Evaluating Computer Games for Language Learning', *Simulation and Gaming* 22: 220–3.

Hunicke, R., M. LeBlanc and R. Zubek (2004), 'MDA: A Formal Approach to Game Design and Game Research', AAAI Workshop – Technical Report, 1.

Jones, G. (1991), 'Some Principles of Simulation Design in Interactive Video for Language Instruction', *Simulation and Gaming* 22: 239–47.

Jones, K. (1982), *Simulations in Language Teaching*, Cambridge: Cambridge University Press.

Jordan, G. (1992), 'Exploring Computer-Based Simulations for Language-Learning Purposes', *Simulation and Gaming* 23: 88–98.

Kern, R. (1995), 'Restructuring Classroom Interaction with Networked Computers: Effects on Quantity and Quality of Language Production', *Modern Language Journal* 79: 457–76.

Lai, C., R. Ni and Y. Zhao (2012), 'Digital Games and Language Learning', in M. Thomas, H. Reinders and M. Warschauer (eds), *Contemporary Computer-Assisted Language Learning*, 183–200, London: Bloomsbury.

Lantolf, J. P., and S. L. Thorne (2006), *Sociocultural Theory and the Genesis of Second Language Development*, Oxford: Oxford University Press.

Lave, J., and E. Wenger (1991), *Situated Learning: Legitimate Peripheral Participation*, Cambridge: Cambridge University Press.

Meskill, C. (1990), 'Where in the World of English Is Carmen Sandiego?', *Simulation and Gaming* 21: 457–60.

Neville, D. (2015), 'The Story in the Mind: The Effect of 3D Gameplay on the Structuring of Written L2 Narratives', *ReCALL* 27 (1): 21–37.

Peterson, M. (2012), 'Learner Interaction in a Massively Multiplayer Online Role Playing Game (MMORPG): A Sociocultural Discourse Analysis', *ReCALL* 24 (3): 361–80.

Peterson, M. (2013), *Computer Games and Language Learning*, New York: Palgrave Macmillan.

Peterson, M. (2016), 'The Use of Massively Multiplayer Online Role-Playing Games in CALL: An Analysis of Research', *Computer Assisted Language Learning* 29 (7): 1181–94.

Phillips, M. (1987), 'Potential Paradigms and Possible Problems for CALL', *System* 15: 275–87.

Rama, P., R. Black, E. van Es and M. Warschauer (2012), 'Affordances for Second Language Learning in World of Warcraft', *ReCALL* 24 (3): 322–38.

Rankin, Y. A., R. Gold and B. Gooch (2006), '3D Role-Playing Games as Language Learning Tools', in *Proceedings of Euro-Graphics 2006*, New York: ACM.

Reinders, H., and S. Wattana (2014), 'Can I Say Something? The Effects of Digital Game Play on Willingness to Communicate', *Language Learning and Technology* 18 (2): 101–23.

Reinhardt, J. (2019), *Gameful Second and Foreign Language Teaching and Learning*, New York: Palgrave Macmillan.

Reinhardt, J., and S. L. Thorne (2016), 'Metaphors for Digital Games and Language Learning', in F. Farr and L. Murray (eds), *Routledge Handbook of Language Learning and Technology*, 415–30, London: Routledge.

Reinhardt, J., and S. L. Thorne (in press), 'Digital Games as Language-Learning Environments', in J. Plass, R. Mayer and B. Homer (eds), *Handbook of Game-Based Learning*, Cambridge, MA: MIT Press.

Scholz, K. (2016), 'Encouraging Free Play: Extramural Digital Game-Based Language Learning as a Complex Adaptive System', *CALICO Journal* 34 (1): 39–57.

Shintaku, K. (2016), 'The Interplay of Game Design and Pedagogical Mediation in Game-Mediated Japanese Learning', *International Journal of Computer-Assisted Language Learning and Teaching* 6 (4): 36–55.

Smolcec, M., and F. Smolcec. (2014), 'Using Minecraft for Learning English', *TESL-EJ* 18 (2). Accessed 15 September 2019 at http://www.tesl-ej.org/wordpress/issues/volume18/ej70/ej70int/.

Suh, S., S. W. Kim and N. J. Kim (2010), 'Effectiveness of MMORPG-Based Instruction in Elementary English Education in Korea', *Journal of Computer Assisted Learning* 26 (5): 370–8.

Sykes, J., and J. Reinhardt (2012), *Language at Play: Digital Games in Second and Foreign Language Teaching and Learning*, New York: Pearson.

Sykes, J., J. Reinhardt and S. L. Thorne (2010), 'Multi-User Gaming as Sites for Research and Practice', in F. Hult (ed.), *Directions and Prospects for Educational Linguistics*, 117–35, Dordrecht: Springer.

Taylor, M. (1990), 'Simulations and Adventure Games in CALL', *Simulation and Gaming* 21 (4): 461–6.

Thomas, K., and R. Kilmann (1997), *Thomas-Kilmann Conflict Mode Instrument*, New York: Xicom.

Thorne, S. L. (2008), 'Transcultural Communication in Open Internet Environments and Massively Multiplayer Online Games', in S. Magnan (ed.), *Mediating Discourse Online*, 305–27, Amsterdam: John Benjamins.

Thorne, S. L., and R. Black (2007), 'Language and Literacy Development in Computer-Mediated Contexts and Communities', *Annual Review of Applied Linguistics* 27: 133–60.

Thorne, S. L., I. Fischer and X. Lu (2012), 'The Semiotic Ecology and Linguistic Complexity of an Online Game World', *ReCALL* 24 (3): 279–301.

van Lier, L. (2004), *The Ecology and Semiotics of Language Learning: A Sociocultural Perspective*, Dordrecht: Kluwer.

Vygotsky, L. (1978), *Mind in Society: The Development of Higher Psychological Processes*, Cambridge, MA: Harvard University Press.

Zhao, J. (2016), 'L2 Languaging in a Massively Multiplayer Online Game: An Exploration of Learner Variations', *International Journal of Computer-Assisted Language Learning and Teaching* 6 (4): 1–17.

Zheng, D., and K. Newgarden (2017), 'Dialogicality, Ecology, and Learning in Online Game Worlds', in S. Thorne (ed.), *The Encyclopedia of Language and Education (Edited by S. May): Vol. 9: Language, Education and Technology*, 345–59, Berlin: Springer.

Zheng, D., M. Young, M. Wagner and R. Brewer (2009), 'Negotiation for Action: English Language Learning in Game-Based Virtual Worlds', *Modern Language Journal* 93 (4): 489–511.

5

Human linguistics as a framework for analysing simulation-gaming

Douglas W. Coleman

Introduction

This chapter presents a brief overview of weaknesses in the foundations of research in simulation-gaming for teaching and learning. By focusing on the construct of realism in sim-games, it shows that the field lacks a framework for real-world models of sim-gaming events, making scientific study of sim-gaming outcomes problematic. Using examples of a lesson that in various versions over time has had both paper-and-pencil and virtual components, it is demonstrated that modelling and analysis of learning sim-games based on the foundations of Human Linguistics (HL) can provide insights that might otherwise be elusive. It is argued that because HL is couched entirely in the real world (in terms of the physical domain) it has the potential to resolve long-standing issues.

Over three decades ago, Wolfe and Crookall brought to light the paucity of scientific underpinnings for simulation-gaming (henceforth, *sim-gaming*):[1]

> Symptomatic and central to this lack of accumulation [of scientific knowledge about sim-gaming] is the fact that, despite many efforts over several years ..., the educational simulation/gaming field has been unable to create a generally accepted typology, let alone taxonomy, of the nature of simulation/gaming. ... Without this road map and underlying framework, the field has been stuck, despite its age, at a relatively low level of development. (1998: 8–9)

In introducing their second edition of *CALL Environments*, editors Egbert, Hanson-Smith and Chao (2007) lay out what they see as the conditions for optimal computer-assisted language learning (CALL) environments, basing their list on conditions identified by Spolsky (1989); his conditions are in turn derived from tradition, common-sense assumptions and a mix of formal and informal observation. Their list was not built upon the foundation of a coherent, real-world view of how people learn to communicate. Such a theory was lacking at the time. Very recently, Yamazaki (2019) has noted that this problem still applies specifically to CALL, citing work by Sadler, and Sadler and Dooley:

> Despite the increasing number of published studies regarding the use of virtual worlds in language learning classrooms today, the paucity of empirical evidence is noted as one of the major issues in the field. (Yamazaki 2019: 227)

Peterson (2013) noted this weakness when he described the relative lack of studies to establish a firm, up-to-date theoretical foundation on which to measure the effectiveness of computer games for language learning. He attributed this to the state of second language acquisition (SLA) theory.

> It is observed that SLA research is subject to limitations, and that there is, at present, no consensus regarding a generally accepted theory. (Peterson 2013: 51)

As Yamazaki's assessment recognizes, there has been no defining moment of change since 2013. In this paper, I argue that the reason for the current state of affairs is straightforward. Sim-gaming as a field lacks a formal theory of people communicating or of how people learn new ways to communicate. This is because SLA, for its part, attempts to use scientific methods to explore something not amenable to science: the abstract concept of *language*. Further, the problem in SLA goes back to a fundamental flaw in general linguistics. As Yngve points out,

> A crucial difficulty is that there seems to be no scientific way of deciding among the many [theoretical] contenders or among the various ways they propose for analyzing linguistic materials. Instead we find positions and methods being promoted like a new movie or defended with withering polemics or taken up as the latest fad. (1996: 11)

The abstractness of language

The underlying problem is that language is not a real-world object accessible to scientific method. Here is a brief demonstration of the fact. Imagine I point to two pennies on a table between us. I ask you, 'Do you see one penny or two different pennies?' Even if the pennies have the same date and mint mark, are equally shiny and are equally lacking in scratches or other wear, you are able to say with confidence, 'They *look* the same, but they're two different pennies.'

'How do you know …', I ask, 'since they look exactly the same?' You answer, 'Because it's physically impossible for one penny to be in two places at the same time!' I next point to the upper right of the face of the coin, above the portrait of Lincoln, and ask, 'What word is this?' You look and say, 'trust'. When I point to the other penny and repeat the question, you will again say 'trust'. I now ask, 'Is it the same word?' You will say, 'Yes'. Notice that at this point you have reported seeing the same word in two places at the same time. Clearly, physical impossibility does not apply to words (just as it does not apply to grammar).

You might object that words and grammar must be carried by the sound of speech, and the sound of speech surely is a physical event. Yet if the sound of speech carried words and their meanings, how could we have homophones with different meanings (like 'bare', 'bear "carry"', 'bear "ursus"' and 'Baer' the surname) that *sound exactly the same*? If the sound of speech carried grammatical structure, how could there be the oft-cited grammatically ambiguous sentences like 'Flying planes can be dangerous' ('planes can be dangerous when they are flying' or 'it can be dangerous to fly planes') that also *sound exactly the same*? How could we have something in Polish ('muj' 'my') and Spanish ('muy' 'very') that sounds the same yet has a completely different meaning? If the sound waves of speech contain a pattern that carries a word or a grammatical structure, how can a very different pattern of light waves from text carry the same grammatical structure? Finally, if words and grammar (and the meanings they contain) are carried by the sound of speech, how could misunderstanding ever occur unless the sound of the speech is misheard? The sound waves of speech have only three real-world properties: (a) *intensity* varying across (b) *frequency* over (c) *time*, none of which is equivalent to 'meaning' or 'grammatical structure', As Yngve explains,

> The sound waves do not carry their interpretations from a speaker to a hearer as ancient theory would have it. To speak of sounds in a scientific context as carrying meanings is to invite continuing confusion and error. (1996: 4)

Surprisingly, perhaps, this recognition of the nonphysical nature of language is not new. As Saussure – often called 'the father of modern linguistics' because he was primarily responsible for shifting the focus of the field away from purely historical studies – said, 'Language is not an entity and exists only in speakers' (1959: 5).[2] He took this assertion even further, saying,

> Far from it being the object [any word or element of grammar] that antedates the viewpoint, it would seem that it is the viewpoint that creates the object; besides, *nothing tells us in advance that one way of considering the fact in question*

takes precedence over the others or is in any way superior to them. (1959: 8; emphasis added)

Bloomfield, perhaps the most influential American linguist of the first half of the twentieth century, acknowledged the non-physical nature of language when he outlined arguments for behaviourism as the proper basis for linguistics (Bloomfield 1933: 22–34).

Interestingly, both Saussure and Bloomfield created their escape hatches, ways to avoid having to give up traditional ideas about words and grammar. Saussure presented an astounding argument (1959: 8–10) that proceeds from an admission that language is 'not an entity' and exists only in speakers to the conclusion that language is a concrete, objective thing. Similarly, after Bloomfield presented his own arguments, he quickly turned away from them; within the same book, he later adopted what he called the 'fundamental assumption of linguistics' (1933: 78).[3] He did this even though his fundamental assumption required directly violating his own arguments about the nature of language and meaning. Chomsky (see the lengthy discussion in Chomsky 1986: 1–50), perhaps taking a cue from Saussure, has repeatedly conflated the physical and mental. This has led him to co-opt the terminology of science in order to apply it to 'mental objects' created by assumption.[4] For some background showing how linguistics has *co-opted*, rather than adopted, the terminology of science, see corpus studies reported by Coleman (2000, 2001, 2003) which compare the use of scientific terminology in texts in theoretical linguistics, applied linguistics and biology.

Realism in sim-gaming

Realism in sim-gaming has been the focus of a great deal of writing on the subject because it is at the heart of the question of the effectiveness of the sim-game for learning. A key problem, which should now be clearly evident, is that we cannot establish a scientific foundation for evaluating sim-gaming if we begin with a set of assumptions that include language, since language cannot be studied scientifically. We need another way to think about how people learn new ways to communicate.

It may be helpful to begin to find this other way of thinking by first examining how realism in sim-gaming has been approached in the past. I will take this in two steps: (1) first by looking at ways sim-games have been distinguished from similar learning events and (2) then by looking at how realism has been defined in regard to sim-games. Garris, Ahlers and Driskell (2002) attempted to distinguish simulations (a broad category into which sim-gaming falls) from games, citing earlier work by Greenblat; Crookall and Saunders; and Crookall, Oxford and Saunders. Garris paraphrased Greenblat this way: 'A simulation is an operating model of some system' or 'a representation of some real-world system that can also take on some aspects of reality for participants or users' (Garris, Ahlers and Driskell 2002: 443). Garris contrasted simulations with games, which he described, based on Crookall and others, by stating that 'a game does not intend to represent any real-world system; it is "real" in its own right' (Garris, Ahlers and Driskell 2002: 443). For various reasons, many in the field do not find this distinction very satisfying. Compare checkers, chess, *xiangqi* ('Chinese chess', the game from which 'modern' Western chess seems to have developed) and the board game RISK. Of the four, checkers is a rather abstract game of movement of pieces which are identical (until one is 'kinged') to engage in capture and control of territory. Chess, in contrast, associates pieces with actual political and martial entities, yet it retains major elements of abstraction: the queen is the most powerful piece, castles race across the board and so on. *Xiangxi*, on which Western chess is said to be based, strongly resembles chess but has a few aspects which make it seem slightly more 'real-world': the king stays in his court, an area of the board to which the king's counsellors are also limited; cannons kill other pieces by moving (firing) over an intervening piece; and so on. RISK, a modern commercially developed game, represents components of armies in a yet more realistic way and requires a mix of diplomacy and military strategy from players as they jockey for position on a game board. I would argue that one can easily extend this emerging continuum until computer-based combat simulations are included and even to war games in the field, with actual soldiers and equipment involved. Representationality as correspondence with a real-world system does not seem to be strictly 'either-or', but a matter of degree. Still, it is clear that sim-games are often seen in terms of their high degree of representationality, or correspondence to a reference system in the real world. Greenblat (in her own words) said 'a simulation is a form of *model*' (1988: 14). Others seem to agree, at least in essence. For example, Kryukov and Kryukova (1986: 394) said, 'Any simulation game always reflects reality.' Peters et al. (1998: 23) refer to realism in terms of validity, asserting, 'A very general definition of validity in relation to [simulation-gaming, even though they use the term "games"] is … the degree of correspondence between the reference system and the simulated model thereof.'

The question of realism also points up a key difference between sim-gaming and role play. If we look at role play in, for example, Di Pietro's *strategic interaction* activities (Di Pietro 1987), we see that role play typically involves less predetermination of the initial *structure* of the event, allowing participants to create the reality as they go (and even argue about what is 'real'). On the other hand, a role play more narrowly constrains the *decision-making power* available to the learner. It does this by assigning not only a functional role and goals but also often assigns attitudes and elements of personal character. Proponents of role play thus face concerns such as what Schick (2008) called 'breaking character', a situation that arises when a participant-learner in a role play references their own life or behaves in a way that is natural to them, but which contradicts an attitude or characteristic imposed on them by the definition of their role. Jones, in arguing for the use of simulation in language learning rather than role play, said that a simulation

> automatically rules out play-acting, or playing games, or playing about, or playing the fool, or playing to please (or provoke) the teacher. There is no play – either in a theatrical or in a gaming sense – in a simulation, and if there were, it would stop being a simulation. (1982: 4)

In short, the students in a simulation 'must mentally accept the function the simulation requires of them. They must ... avoid standing one step away from their own activities' (Jones 1982: 4), a posture students sometimes are *required* to adopt in a role play.

The nature of communication

The traditional way of thinking about human communication is in terms of what Reddy (1979) called the *conduit metaphor*. The conduit metaphor is a view of speech communication in which a speaker A has in her head a representation of an idea that she is trying to communicate, which she encodes into a speech signal, which crosses the space between her and another person B; B is able to decode the signal because he has identical (or very similar) knowledge of language so that he ends up with a representation of her idea in his head. As many have demonstrated, there are a number of insurmountable problems with this way of thinking about communication.

- The first faulty assumption is that meanings are in words.
- The second faulty assumption ... is that the message sent equals the message received.

- The third faulty assumption is that communication equals the transfer of information. (Lederman 1992: 92–3)

For a brief discussion of some of the major problems with the conduit metaphor as cast against a background of the neurology of speech and hearing, see Balconi and Amenta (2010). Reddy (1979) proposed the *toolmaker's paradigm* as an alternative way of thinking about human communication. In the toolmaker's paradigm, the speaker A uses her knowledge of B in order to construct the appropriate speech; the hearer's knowledge allows him to create the response that constitutes an appropriate reaction to A's communicative behaviour. Reddy, by the way, did not assume this occurs through any kind of conscious analysis or figuring out. The toolmaker's paradigm avoids all of the faulty assumptions above that the conduit metaphor falls prey to.

Maturana and Varela (1992) put forward a view very similar to Reddy's, but state it in terms of neurobiology. They diagrammed an organism in its environment as shown in Figure 5.1a. The outer circle represents the unity of the organism, its coherence as a continuing living thing. The inner loops with their arrows represent the activity of its nervous system. The single-headed arrows pointing up and down represent inputs and outputs to/from the organism's

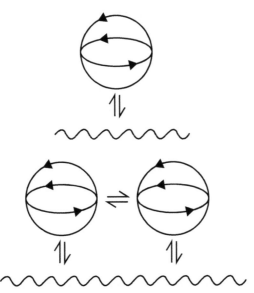

Figure 5.1 Diagrammatic view of organisms in their environment (adapted from Maturana and Varela 1992: 180). (a) A single organism in its environment. (b) Two organisms with structural coupling (in communication).

environment, which is represented by the wavy line. The upward arrow indicates how the environment affects the structure of the organism; the downward arrow represents how the organism affects its environment. Figure 5.1b represents two organisms in communication. Maturana and Varela call this 'structural coupling' (1992: 75). The organisms each are not only affected by their shared environment but also directly affect each other (the latter as represented by the horizontal pair of single-headed arrows). The structures of the two organisms (their nervous systems in particular) are each affected by changes in the other's.

This may seem like an exotic way to express the same thing as the more traditional conduit metaphor, but it is not. None of the faulty assumptions enumerated by Lederman, above, are incorporated in the concept of structural coupling.

A groundbreaking experimental study by Galantucci (2005) showed that none of the assumptions of the conduit metaphor are warranted, as commonsense as they might seem. He used a carefully constructed video game environment to examine the emergence of human communication systems. Players, physically isolated from each other in the experiment, could communicate only through the game interface. Their screens were divided into three sections, the majority of the screen on the left side dedicated to a 'map' of the virtual environment from that participant's point of view, with two smaller panels on the right, one for marks made by the participant, one for marks made by the other participant. Participants were prevented from using conventional signs to communicate. As a participant moved a pen on a graphics tablet, only the pen's horizontal movement was registered; as the mark appeared on the screen, the display in the corresponding panel scrolled upward at a constant rate. Participants' marks were thus limited to the kind of back-and-forth lines on a polygraph or electrocardiogram, or short segments of such lines. There were three different games in the experiment: in game 1, the two participants had a total of two moves in which to find each other in a 2 × 2 virtual maze of four rooms. In games 2 and 3 they had to seek a prey or avoid a predator in a larger (3 × 3, nine-room) maze. Different pairs of participants established different mappings of sign to referent in order to accomplish the same moves. In fact, Galantucci found that the two participants in each pair, when cooperating to 'win' a game, did not need to have the same conscious understanding of the meaning of a shared sign they had adopted for communication.

In Maturana and Varela's terms, the pair needed only to 'know' in the sense of being able to engage in *effective action* (1992: 29), or as Winograd and Flores put it, 'Practical understanding is more fundamental than detached theoretical understanding … we do not relate to things primarily by having representations [or conscious understanding] of them' (1986: 33). Winograd and Flores invoke Heidegger's concept of 'thrownness' to help explain this. Here is my own example adapted from one of theirs. Suppose you are a foreign language learner and are faced with a situation in which you do not understand a native speaker. You wonder, 'What does he mean?' and start to reflect on vocabulary and grammatical rules you learned in class. You may think you are doing this in order to come up with an appropriate response. But the fact is that by stopping to reflect on what to do next, you have not been able to avoid taking action. Your silence will itself have a communicative effect on the native speaker. In Heiddeger's terms, you experience 'thrownness' in the situation in which you find yourself; this happens because real life does not have a pause button like some single-player video games.

Thus, if the signals transmitted back and forth from one participant to the other in Galantucci's experiment cause changes of state in them that maintain the stability of the pair's structural coupling (i.e. allow them to successfully *take action* in the game cooperatively over time), then this is what really matters. Their conscious understanding of the meaning of the marks they shared does not matter. This illustrates the essence of the toolmaker's paradigm and shows the toolmaker's paradigm to be an essentially *social* statement about how communication occurs.

While communication involves changes in the state of participants, a coherent view of it requires that we step back and look not only at the physical reality of individuals involved but also at the larger real-world system of which they are both part. This supports a very important idea about realism in sim-gaming: it is important to view realism in terms of *functional social processes* involving participants, not merely the structural aspects of the sim-game. This realization is not new; scattered references to it go back at least two or three decades; see, for example, Crookall et al. (1986: 346), Christopher and Smith (1990: 3) and Hubbard (1991: 222). The idea that social function matters more than structure in determining realism also accords with recent research showing that the human brain has evolved as an organ possessing a largely social function (Franks 2010: 39–61).

The focus of linguistics on language is a problem not only because it chooses as its foundation an object of study that is not amenable to scientific method. Because language is an abstraction rather than a real-world entity, the idea of *contextualizing language in a real situation* is oxymoronic. A thing that is not physically real cannot be placed in a real-world context. This is why linguistic theories which focus on language cannot extend their formal apparatus (grammar) to deal with communication at a social level. People communicating are in the real world, and thus are of a different order of existence from language.

Human Linguistics

HL is a theory of people communicating, so it begins with *people as living beings* instead of with the *ancient philosophical construct of language*. The theory is still being developed, but its foundations were laid out by Victor H. Yngve in several papers and books, especially in Yngve (1996) and Yngve and Wąsik (2004).[5] HL studies physical systems at two different levels: individual and social. HL's model of the individual level – containing all of the properties of the person relevant to a general ability to communicate – is the *communicating individual*; when the communicating individual takes part in an interaction, the relevant part of the person is modelled as a *participant* in the interaction. Communicative interactions are modelled as *linkages*, which include not only as their subparts the participants but also *props* (which model relevant objects and their properties), the *setting* (which models the relevant properties of the environment in which the communication takes place) and *channels* (which model the relevant energy flow and means of energy flow among people and objects). See Yngve (1996: 126–33).

Suppose you are in a bakery and, when it is your turn, you point to a pile of cheese Danish and say, 'Five, please.' The employee will interpret your request as a quantity. Suppose you enter an elevator that already has a fellow passenger who happens to be standing next to the control panel; you point to the control panel and say, 'Five please.' The other person will interpret your request as a floor number. The difference is due primarily to the effect of the setting (bakery vs. elevator) and a prop (the pile of cheese Danish vs. the control panel). Such differences in interpretation are ubiquitous in real-world communication; further, *there is absolutely no evidence that either person treats the speech as ambiguous.* Unlike theories of language which would treat 'Five, please' as an ambiguous utterance, HL models are designed to describe the interpretation on the basis of the real-world environment in which communication occurs.

HL also models both structural and functional aspects of each system within its scope. For example, the structural properties of a person in a communicative interaction are modelled as a *participant*, but the functional aspects of that person are modelled as a *role part*. Similarly, the functional aspect of energy flow corresponding to a channel sometimes needs to be modelled separately from its structural aspect; so in addition to the *channel*, an HL description may also refer to a *channel part*, the functional aspect of the energy flow. HL also models *prop parts* and *setting parts*. Suppose you are in a checkout line and, when it is time to pay, the cashier says, 'That'll be one twenty-five.' Whether you hand the cashier (a) a one dollar bill printed in 2009 and a quarter or (b) a dollar bill printed in 2013, two dimes, and a nickel, the outcome is the same. Either combination of bill and coin(s) has exactly the same functional aspect with regard to your communicative interaction, that is, the same prop part. Suppose you are in a fast food restaurant, you complete your order and the employee asks, 'Anything else?' If (a) you say 'No, thanks' or (b) you just smile and shake your head, the outcome is the same. 'No, thanks' and the smiling head shake have the same channel part in this case.

A very powerful theoretical construct of HL was introduced by Yngve and elaborated later (Yngve 2006, 2007; Yngve and Burazer 2009), the *orthoconcept*, a functional property of a person which represents their understanding of an interaction, another person, or of a prop, setting or channel. The orthoconcept as a theoretical construct has been shown to be central to the analysis of understanding versus misunderstanding, misspeaking versus lying and other phenomena traditionally considered peripheral to linguistics or even 'nonlinguistic' in nature (see e.g. Brezar 2004; Coleman 2006; Sypniewski and Coleman 2011; Coleman forthcoming).

HL has a formal notation for describing structural and functional systems, their properties and the cause–effect relations among them. Because the notation is based on a temporal Boolean logic (Yngve 1996: 246–74), it is theory-neutral in the sense that it does not begin with assumptions about linguistic elements such as phonemes, morphemes and so on. Rather, it allows the researcher to infer the relevant structural and functional elements of systems based on observation of real-world cases.

Example analysis: Two maps used for a street directions lesson

Because they so clearly show the connection between understanding and effective action, I will examine examples from an ESL lesson on street directions; these materials developed over a period of a number of years, changing significantly. The lesson was part of a teacher-training course in which graduate student

Figure 5.2 Two views of a three-dimensional map used for a street directions lesson: (a) At left, the map seen from above, looking down; (b) at right, the same area of the map seen from a sitting position as if viewing it during a lesson. Note the effect of 3D objects blocking the view of signage and even of the streets themselves.

Figure 5.2 *Continued*

interns practice-taught a public-service ESL class for adult students from the community around the university. Every version of the lesson incorporated a physical (i.e. not virtual) map for demonstration of communication behaviours and for briefing of the street directions task, so I will first consider the form of that map.

At one point in the history of the lesson's development, it was suggested that a more realistic-looking map would better engage and motivate students. Discussion with graduate student interns led to the idea of making the map a three-dimensional architect's model kind of representation, with 3D landscape, buildings, trees and so on. The landscape was formed from papier-mâché over screen stapled to a thin plywood base, to produce a slightly hilly effect. Buildings (and a bridge) were cut from wood scraps, and trees (about 1" tall) were purchased from a hobby outlet. Signage (street names, stop signs, yield signs, RR crossing signs) and traffic lights were on flat markers attached to road surfaces. Some buildings to be used as landmarks were identified with decals on their roofs. See the left side of Figure 5.2 for an overview of a portion of the map.

The left-hand image in Figure 5.2 is based on a photo taken of the map while standing and looking down at it. Note what happens to the readability of the map, however, for viewers sitting at a table, as they are when actually engaged in the lesson. Although the contours of the landscape and the 3D quality of buildings and trees seem to contribute to realism, that *feeling* of realism is dependent on *structural* correspondence between the map elements and the reference system. However, restrictions on the ability to see and actually navigate the map make the 3D map functionally *less* realistic than a flat one, not more so. Students taking the lesson remarked that they found the 3D map more realistic compared to an older, flat map used for the same lesson, but their task behaviour also showed they had a harder time navigating it.

HL might label the overall physical system, or linkage, involved in the use of this map in the lesson as [Map Lesson]. If two teaching interns and eight students were involved, [Map Lesson] would be described in terms of its subsystems as [Map Lesson] = [Intern1] + [Intern2] + [Student1] + [Student2] + [Student3] + [Student4] + [Student5] + [Student6] + [Student7] + [Student8] + [City] + [Marker]. The subsystem [City] is a prop which models the map, and [Marker] is a prop which models a small figure made to resemble a person used to indicate movement on the map, much like a game piece on a game board. In addition to the above, [Speech] and [Gesture] could indicate two relevant channels, and [Classroom] could label the setting. Corresponding to each of these is the functional part of that system, usually also labelled with square brackets []. Perceived realism from the point of view of any given participant must be kept distinct from the functional realism of the system. The functional realism of the system depends on the correspondence between a map element and a corresponding element in the real world in terms of how participants orient their representation to the map element versus how they later orient themselves to some aspect of the real world. So, to take a simple example, suppose a stop sign is shown in an appropriate location on the map as a red octagon and a participant is told, 'Turn right at the stop sign.' If the student moving the marker turns right onto the image of the cross street at the stop sign, and, when told the same thing in the real world, can perform an analogous action, then we can say the simulation has functional realism. Functional realism arises from a comparison of the properties of two linkages, one in a sim-game, the other in the real world.

In contrast, *perceived* realism is not a property of a linkage, but of a participant. Participants in a linkage are also observers of the linkage in which they are a part. HL represents this in terms of an *observing linkage*, which consists of a participant and the linkage being observed: [Map Lesson Obs] = [Observer] + [Map Lesson]. Here, [Learner] is a role part associated with one of the learners ('Obs' is a shorthand way to indicate that the linkage being defined is an observing linkage, not a 'regular' one). HL describes the property of perceived realism for that observer as [Learner]<[Map Lesson]<realistic>>. This identifies the system, [Learner], which has the property. The pointed < > brackets identify all that follows, <[Map Lesson]<realistic>>, as a property of the observer. In this case, [Learner]<[Map Lesson]<realistic>> describes the observer's understanding that the map lesson is realistic. It does not describe the realism of the lesson or of the map itself. HL also allows the modelling of an observer's understanding of individual elements of [Map Lesson] such as [Learner]<[City]<realistic>>, which assigns the property <[City]<realistic>> to the learner.

Chapelle and Liu (2007) correctly argued that learner perception of realism cannot be equated with task authenticity, but that it is the correspondence between a learning task and a real-world task to be faced later outside the classroom that matters most. In this way, they defined realism in terms of functional properties related to *effective action* rather than superficial structural factors which might affect learners' *consciously reported perceptions*. HL notation is not needed in order for such insights to arise. However, it does provide a way to make them explicit. It also provides a formal mechanism to describe cause–effect relations within complex systems, based on their properties and how these properties interact. Suppose that we confirm experimentally that perception of realism of the map prop triggers (::) an increase in learner motivation. We could then make a predictive statement like [Learner]<[City]<realistic>>:: [Learner]<motivation+>, where <motivation+> is a procedural property of the learner which increases motivation from its current level to a higher threshold. The formal statement [Learner]<[City]<realistic>>:: [Learner]<motivation+> has no effect if [Learner]<[City]>hastheproperty<realistic>,thatis,if[Learner]<[City]<realistic>> is TRUE. Its effect depends on [Learner]<[City]<realistic>> being TRUE.[6]

Example analysis: Flat map versus a 3D game environment

Early on, it was discovered that there were problems in functional realism with any two-dimensional map. In a segment of the lesson to assess learning, an intern directed the learner from an arbitrary location on the board to a destination. The learner could see the destination, which made the task completely artificial. (If a person knows where they are going, they do not need directions.) This issue became obvious immediately, so the interns took up the markers that labelled buildings and replaced them, in new locations, face down. This reduced the problem but did not eliminate it; as the learner moved across the board in accordance with directions from the intern, the number of face-down building markers in the appropriate direction was quickly reduced. Combined with the layout of the roads, it became more and more possible for the learner to guess correctly where to go without adequate understanding of the intern's speech. It was soon realized that the 'God's-Eye' point of view of a flat map gave the learner too much information, making a large part of the intern's directions moot. Because it was still in the later 1990s, options for appropriate immersive 3D environments were limited. Online possibilities tended towards fantasy scenarios, such as *Neverwinter*, or ran too slowly on institutionally available computers, such as *ActiveWorlds*. Eventually, *Sim Copter* was chosen on an experimental basis, as it was designed to allow a player to exit the helicopter and walk around in any city created in the format used for *Sim City*, a city-building/simulation game still popular at the time. Having been designed as a single-user game that did not require communication over the internet, *Sim Copter* ran very well on basic PCs that were available at the time.

   Sim Copter resolved the problem of the person receiving directions having a 'God's-Eye' view of the streets. Because the player's view was limited to street level, it was impossible for them to see the destination, and, usually, impossible for them to see more than a block or two ahead unless they were on a hill looking down across an open area. We could describe the new linkage in more or less the same terms as the linkage involving the flat map, but with [City] being a HL model of the virtual environment in *Sim Copter*. If we see that learner behaviour when hearing directions more closely resembles the appropriate behaviour in the real world, then we could say that the three-dimensional, immersive nature of the *Sim Copter* environment <3D immersive> caused an actual increase in realism <realistic+>. In HL notation, this would be [City]<3D immersive>:: [City]<realistic+>. It is important to note the difference between the properties [City]<realistic>, which is a property of the map, and [Learner]<[City]<realistic>>, which is a property of the learner, that is, the learner's perception of the map. Similarly, if increasing the realism of the representation of the city (by map vs. 3D environment) increases realism in the task overall, we need to be careful to distinguish [Map Lesson]<realistic>, which is a property of a linkage (the realism of the task), from [Learner]<[Map Lesson]<realistic>>, which is a property of the learner (the learner's *perception* of its realism).[7]

Example analysis: An OpenSim city as follow-up to a map

Some years later, the author acquired *OpenSim*, an open-source platform created to look and function like *Second Life*, and also acquired the use of a campus server on which to install it. In this later version of the street directions lesson, a map was still used to provide input and to make initial comprehension checks. The immersive environment served as a way to check for the validity of the simulation by placing the learner in an environment where viewpoint and mobility closely resembled those of the real world. Figure 5.3 shows a screen capture of an avatar in the city (New Victoria) created using the Open Sim platform. Realistic details included street name signs, stop signs, traffic lights, crosswalks, sidewalks and so on. The scenario included dead ends, roundabouts, hilly terrain, bridges and other realistic features as well.

The teaching intern would locate their avatar somewhere within the one square kilometre space of the simulated environment. The learner's avatar would be initialized inside the heliport terminal in one corner of the region. Using the conceit that the learner and intern were in touch by mobile phone, the intern gave directions by voice to the learner. The learner used a computer at the front of the room which was connected to a projection/speaker system so that other learners could also see and hear what the learner-participant heard and saw, as well as what actions the learner-participant was performing. The design of the lesson stipulated that the intern would be in another room and

Figure 5.3 OpenSim street-level view.

that the conversation with the learner would be by OpenSim voice chat. One intern, however, decided that it would make no difference if she were in the same room with the learner. She reported that she wanted to see better what was going on. This decision was a mistake, predicted ahead of time by a preliminary HL analysis of the design. If the intern had been out of the room, she would not have seen what the learner-participant was doing; in short, she would not have seen if that learner took a wrong turn, went too far or did not go far enough. Seeing the learner make errors affected the intern's behaviour. She would say things like 'Stop! You're going the wrong way!' or 'You passed it. Go back and turn left.' HL predicted that the intern being in the room gave the intern knowledge she should not have possessed in a real situation, which we would model as properties (specifically, orthoconcepts) associated with her role part. From those properties that differed drastically from ones she would have in the real world, we could predict unrealistic behaviour on her part.

Concluding remarks

Simulation-gaming has suffered from the lack of a rigorous, formal framework of analysis. With a discussion centred on the construct of realism, particularly on functional, as opposed to structural, realism, I have laid out the basics of a HL approach to the description and analysis of sim-games. Elsewhere, HL has been shown already to be applicable from the individual level to the social level (from the description of speech mechanisms – in Coleman 2004 or Honorof 2004, for example – to how groups interact – in Yngve 2004 or Brezar 2004, for example). HL can also provide the foundation for research in simulation-gaming that so far has eluded the field of sim-gaming and learning how to communicate.

Notes

1   I will use the term 'simulation-gaming', usually shortened to 'sim-gaming', to refer to a particular type of activity. The term is essentially interchangeable with 'simulation/ gaming', 'simulation game' or 'gaming simulation'. It is distinct from 'game', 'gaming', 'role play' and variants such as 'role-play game'. See below for more about this.

2   It is important to note that, although *Saussure's Course in General Linguistics* carries a date of 1959 for its English translation, the original was published in French in 1915, over a century ago.

3   Bloomfield's fundamental assumption of linguistics states, 'In every speech-community some utterances are alike in form and meaning' (1933: 78). The assumption requires that 'meaning' be determined from the linguist's intuition, even though his earlier arguments (22–7) showed this approach to be unscientific.

4   Chomsky has explicitly asserted that theories of I-Language (supposedly an internal property of the 'mind/brain') are theories of something 'real and definite', while theories of 'E-Language' (observable speech behaviours) 'if sensible at all, have some different and more obscure status *because there is no corresponding real-world object* [emphasis added]' (1986: 27). In Chomsky's view, the abstract (mind) is more real than the physical (speech).

5   Human linguistics is also sometimes called 'hard-science linguistics' (thus 'HL' or 'HSL'). The former term focuses on the object of study – people communicating – while the latter focuses on its methods – those of science rather than those of philosophy. In the context of a discussion of teaching and learning (rather than on linguistic metatheory), 'HL' seems the more appropriate label.

6   [Observer]<[City]<realistic>>:: [Observer]<motivation+> is termed a *setting procedure* in HL. A setting procedure in the form *a:: b* means that *b* will become Boolean TRUE if the value of *a* changes from FALSE to TRUE. If *a* later changes back to FALSE, the setting procedure has no additional effect; *b* stays TRUE. This is why a setting procedure can be thought of as being like a trigger (letting go of a gun's trigger does not draw the bullet back into the gun). A setting procedure is not exclusive: there may be another cause of *b* becoming TRUE; if such were the case, another additional setting procedure might be needed.

7   There are other, more subtle ways structural realism interferes with functional realism. In the input/briefing component of the lesson, consider directions such as 'Go two blocks', 'Turn left at the third traffic light', 'Continue on to Broad Street' (which happens to be four blocks away) and so on. Picture moving a marker on a game board-style map; then, picture moving a walking avatar in a 3D environment. The 3D environment gets in the way of the teacher's ability to provide adequate quantities of input (by slowing down the pace and restricting the view – exactly the same characteristics which in an assessment phase make the 3D environment more realistic).

References

Balconi, M., and S. Amenta (2010), 'From Pragmatics to Neuropragmatics', in M. Balconi (ed.), *Neuropsychology of Communication*, 93–109, New York: Springer Verlag.

Bloomfield, L. (1933), *Language*, New York: Henry Holt.

Brezar, M. S. (2004), 'Analysis of a Business Negotiation', in V. H. Yngve and Z. Wąsik (eds), *Hard-Science Linguistics*, 142–73, New York: Continuum.

Chapelle, C., and H.-M. Liu (2007), 'Theory and Research: Investigating Authenticity', in J. Egbert and E. Hanson-Smith (eds), *CALL Environments*, 111–30, Alexandria, VA: Teachers of English to Speakers of Other Languages.

Chomsky, N. (1986), *Knowledge of Language: Its Nature, Origin, and Use*, New York: Praeger.

Christopher, E. M., and L. E. Smith (1990), 'Shaping the Content of Simulation/Games', in D. Crookall and R. L. Oxford (eds), *Simulation, Gaming, and Language Learning*, 47–54, New York: Newbury House/Harper and Row.

Coleman, D. W. (2000), 'Linguistic Data and Its Uses: The Problem of Conflating "Data" and "Examples"', *LACUS Forum* 26: 71–80.

Coleman, D. W. (2001), 'DATA and SCIENCE in Introductory Linguistics Textbooks', *LACUS Forum* 27: 75–85.

Coleman, D. W. (2003), 'A Series of Corpus-Based Studies on the Scientific Status of Linguistics', in B. Lewandowska-Tomaszczyk (ed.), *PALC 2001: Practical Applications in Language Corpora*, 251–62, New York: Peter Lang.

Coleman, D. W. (2004), 'Moving a Classic Applied Linguistics Study into the Real World', in V. H. Yngve and Z. Wąsik (eds), *Hard-Science Linguistics*, 191–213, New York: Continuum.

Coleman, D. W. (2006), 'A Formal Integrated View of Speech, Gesture, Gaze and Its Implications for Learning', *LACUS Forum* 32: 163–72.

Coleman, D. W. (forthcoming), 'How Readers Understand Characters in Fiction: Human Linguistics and Theory of Mind (TOM)' *LACUS Forum* 43.

Crookall, D., A. Martin, D. Saunders and A. Coote (1986), 'Human and Computer Involvement in Simulation', *Simulation & Games* 17 (3): 345–75.

Di Pietro, R. J. (1987), *Strategic Interaction: Learning Languages through Scenarios*, New York: Cambridge University Press.

Egbert, J, E. Hanson-Smith and C.-C. Chao (2007), 'Introduction: Foundations for Teaching and Learning', in J. Egbert and E. Hanson-Smith (eds), *CALL Environments*, 2nd edn, 1–15, Alexandria, VA: Teachers of English to Speakers of Other Languages.

Franks, D. D. (2010), *Neurosociology: The Nexus between Neuroscience and Social Psychology*, New York: Springer Verlag.

Galantucci, B. (2005), 'An Experimental Study of the Emergence of Human Communication Systems', *Cognitive Science* 29 (5): 737–67.

Garris, R. R. Ahlers and J. E. Driskell (2002), 'Games, Motivation, and Learning: A Research and Practice Model', *Simulation & Gaming* 33 (4): 441–67.

Greenblat, C. S. (1988), *Designing Games and Simulations: An Illustrated Handbook*, Newbury Park, CA: Sage.

Honorof, D. N. (2004), 'Articulatory Events Are Given in Advance', in V. H. Yngve and Z. Wąsik (eds), *Hard-Science Linguistics*, 67–86, New York: Continuum.

Hubbard, P. (1991), 'Evaluating Computer Games for Language Learning', *Simulation & Gaming* 22 (2): 220–3.

Jones, K. (1982), *Simulations in Language Teaching*, New York: Cambridge University Press.

Kryukov, M. M., and L. I. Kryukova (1986), 'Toward a Simulation Games Classification and Game Dialogue Types', *Simulation & Games* 17 (3): 393–402.

Lederman, L. C. (1992), 'Debriefing: Toward a Systematic Assessment of Theory and Practice', *Simulation & Gaming* 23 (2): 145–60.

Maturana, H. R., and F. J. Varela (1992), *The Tree of Knowledge: The Biological Roots of Human Understanding*, Boston, MA: Shambhala.

Peters, V. G. Vissers, and G. Heijne (1998), 'The Validity of Games', *Simulation & Gaming* 29 (1): 20–30.

Peterson, M. (2013), *Computer Games and Language Learning*, New York: Palgrave Macmillan.

Reddy, M. J. (1979), 'The Conduit Metaphor', in A. Ortony (ed.), *Metaphor and Thought*, 284–324. New York: Cambridge University Press.

Saussure, F. de (1959), *Course in General Linguistics*, trans. Wade Baskin, New York: Philosophical Library (orig. pub. in French, 1915).

Schick, L. (2008), 'Breaking Frame in a Role-Play Simulation: A Language Socialization Perspective', *Simulation & Gaming* 39 (2): 184–97.

Spolsky, B. (1989), *Conditions for Second Language Learning*, New York: Oxford University Press.

Sypniewski, B., and D. W. Coleman (2011), 'Lies and Lying in Hard-Science Linguistics', *LACUS Forum* 36: 291–8.

Winograd, T., and F. Flores (1986), *Understanding Computers and Cognition: A New Foundation for Design*, Reading, MA: Addison-Wesley.

Wolfe, J., and D. Crookall (1998), 'Developing a Scientific Knowledge of Simulation/ Gaming', *Simulation & Gaming* 29 (1): 7–19.

Yamazaki, K. (2019), 'The Effective Use of a 3D Virtual World in a JFL Classroom: Evidence from Discourse Analysis', in E. Zimmerman and A. McMeekin (eds), *Technology Supported Learning In and Out of the Japanese Language Classroom: Pedagogical, Theoretical, and Empirical Developments*, 227–51, Bristol: Multilingual Matters.

Yngve, V. H. (1996), *From Grammar to Science: New Foundations for General Linguistics*, Philadelphia, PA: John Benjamins.

Yngve, V. H. (2004), 'An Outline of Hard-Science Phonetics-Phonology', in V. H. Yngve and Z. Wąsik (eds), *Hard-Science Linguistics*, 87–112, New York: Continuum.

Yngve, V. H. (2006), 'Formalizing the Observer in Hard-Science Linguistics', *LACUS Forum* 32: 267–76.

Yngve, V. H. (2007), 'People, Orthoconcepts, and Dialog', *LACUS Forum* 33: 313–19.

Yngve, V. H., and L. Burazer (2009), 'Further Rewards from Formalizing the Observer', *LACUS Forum* 33: 405–13.

Yngve, V. H., and Z. Wąsik, eds (2006), *Hard-Science Linguistics*, New York: Continuum.

Part Two

Development and implementation of digital games in computer-assisted language learning

6

Playing with digital game pedagogies

Alex Bacalja and Kate Euphemia Clark

Introduction

English classrooms represent an important source of language learning for a diversity of students. This work has always been supported by texts which mediate classroom teaching that engages with identity, subjectivity and the cultivation of dispositions, attitudes and values (Beavis 2018). In recent times, debates about what constitutes a text, worthy of study, have manifest into curricula and practice that increasingly includes digital games as forms of literature through which the objectives of English teaching can be achieved. This has raised questions about how teachers employ pedagogy to support all learners facing these new ways of working with texts.

This chapter explores two ways that digital games might be used as texts in the English classroom. The first is a case study using the game *Never Alone* (Upper One Games 2014), alongside traditional texts in an Australian English language arts classroom. The game's story, themes, characters and textual features were aligned with curriculum demands in order to support student understanding regarding how different text types construct indigenous stories. Data were collected which related to the design and implementation of the unit of work, which was taught to almost three hundred students across two campuses, teacher interviews, curriculum materials, student focus groups and student work samples.

The second approach details the importance of allowing for the experience of playing digital games, and a pedagogy of play more closely aligned with experiential reading. Privileging experiential and embodied ways of knowing and learning, which are less constrained by traditional school-based approaches to pedagogy, it focuses on *No Man's Sky* (Hello Games 2016), a space-exploration game.

What follows is an analysis of how pedagogies of play across both case studies opened and closed opportunities for learning, impacting how students experienced the games at the centre of each study, and demonstrating that what we do with games when we seek to use them as objects of study has a significant impact on what they have to offer for students.

Why use digital games?

The digital age has been responsible for significant social, cultural and technological change, especially among today's youth (Prensky 2001; Steinkuehler 2006; Gee 2007b). Much of this change has resulted in both increased anxiety about the types of texts occupying young people's lives and unbridled optimism for the learning potential associated with new technologies (Beavis 1998; Donnelly 1998; Luke and Luke 2001). Research into the ways that students participate, connect and learn in online environments has often revealed the affordances of such spaces (Squire 2005; Gee 2007a; Coiro et al. 2008), and there is increasing interest in the pedagogical issues associated with bringing new media texts into formal learning contexts (New London Group 1996; Cope and Kalantzis 2009). Digital games are but one manifestation of this new media age, and one which is attracting significant attention from teachers and researchers alike. In terms of second language acquisition (SLA), digital games have great potential, as they are engaging and motivating for students (Reinders and Wattana 2012). Current research suggests that playing a variety of digital games is beneficial to SLA learning (Peterson 2013); however, the novelty of these texts necessitates close attention to the ways teachers are integrating them in classrooms.

In digital game studies there has been a push towards the recognition of the immersive potential of digital games and the unique affordances that digital games offer (Galloway 2004; Bogost 2006, 2007; Condis 2015; Wilde and Evans 2019). This includes the social and contextual elements of digital games that are of particular importance to SLA learners (Thorne, Black and Sykes 2009). While game-based learning which utilizes games to teach specific curriculum context has become increasingly prevalent (Perrotta, Aston and Houghton 2013), far less attention has been dedicated to using digital games in formal learning environments in ways that provide the player-student with possibilities to experience a different way of perceiving themselves and the environment (Condis 2015).

Megan Condis urges us to look at how digital games that are not explicitly educational can engage students in ways that traditionally educational games cannot. This is because games that are designed with an explicit message can make players feel as though they are being manipulated and, as a result, are less invested in the learning outcomes intended from looking at the text (2015: 93). This is particularly important for English language arts contexts, and specifically the SLA students within them, as motivation to learn a second language is a large factor in success (Pfenninger and Singleton 2016). As Condis suggests, 'Through play, our students can experience how that language compels and instructs their movements through those environments, and they can compare how different descriptive rules create different incentives for them as actors in those worlds' (2015: 91). In order to open up this immersive potential when using digital games as texts in the classroom, we must consider the pedagogical options available to teachers and the implications of the decisions they make.

Any attempt to bring digital games into school contexts will need to recognize the institutional ways of knowing and doing that are tied up in school subjects. Young (1998) describes how curriculum knowledge is socially and historically produced: what individual teachers do, and the assumptions they make about knowledge, matter in terms of the learning they encourage in the classroom. Curriculum is not ideologically neutral; rather it represents history and the competing interests and values of modern society that become expressed in the school curriculum (9). Importantly, Young argues that curriculum is always organized to preserve vested interest and maintain the status quo. Any attempt to change this curriculum, and therefore disrupt the status quo, is met with fierce resistance by those who perceive that such change will undermine the values, relative power and privileges of the dominant groups involved. However, it is also worth remembering that disciplines are not static (Yates et al. 2017). Over time, their boundaries change.

Likewise, the dispositions of teachers, a product of historically and social situated practice, is not equally orientated towards all forms of texts, nor all forms of textual study. As Bourdieu has explored extensively, every field, be they classrooms, book clubs or libraries, are historical products which set the conditions for what is deemed appropriate practice in such spaces (Bourdieu 1977). The teachers who choose to use digital games for language and literacy learning are themselves products of their time in these fields. However, as fields change, so do the conditions that dictate what is acceptable in social spaces. The inclusion of digital games, and especially games designed for entertainment, into classroom environments has the potential to disrupt the nature of learning and teaching which all students will experience in such spaces.

Existing approaches

Models have been developed which conceptualize pedagogies for gameplay and study in English language arts and literacy contexts (Apperley and Beavis 2013; Burn 2016; Bacalja 2017). Apperley and Beavis's Games as Text, Games as Action model (2013) includes two interwoven conceptual wheels (see Figure 6.1). The first, games as action, has three elements: *Actions*, whereby games are enacted by the actions of players and by the console or computer on which the game is played; *Designs*, the elements of production enacted during gameplay or through participation in online communities and paratexts; and *Situations*, the contexts within which games as action takes place. The second conceptual wheel, games as text, outlines four textual components of games (the world around the game, the game player, knowledge about games and the learning associated with playing the game). The framework recognizes the interconnectedness between the action associated with gameplay and the textual features of the game. Through

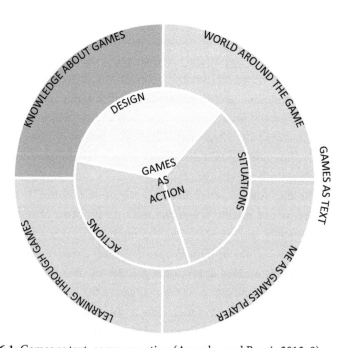

Figure 6.1 Games as text, games as action (Apperley and Beavis 2013: 9).

Analytical approaches			
Play, avatars and person	Modality	Coherence and cohesion	Code as mode

Figure 6.2 Frameworks for multimodal analysis (adapted from Burn 2016).

these connections, the model highlights the importance of going beyond purely textual approaches to studying games, for example, characters, setting, plot or vocabulary, and reminds us that games are about action, and that this action cannot be neglected. In some respects, the model helps educators and others make sense of what Beavis calls the 'undomesticated and untamable' (2013: 59) nature of video game play which, through each iteration of the game, contributes to the changing nature of this textual experience.

Burn (2016) applies several frameworks for multimodal analysis to digital games and other media texts to show how teachers might support students to analyse these texts. He brings together four analytical frames (see Figure 6.2), drawing on theories of social semiotics to demonstrate how different modes and media serve particular social functions, to represent the world, or to communicate particular interest and ideas, and that each analytical approach contributes to understanding how different modes (language, visual, music, etc.) construct meaning individually as well as collectively.

Bacalja's (2017) framework for video game literacies in subject-English (see Figure 6.3) is more closely situated within historical orientations towards subject-English, seeking to make connections between these dominant discourses and the play and study of games within the confines of the subject.

The framework draws on four dominant paradigms, skills, personal growth, critical literacy and cultural heritage, to show how each can be adopted, and adapted, to suit textual characteristics of digital games. Bacalja's framework recognizes the disciplinary forces which structure the English classroom, while also demonstrating how possibilities for play must negotiate the competing demands of traditional ways of understanding texts and the unique ways of realizing digital game stories.

These three evolving approaches to the challenge of bringing games into language and literacy contexts reveal tensions for educators seeking to use digital

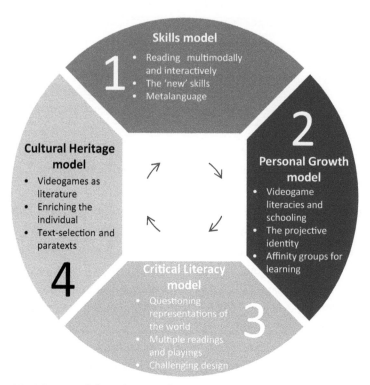

Figure 6.3 A framework for video game literacies in subject-English (Bacalja 2017: 196).

games in their classrooms. What follows below are two contrasting responses to the question: how can pedagogies of play support game-based learning? The two case studies utilized digital games as the central objects of study to explore how pedagogical decisions mediate the ways games shift from binary code into lived realities, the first through a whole-school approach whereby teachers drew closely on teacher-centred ways of studying texts, and second, an experiential reading which resists subject-specific ways of knowing and doing.

Learning with games in the English classroom and *Never Alone*

The first case study involves the use of one digital game, *Never Alone* (Upper One Games 2014), as the central text for study in an English classroom. Over three hundred students across two middle-year campuses of a regional Australian secondary school were involved in the study, with classes taught by approximately fourteen teachers. The unit of work focused on indigenous storytelling across multiple text types: a digital game, a series of animations and a print-based short story. The common theme across all texts was their exploration of indigenous stories of Aboriginal Australian and Canadian Iñupiat origins. *Never Alone* is a side-scroller game[1] steeped in traditional Alaskan native stories associated with the culture and values of the Iñupiat community. Designed in consultation with Cook Inlet Tribal Council, a pioneering Alaska native tribal organization, and E-Line Media, a leading developer and publisher of digital games that engage and empower, players take on the roles of Nuna, a young Iñupiat girl and her companion, an arctic fox, as they search for the source of an endless blizzard that is threatening her village.

The teaching unit relied closely on the aforementioned paradigms of teaching subject-English, namely personal growth, skills and critical literacy. Curriculum design was mapped against the imperatives of these three paradigms, with each classroom teacher determining how play would be utilized to complete teaching and learning activities. While the analysis below will focus on issues of play, there is value in briefly outlining how each paradigm of English teaching informed classroom activities.

Personal growth approaches to English begin with an interest in students' experiences, and ways of talking and creating texts. Students' selves are at the heart of this model, where the classroom comes to represent a language community focusing on personal engagement. During the study, students' at-home literacies were valued through a privileging of the gaming knowledge, in the form of gaming capital that they possessed. Students were given opportunities to discuss their developing understanding of the textual features of *Never Alone*.

A skills approach to English seeks to develop mastery over a specific set of competencies which tend to have a practical quality. More traditionally associated with reading comprehension and print-based writing practices, this approach now includes a range of visual literacy abilities, as well as reading practices that go beyond the literal interpretation of the printed word. In the study, the range of semiotic systems used across the three texts, the digital game, the animation and the short-story, were a focus of teaching, with students expected to explain how different modalities, in combination with authorial linguistic and non-linguistic choices, impact how each story is realized by the audience.

Critical literacy captures learning orientated towards supporting students to ask questions, challenge assumptions and adopt a resistant reading position to texts. Teaching focuses on the constructed nature of texts and how design features position their audiences in particular ways. Activities designed for

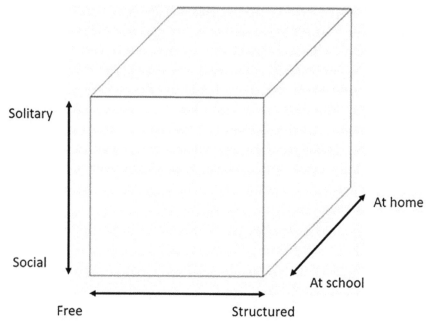

Figure 6.4 Pedagogies of play continua.

critical understanding included discussion of narrator voice, learning about the cultural background of the game's protagonist, story mapping and comparing the game story with the original indigenous story.

While all teachers in the study had access to the same pre-prepared teaching and learning activities, each individual teacher was empowered to make their own decisions about how gameplay would be managed with their students. Though every student in the study had their own device for playing the game, and all classes relied upon the same technological infrastructure, interviews with teachers post-unit revealed vastly different approaches to play, both inside and outside of the classroom. The types of play which manifest as a result of decisions made by teachers can be visualized and analysed in terms of three linear scales, as evident in Figure 6.4.

Free play and structured play

The control of play as a pedagogical device was organized between time dedicated to structured play and time dedicated to free play. Structured play referred to time spent playing the game that was tied to specific teacher-dictated learning goals. Free play described activities whereby play was not hindered by any explicit learning activities.

Many teachers structured or controlled play so that it operated in collaboration with other learning activities. These teachers tended to treat play as an activity not worthy of study in its own right, but rather as a means to achieve other outcomes. Anthony described how he started the unit by talking about *Never Alone* and the unit's learning goals. Discussion about stories and how they evolve preceded any gameplay. When play was allowed during class time, it was tied to the completion of chapter summaries. As Anthony said, 'I think the chapter summaries was something that needed to be constantly reinforced because the kids just got so addicted to the game, which was good. Some of them just absolutely love the games that they just forgot to do chapter summaries.'

Explicit teaching to guide play took various forms. One teacher used discussion prior to play to inform how students 'read' the game during play. Another reported using teacher talk during gameplay as they moved around the room, drawing students' attention to relevant features of the game. Written summaries that captured students' experiences of play and were completed at the end of some lessons to synthesize new understandings emanating was a strategy reported by numerous teachers. For these teachers, the purpose of play was to develop the content that was being explicitly taught, content about the indigenous peoples and their stories, the development of the protagonist and the use of multimodal elements to communicate the story. Play was perceived as important because it helped establish connections to the learning focus of the unit. Students who struggled to use play to progress through the game 'couldn't make those connections because they hadn't been there to learn them' (Cadence).

Free play was rarely employed as a pedagogical tool. Few teachers saw free play as a tool for exploring the game. Those teachers who did engage this pedagogical option tended to be more experienced with digital games and recognized this form of textual practice as legitimate.

Kellie describes how she began the unit with free play, because 'some of it, you couldn't really do some of the lessons without them knowing the character and knowing the setting a little bit, so some of it was just purely go in and play'. In these instances, students were not given specific goals to guide their play, even though the teacher planned for this play with the justification that it would enhance the ability of students to know the characters and setting. Wesley similarly used free play at the start of the unit so that students could learn about the characters: 'I gave them free play to introduce the actual game, give them a chance to learn about the characters.'

A rhetoric of play as a threat to more meaningful learning was common and in pedagogical terms manifest as limited opportunities for play not explicitly tied to particular reading and writing activities. Beavis has cautioned those seeking to work with games in formal learning contexts due to their 'wildness' (2013: 59), a sense that they cannot be contained or even fully accounted for within the formal parameters of school. This sentiment was shared by numerous teachers in the study. Carson reported trying free play, 'I did try it at the start a couple of times and it was just too hard to bring them back. ... "Okay, all right, guys. Off your iPads. Put them in our smart box. It's now time to learn."' For Carson, 'taming' the playing of *Never Alone* so that it could be leveraged for formal classroom learning was a challenge. Anthony shared similar sentiments, reporting how 'immersing them in the game unit too early actually distracted a lot of them from the unit's core goals'. There was a belief among participating teachers that classroom gameplay represented an activity that must be carefully managed and controlled.

Interestingly, many teachers used play as a reward for student participation in other, seemingly more worthwhile, activities. Completion of non-play-related classroom activities was prioritized, with the reward of free play offered as a carrot. Teachers relied on students' desires to play the game to compel them to complete more traditional literacy activities:

'I thought that playing the Never Alone game was definitely something they looked forward to, and we even used that as a bit of an incentive. We'd teach content and then if you got all that done, they could have 20 minutes on the game at the end.' (Cadence)

'I also used it [play] as a bit of a carrot, you know, if we get our work done, we're going to spend the last 15 minutes playing on the game.' (Carson)

'I was able to use it as a bit of a reward at different times. Which was good. I was like right, you've gotten all this stuff done, or if you get all this stuff done you got 10 minutes to play the game.' (Molly)

These comments suggest a disconnect between how these teachers perceive the role of play in realizing *Never Alone*'s story and how they perceive students will learn the content necessary to complete the goals of the unit. They tend to privilege the teacher's role as arbiter and mediator of knowledge and minimize the power of the interactions between student and game as a tool for knowing and doing.

Social play and solitary play

Teacher decisions about organizing play as a social or solitary activity similarly impacted on how students came to engage with the game. Social play, as we use the term here, refers to instances when two or more students engaged in the game together. We place this term in juxtaposition to solitary play, which describes moments when students played *Never Alone* on their own.

Almost all teachers constructed classroom gameplay as a social activity. Kellie described play in her classroom as a collective activity: 'You'd have kids going around and helping each other, especially those kids who finished the game and knew what they were doing. You'd have them go around helping each other. They'd usually sit in little groups and sort of talk about it as they're playing.' Gretal's classroom description might appear to an outsider as a site of chaos and disorder but reveals more complex levels of peer support and productive student talk for the purposes of engaging with the game. She said,

> Oh, they were sort of yelling at each other 'Oh, have you gotten to this bit yet?' Or 'No, how do you do it? I can't get passed the polar bear! What's happening?' And I will also be a bit like 'You know, with something like that, I have no idea how to get passed this level,' 'Oh, Miss, you need the bow.' And one of the students actually was like 'Yeah I knew what a [inaudible] was and you know, I learnt it from here and here.' So they start sharing and trying to make connections with some things they came across in the game. It was really good in that way.

In these instances, a combination of teacher anxiety about their own level of play proficiency with support for Vygotksy's (1978) principle of the more knowledgeable other allowed them to utilize experienced gamers, as well as those who had completed the game at home, as resources to support teaching. As a result, not only were students asked to support each other's progress, for example, Carson reported deferring student requests for help to other more experienced gamers in the room, but students were also allowed to help each other negotiate challenging moments of play.

Play as a solitary activity was almost totally absent from in-class pedagogical activity. One teacher, Bryan, discussed what happened when he asked students to bring headphones to class for use during a single lesson. He explained how the use of the headphones acted as a barrier to social activity, with students engrossed in their own play and minimizing the amount of talk in the room. However, this example of a teaching decision which favoured solitary play was the exception.

Given the case study worked with teachers who had never used digital games as objects for study, it should not be surprising that most favoured an approach to social play which enabled students to work collaboratively. Bourgonjon and Hanghoj's (2011) work investigating the characteristics of teachers engaged in game-based learning reveals the complex factors impacting on teaching and learning in these contexts. They use the following questions to explore the idea of a game-literate teacher: does it suffice to acquire expert knowledge about video games in order to be a game-literate teacher? Is video game expertise a prerequisite for using games in the classroom? And is the successful implementation of video games in the classroom proof for being a game-literate teacher (70)? In our *Never Alone* case study, it is interesting to observe teachers whose lack of game-specific knowledge was mediated by their institutionalized knowledge, specific to pedagogy, to resolve the challenge of constructing a learning environment, demonstrating what Hanghoj refers to as 'the interplay of knowledge forms in educational gaming' (2011: 22).

At-school and at-home play

Teachers differed in terms of how they valued and made use of out-of-classroom play and at-home play. Attitudes towards at-home play included the belief that the engagement factor associated with digital game play, coupled with the absence of a teacher, limited the ability of students to take much from their unsupervised out-of-classroom play practices. In contrast, there were also those who believed that all engagement with the game world was valuable, and therefore, at-home play, whether tied to specific homework activities or not, should be encouraged.

One opposition to at-home play relied on a belief that students were not capable of distinguishing between play for learning and play for entertainment. This position is captured by Anthony's statement: 'I found when they got home they just played the game and didn't do a lot of homework. So, they needed someone to constantly be there to remind them.' This statement reveals a number of insights about how teachers in the study viewed the value of play, as well as their own roles in facilitating learning. There is a clear negative attitude towards playing *Never Alone* without the support of additional learning activities. 'Just' playing the game is juxtaposed to more valuable activity, such as homework. Despite familiarity with the story's characters, themes, narrative and setting requiring engagement with the game, unsupervised and at-home 'play' was not a form of textual practice that was respected. Many teachers could not reconcile the possibility for unsupervised play, often influenced by desires for fun and entertainment to support structured homework for the purposes of formal classroom learning.

Another criticism of at-home play came from those teachers who allowed students to play the game at home, which resulted in students returning to class having achieved different stages of progression through the story. Some students who were encouraged to play at home reported finishing the game in a single evening, while other students given such opportunities chose not to engage in at-home play. The consequence for many teachers was a room of learners with vastly different knowledge about the game. This produced two challenges for teachers in the study. First, differentiating classroom activities to compensate for students who were at different stages of the text was more challenging than having a room of learners all progressing at the same pace. It was interesting to hear teachers raise this dilemma given it captures a legitimate challenge of all teaching. Second, teachers reported frustration at their reduced ability to control student progression through the text. Claire recounted giving her class strict instructions limiting gameplay to classroom time, seeking to control the speed of progress through the game. However, several students ignored these instructions and finished the game quickly at home. This disrupted Claire's control over the pace of exposure to the game.

Parental acceptance of games as texts worthy of study and play also impacted the ability of some teachers to use at-home play as a way to build exposure and familiarity. Teachers reported some parents not allowing the game to be played at home, while others reported students losing access to their iPads due to misuse. A lack of access to devices at home was reported by one teacher as a factor limiting learning, as some students could not complete the game and therefore were less familiar with key concepts from the text.

There are clearly concerns among teachers about what exactly students do with play and how it functions to improve their participation and performance in formal learning. The main concern expressed by teachers being that students not provided with structure for their gameplay would be negatively impacted. Interestingly, this is the opposite attitude to recommendations regarding structuring teenage reading. There is a strong movement in the literature rejecting at-home reading practices that tie reading to specific school-orientated learning objectives. Termed 'readicide' by one researcher (Gallagher 2009), the concern is that school-based reading practices are killing the love of reading. When combined with research literature identifying the relationship between the time young people spend reading for pleasure and literacy performance

(OECD 2003), there has been a shift towards encouraging at-home reading which favours reading for pleasure (Guthrie 2008; Duke et al. 2011). Yet, most of the teachers in this study tended to be critical of allowing students to enact the game in at-home environments which lacked teacher-directed activities.

What the above analysis of play pedagogies, free/structured, social/solitary, at-home/at-school, reveals is that the realization of key textual features of the game at the centre of this learning unit tended to be closely tied to teacher-centred approaches to learning and texts. These approaches are grounded in the discipline of English teaching, whereby teachers are active agents in determining how students experience texts, and how pedagogy will act as a force to control the manner in which the game can provide learning possibilities. Despite the unique nature of digital games, in terms of the active role a player must take in order to negotiate the real and virtual world of the game, play was perceived, for the most part, as an obstacle to be overcome.

Experiential reading and *No Man's Sky*

Our second case study offers an alternative approach to games-based language learning that resists the constraining impact of disciplinary approaches to education and embraces the affordances of play and informal learning possible in immersive open-world games, as a way to avoid the foreclosure of students' experiences with texts. In the above study on *Never Alone*, we can see that free play was largely seen by teaching staff as a distraction or impediment to learning, rather than a vital component of it. The active, immersive and educational role of play was largely ignored by teachers.

However, as Snaza, Sonu, Truman and Zaliwska contend, classroom objects 'participate in learning' (2016: xx). In other words, digital games are not merely the background or delivery system of a student's learning experience. Rather, objects, such as digital games, are active participants in the construction of learning. Moving beyond merely acknowledging the role that digital games play in the classroom, this second case study of *No Man's Sky* emphasizes and deconstructs the tension, as described by Bacalja (2017: 196), that arises from the relationship between discipline and the structure of a classroom. Consequently, instead of starting at the outcomes and working backwards to develop pedagogy and curriculum (Snaza et al. 2016: xxii), we investigate how English teachers might begin with a reading of digital games that foregrounds the playthrough experience in the classroom, an approach that requires us to rethink the pedagogies that accompany the games-based English language classroom that take seriously students' experiences of play.

No Man's Sky

This case study centres around *No Man's Sky*, an open-world[2] survival game. The open-world aspect of *No Man's Sky* is in stark contrast to the side-scroller *Never Alone*, as the player is able to explore the world in any direction that they see fit. This is compounded by the fact that *No Man's Sky's* universe is filled with eighteen quintillion planets that are procedurally generated, each filled with their own procedurally generated animals, plants, atmospheres and colour schemes (Kharpal 2016). Instead of creating each planet by hand, procedural generation allowed the developers to build the game universe by providing parameters of what the game would look like and what would populate the universe through algorithms that structured the random generation of the game universe. The procedural generation utilized by *No Man's Sky* is unique in the game development world and therefore garnered a lot of attention. The scale of the game is overwhelming and, at first glance, seemingly infinite.

Our approach to enacting the game utilizes a first-person narrative which bridges iterations of experiential reading. This requires us to pay close attention to how the game unfolds, our role enacting this activity and how we feel about this experience. This form of analysis is not possible through watching the game, or through description of the game, which also emphasizes the importance of playing the game in the classroom. It is through play that the emotive potential of digital games that student experience can be scaffolded and utilized in the classroom.

Affect and digital games in the classroom

Although mainstream or digital games designed to entertain are most readily associated with fun, the emotive experiences that arise from playing digital games cannot be so easily discounted if we are to learn from/with digital games as texts. As Alenda Chang suggests, emotion is of vital importance to the experience of playing digital games (2011). Emotions are an aspect of how we negotiate virtual environments. In Chang's research she discusses the ways that games that deal with ecological disaster have the potential to 'impress themselves forcefully on our psyche' (2011: 75). It is in this sense that media texts, such as digital games, not only reflect reality but also play a part in our construction of reality (Fiske 2010). Therefore, the emotional experiences of playing digital games cannot be disentangled from other aspects of digital gameplay, as they are an important aspect in negotiating gameplay. This is further demonstrated by the fact that game design can only account for choices that a player makes to a certain extent. In fact, players often make choices that feel right for the character they are playing, even if these are not the choices that will produce the most advantageous outcome (Consalvo, Busch and Jong 2019: 221).

In light of the importance of emotion in decision-making in games, we caution against ignoring the affective reactions that players have to digital games, and reconsider how affective relationships to digital games can be used as pedagogy in the classroom. Affect is the term given by theorists to forces that exist before our conscious thought turns them into emotions (Tomkins 1963; Gregg and Seigworth 2010). Affects can be described as currents that exist before our rationalizing thought processes that influence how we think and feel about a certain situation. In other words, affect refers to the flows or currents that feed into and influence our emotions (Hemmings 2005; Gregg and Seigworth 2010; Wetherell 2012). For example, when walking into a room we can innately sense tension, or excitement, or nervous energy, that dictates how we then go to interact with that environment (Ahmed 2010). Digital games are designed to make us emote in certain ways. The affective potential of digital games is expressed by one teacher, Jason, in the *Never Alone* case study analysed above:

> I got to have those conversations with the students around, hey, when you were watching Blind Side [a film studied by students in a previous term], did you feel the challenges that the character felt? Did you feel like you were going through the experience that the protagonist of that text was going through? And the answer was generally, well, no … How about with any other text we've studied in a high school? Did you feel the frustration that, that character must've felt? And the answer was almost always, no. … [S]o do you think that game makers are making a deliberate choice here, to put these challenges in your way so that you experience the events of the text, the way the character must be? Is this not a part of the experience of the game? All of the responses to that prompt were essentially, yes, that makes sense.

Jason's conversation with students about how digital games open us up to affects is an important element of digital games in the classroom that is often neglected. However, it should be acknowledged that the emotive reaction that we experience may be wildly different from the intended player's experience.

Despite the potential for unintended consequences in our emotive reaction to games, affect is still guided by the structure of the game. Clare Hemmings details how affective currents are constrained by the social world. That is, the potential affective connections that we make with the world around us are often constrained by the perceptions we have of the world. For example, if teachers think of play as distraction, the affective potential of play in the classroom is constrained. The affective possibilities of digital games in the classroom highlighted by Jason's discussion with his student demonstrates this. The student's inability to connect with the characters in the films and books that they read in class is dependent on how these stories relate to their own experiences, and how they have been explored in class. Moreover, as Margaret Wetherell posits, 'Flows of affect can tangle, mesh with the media – there are a wide range of potential connections' (2012: 13). This can also be seen in Apperley and Beavis's *Games as Text, Games as Action* model (2013: 9) (see Figure 6.1) which recognizes the importance of understanding elements outside of the control of the player, as well as student responses to the digital game. In the context of SLA classrooms, there are a vast array of potential connections between student experiences, teachers, game-designers and curriculum designers. In *No Man's Sky*, the affective experience is shaped by not only the coding or possibilities for action within the game but also the perspective that the student-player, teacher and the curriculum bring to the game. In this context, we can talk about these elements of digital gameplay as affect tangling and meshing with the world around it. Affect is disrupting and reembedding the structure of the classroom. Experiential reading requires us to consider these affective flows and how they shape students' experiences and learning capabilities.

Experiential reading as pedagogy

Experiential reading foregrounds the player's experience and allows room for the digital game to be an active participant (Snaza et al. 2016) in student's learning. This example of an experiential reading of *No Man's Sky* is certainly guided by the player's emotional reaction to a digital game. It is important to note that experiential reading is not without direction, or scaffolding. What is of importance in this example is that, when dealing with digital games in the classroom, if the path forward is fully realized before the term begins these moments of affective immersion are foreclosed. Instead, affective, experiential readings can be partially constructed, as long as the experience can still lead us, rather than clearly structuring cause and effect. This will still move class discussion to unexpected and rewarding places.

There are two key stages that make an analysis of a digital game an experiential reading that provides the foundation for the pedagogy of experiential reading in the classroom. In the first stage, immersion in the digital game is a central tenant to experiential reading. This means that the teachers and students involved in the classroom should spend time with the game and be given enough room to play through the game and let themselves experience the affective connections that are produced by digital games. In the second stage, close attention should be paid to affect and how digital games make us feel. This stage allows the student-player to begin to document how the game made them feel, and what aspects of the game were particularly important to the experience of playing the game. This can be developed in the classroom along certain key themes, relevant to the classroom's outcomes, that structure the responses to immersive experience. By providing questions that guide the experience of playing the game, teachers are able to direct the gameplay in the classroom, while still giving room for the students to experience the game in their own way. It is in this way that the affective not only has the potential to disrupt traditional modes of thought in relation to the structure of the classroom but can also be linked to key themes of the curriculum.

In the case study of *No Man's Sky*, the starting point was to focus on how the digital environment of the game both reflected and subverted the West's understanding of its relationship to the environment. There were key themes (such as climate change and how the size of the universe made the player feel) that structured the analysis. These questions scaffolded the experiential reading, while also allowing for the game to 'speak back' and to play a role in learning. What was surprising in this research was the way that the position that the player viewed the game world from, where the avatar was almost completely out of frame, meant that the environment took up much more of the players attention, when compared with other digital games. Therefore, the narrative that centred around the avatar began to seem much less important, which increased the importance placed on the game world's environment. This reading of a particular digital game demonstrates not only the ways that teachers can acknowledge digital games as active participants in the classroom but also provide opportunities for immersive learning that allows students to be creative, engaged and active participants in learning outcomes.

The tension between *No Man's Sky* as a digital game and the expectations for what a video game should be mirrors the difficulty of applying certain frameworks to digital games. In the classroom, this means that the moment we choose to apply a strict framework or pedagogy to a digital game, we obscure other potentialities for learning. Moreover, if we only use games that we consider 'educational' in classrooms, we limit what we can do with them, as students often feel reluctant to deeply engage with digital games that are explicitly educational (Condis 2015).

In this example we have explored how teachers in the classroom can open up the possibilities of video games as texts through a pedagogical framework that centres an experience of affective reactions to digital games. This can lead educators to unpack how our pedagogical tools can inadvertently close off valuable learning experiences. Those working with digital games in formal learning environment often underestimate the importance of free play and therefore close off the value of emotional learning experiences. It is important to consider the role that emotions play in SLA, as emotions mediate development in SLA classrooms (Imai 2010).

Conclusion

This paper has dealt with two cases studies that detail two very different methodologies and pedagogies of bringing digital games to the classroom. The *Never Alone* case study detailed how bringing a new textual medium in a classroom is not enough in and of itself to open up new forms of learning, pedagogy and engaging students. Utilizing *Never Alone* in classrooms demonstrated how the possibilities for learning were often constrained by teachers' perceptions of digital games, what constitutes learning and what counts as a text. In contrast, the *No Man's Sky* case study took an immense, open-world digital game and acknowledged its role as an active participant in the construction of learning. This case study eschewed traditional disciplinary approaches to education, instead focusing on several key themes, using these as guiding principles in learning. This pedagogy does not use desired learning outcomes to structure classroom activities, instead privileging novel engagement with classroom texts.

These two case studies, when presented together, demonstrate that digital games go beyond a tool for learning – they become a learning experience, where the role of play is central to their classroom experiences. Curricula that do not give forms of play adequate room close off potential avenues for learning. In SLA classrooms, there are many different, sometimes competing perspectives, not only from the students but also from the teachers, curriculum designers and digital game designers. Paying attention to the experience of using digital games in an SLA classroom context would aid in both centring student experience and also engaging with emotional connections to digital games and language development that would provide rich experiences for study. In the *Never Alone* case study, we saw that teachers' expectations sometimes overshadowed how students were engaging with the class material. Whereas with *No Man's Sky*, we can see how student experiences in the classroom are taken seriously, and are given room to be addressed, critiqued and developed in an environment that gives room to students' emotions.

The newness of digital games provides us with an opportunity to re-evaluate how we bring texts into the classroom and the ways that we structure learning around these texts. This is of particular importance to SLA classrooms, as the variety of experiences bring different potentialities to the classroom, and it is important not to restrict possibilities for learning.

Notes

1 Side-scroller games, or horizontal scrolling games, typically involve gameplay viewed from a side-view camera angle, where the on-screen characters generally move from left to right on the screen, as they move across the game world.
2 An open-world digital game is a game that allows the player to explore the game in any order that they wish, rather than a game that can only be played in one way.

References

Ahmed, S. (2010), 'Happy Objects', in M. Gregg and G Siegworth (eds), *The Affect Theory Reader*, 29–51, Durham, NC: Duke University Press.

Apperley, T., and C. Beavis (2013), 'A Model for Critical Games Literacy', *E-Learning and Digital Media* 10 (1): 1–12.

Bacalja, A. (2017), 'Videogames, Distinction and Subject-English: New Paradigms for Pedagogy', PhD thesis, University of Melbourne, Melbourne, Australia. Retrieved from http://hdl.handle.net/11343/194245 (accessed 13 November 2018).

Beavis, C. (1998), 'Pressing (the Right?) Buttons: Literacy and Technology, Crisis and Continuity', *English in Australia* 123: 42–51.

Beavis, C. (2013), 'Multiliteracies in the Wild: Learning from Computer Games', in G. Merchant, J. Gillen, J. Marsh, and J. Davies (eds), *Virtual Literacies: Interactive Spaces for Children and Young People*, 57–74, London: Routledge.

Beavis, C. (2018), 'Literature in Subject English in Australia: Purpose, Identity and Mode', in C. E. Loh, S. S. Choo and C. Beavis (eds), *Literature Education in the Asia-Pacific*, 24–38, London: Routledge.

Bogost, I. (2006), 'Videogames and Ideological Frames', *Popular Communication* 4 (3): 165–83.

Bogost, I. (2007), *Persuasive Games: The Expressive Power of Videogames*, Cambridge, MA: MIT Press.

Bourdieu, P. (1977), *Outline of a Theory of Practice*, Cambridge: Cambridge University Press.

Bourgonjon, J., and T. Hanghøj (2011), 'What Does It Mean to Be a Game Literate Teacher? Interviews with Teachers Who Translate Games into Educational Practice', *Paper Presented at the Proceedings of the 5th European Conference on Games Based Learning.*

Burn, A. (2016), 'Games, Films and Media Literacy: Frameworks for Multimodal Analysis', in M. Knobel and C. Lankshear (eds), *Researching New Literacies: Design, Theory, and Data in Sociocultural Investigation*, 169–94, New York: Peter Lang.

Chang, A. Y. (2011), 'Games as Environmental Texts', *Qui Parle: Critical Humanities and Social Sciences* 19 (2): 57–84.

Coiro, J., M. Knobel, C. Lankshear and D.J. Leu, eds (2008), *Handbook of Research on New Literacies*, New York: Lawrence Erlbaum Associates.

Condis, M. (2015), ' "Live in Your World, Play in Ours": Video Games, Critical Play, and the Environmental Humanities', *Resilience: A Journal of the Environmental Humanities* 2 (3): 87–104.

Consalvo, M., T. Busch and C. Jong (2019), 'Playing a Better Me: How Players Rehearse Their Ethos via Moral Choices', *Games and Culture* 14 (3): 216–35.

Cope, B., and M. Kalantzis. (2009), 'Multiliteracies: New Literacies, New Learning', *Pedagogies: An International Journal* 4 (3): 164–95.

Donnelly, K. (1998), 'Pushing Buttons … A Reply', *English in Australia* 123: 52–6.

Duke, N. K., P. D. Pearson, S. L. Strachan and A. K. Billman (2011), 'Essential Elements of Fostering and Teaching Reading Comprehension', in S. J. Samuels and A. E. Farstrup (eds), *What Research Has to Say about Reading Instruction*, 286–314, Newark, DE: International Reading Association.

Fiske, J. (2010), *Television Culture*, London: Routledge.

Gallagher, K. (2009), *Readicide: How Schools Are Killing Reading and What You Can Do about It*, Portland, ME: Stenhouse.

Galloway, A. R. (2004), 'Social Realism in Gaming', *Game Studies* 4 (1).

Gee, J. P. (2007a), 'Pleasure, Learning, Video Games, and Life: The Projective Stance', in M. Knobel and C. Lankshear (eds), *A New Literacies Sampler*, 95–113, New York: Peter Lang.

Gee, J. P. (2007b), *What Video Games Have to Teach Us about Learning and Literacy*, rev. and updated edn, New York: Palgrave Macmillan.

Gregg, M., and G. J. Seigworth (2010), *The Affect Theory Reader*, Durham, NC: Duke University Press.

Guthrie, J. T. (2008), 'Reading Motivation and Engagement in Middle and High School: Appraisal and Intervention', in J. T. Guthrie (ed.), *Engaging Adolescents in Reading*, 1–16, Thousand Oaks, CA: Corwin Press.

Hanghøj, T. (2011), 'Clashing and Emerging Genres: The Interplay of Knowledge Forms in Educational Gaming', *Designs for Learning* 4 (1): 22–33.

Hello Games (2016), *No Man's Sky* [PlaySation], Guildford: Hello Games.

Hemmings, C. (2005), 'Invoking Affect: Cultural Theory and the Ontological Turn', *Cultural Studies* 19 (5): 548–67.

Imai, Y. (2010), 'Emotions in SLA: New Insights from Collaborative Learning for an EFL Classroom', *Modern Language Journal* 94 (2): 278–92.

Kharpal, A. (2016), ' "No Man's Sky": Would You Play a Game That Takes 584 Billion Years to Explore?', *CNBC*, 10 August. Available online: https://www.cnbc.com/2016/08/10/no-mans-sky-release-would-you-play-a-game-that-takes-584-billion-years-to-explore.html (accessed 1 July 2017).

Luke, A., and C. Luke (2001), 'Adolescence Lost/Childhood Regained: On Early Intervention and the Emergence of the Techno-Subject', *Journal of Early Childhood Literacy* 1 (1): 91–120.

New London Group (1996), 'A Pedagogy of Multiliteracies: Designing Social Futures', *Harvard Educational Review* 66: 60–92.

OECD (2003), 'Literacy Skills for the World of Tomorrow', OECD. Available online: www.pisa.oecd.org/dataoecd/43/9/33690591.pdf (accessed 1 August 2019).

Perrotta, C., G. Featherstone H. Aston and E. Houghton (2013), 'Game-Based Learning: Latest Evidence and Future Directions', NFER Research Programme: Innovation in Education, Slough: NFER.

Peterson, M. (2013), *Computer Games and Language Learning*, New York: Palgrave Macmillan.

Pfenninger, S. E., and D. Singleton (2016), 'Affect Trumps Age: A Person-in-Context Relational View of Age and Motivation in SLA', *Second Language Research* 32 (3): 311–45.

Prensky, M. (2001), 'Digital Natives, Digital Immigrants', *On the Horizon* 9 (5): 1–6.

Reinders, H., and S. Wattana (2012), 'Talk to Me! Games and Students' Willingness to Communicate', in H. Reinders (ed.), *Digital Games in Language Learning and Teaching*, 156–88, New York: Springer.

Snaza, N., D. Sonu, S. E. Truman and Z. Zaliwska (2016), *Pedagogical Matters: New Materialisms and Curriculum Studies*, New York: Peter Lang.

Squire, K. (2005), 'Changing the Game: What Happens When Video Games Enter the Classroom?', *Innovate* 1 (6).

Steinkuehler, C. A. (2006), 'Why Game (Culture) Studies Now?', *Games and Culture* 1 (1): 97–102.

Thorne, S. L., R. W. Black and J. M. Sykes (2009), 'Second Language Use, Socialization, and Learning in Internet Interest Communities and Online Gaming', *Modern Language Journal* 93: 802–21.

Tomkins, S. (1963), *Affect Imagery Consciousness: Volume II: The Negative Affects*, New York: Springer.

Upper One Games (2014), *Never Alone* [iOS], Anchorage, AK: E-Line Media.

Vygotsky, L. S. (1978), *Mind in Society: The Development of Higher Mental Processes*, Cambridge, MA: Harvard University Press.

Wetherell, M. (2012), *Affect and Emotion: A New Social Science Understanding*, Thousand Oaks, CA: Sage.

Wilde, P., and A. Evans (2019), 'Empathy at Play: Embodying Posthuman Subjectivities in Gaming', *Convergence* 25 (5–6): 791–806.

Yates, L., P. Woelert, V. Millar and K. O'Connor (2017), *Knowledge at the Crossroads?: Physics and History in the Changing World of Schools and Universities*, Singapore: Springer.

Young, M. (1998), *The Curriculum of the Future: From the 'New Sociology of Education' to a Critical Theory of Learning*, London: Falmer Press.

7

The use of avatars in digital role-playing games (RPGs) in computer-assisted language learning (CALL)

Charly Harbord, Euan Dempster and Darshana Jayemanne

Introduction

This chapter provides an overview of the relationship between digital games and second language acquisition (SLA). The discussion examines the major game types utilized in computer-assisted language learning (CALL) and then focuses on providing a theoretically informed rationale for the use of digital role-playing games (RPGs) to enhance second language learning in conjunction with the material used within the classroom. The chapter reports on an ongoing learner-based project in which a purpose-built RPG has been created to investigate the role of this type of digital game in facilitating SLA.

This chapter further reports on a small-scale pilot project that forms part of the above research. This investigates the potential effects of avatar choice on perceptions of learning in a group of Chinese English as a Foreign Language (EFL) learners. The findings on learner avatar preferences are examined, demonstrating the relevance of the 'thin-slice effect' (Shin, Kim and Biocca 2019) in learner's avatar choice. With this bias, players judge other avatars based on how honestly they have represented themselves as an avatar. This would seem to imply that if the player has chosen an avatar that is more culturally representative of the target language (TL), they would assume the same of other players' avatars. The chapter closes with a discussion of the influence of the findings on the wider research into the use of RPGs in CALL and identifies areas of likely interest for future research.

Background

The ideas behind this chapter originally came from the literature on the use of digital games in CALL (Peterson 2013; Reinhardt 2019) and from the personal experiences of one of the authors who observed her son learning Japanese through playing games on a regionally locked Nintendo 3DS. As a language teacher and gamer, this author was more than aware of the difference between the motivation to do homework and the motivation to play.

Additionally, while working as an English foreign language teacher in China the above author noted how the level of English produced in the classroom compared to the astonishingly fluent language produced during the breaks from the students who went to play games online. It appeared that the motivation derived from gaming had aided the students in learning English without them even realizing it (implicit learning).

The notion that implicit learning was taking place was further evidenced when teaching on a masters of professional practice orientation programme (MPPOP) in Beijing. This afforded the creation of a close working relationship and knowledge exchange with the School of Design and Informatics from Abertay University who supplied lecturing staff. It is a programme where games design, professional behaviours and English for Specific Purposes (ESP) were combined in order to create the complete Scottish university preparatory experience. Thereby creating a unique opportunity for research into SLA and games, especially as the students involved were both English as second language learners, designers and players familiar with RPGs. Again, the disparity between the English language produced within the classroom activities and the language produced in games design discussions and gameplay appeared highly significant. The following discussion provides an overview of the relationship between gaming and SLA.

Digital games and SLA

There is a distinct difference between 'SLA', characterized by the implicit gaining of a second language knowledge through gradual exposure, and 'second language learning', characterized by the conscious learning of a second language through explicit teaching (Krashen 1989). The Confucian style of language education implemented in China prescribes rote repetition and memorization of grammatical functions, creating a disconnect to SLA (Suzuki, Nakata and

Dekeyser 2019). This produces a mechanical understanding of the TL but not necessarily the ability to use it in a confident and improvised manner – for example, in real-life conversation (Mokhatar et al. 2017). SLA may be enhanced by active participation in activities with structured goals in the TL. Activities such as group quests, team battles and in-game interactions, including those with non-player characters (NPCs), foster the immersion and interactivity of the game. These form the basic aspects of game mechanics, yet are so hard to replicate in a convincing and genuine manner within an educational setting (Cheng et al. 2017). Peer cooperation during RPG-based gameplay between native and second language learners has the ability to inform the collaborative scaffold around the language learning experience, with the TL and the game itself acting as a mediator. As result of paradigms shifts in modern education, L2 learners are now viewed as social beings as opposed to individual learners (Lee and Pass 2014). By working together with a native speaker to achieve a goal, the learner of the TL will progress further than they would have been able to do working by themselves (Zhang 2009).

According to Hadfield (1984) language games can be compartmentalized into two fields: linguistic and communicative. Games with a linguistic focus concentrate more on fluency and accurate grammar, whereas communicative games are aimed at building rapport and transference of information. As will be noted at a later stage of this discussion, the aim of this current research places the focus firmly on 'language for use' and the learner's ability to implement it into new contexts and situations (Ellis 2019; Suzuki, Nakata and Dekeyser 2019). Motivation is intrinsic with regards to learning, but is an intangible concept which is challenging to quantify. Topirceanu (2017) created a motivational spectrum with a sliding scale of motivation. At one end of the spectrum there is less self-motivation and externally regulated motivational factors form the basis of decision-making and learning – for example, rote learning grammar for a test (a form of dependent learning). The opposite end of the sliding scale represents intrinsic motivation (autonomous learning), where a person carries out an action or learns something purely for the personal gain and enjoyment not due to outside pressure (Felicia 2011). This is the goal for educational games, where a student actively chooses to play the game and thereby learn outside the classroom context (Blumberg and Altschuler 2011). Games such as *Minecraft* and *The SIMs* may be seen to have crossed the education/fun divide. Both games have been used for educational and specifically second language research (Ames and Burrell 2017) and have proved valuable tools for such projects. However, it should be noted that while both of these games (and others like them) may be being used outside the research/educational scenario, it is challenging to prove if they are still being played within the educational context of the classroom/research project. In the following section the discussion provides an overview of the major game types utilized in CALL.

Major game types utilized in CALL

Research on CALL relating to gaming can be observed to focus on two main types of game: commercial off-the-shelf (COTS) games and serious games or games designed specifically for learning rather than for entertainment (Connolly et al. 2012). Both types of game have the potential to support effective language learning by increasing motivation, offering real-time feedback and increasing exposure to the TL. The serious games genre focuses on an educational agenda first and entertainment second (Sorensen and Meyer 2007). One aspect that requires consideration when designing such games is the balance between formal and informal learning. Formal learning, such as that carried out within a school setting, primarily focuses on a quantifiable educational goal. Informal learning, which often takes place outside of the classroom setting, focuses on entertainment first and gaining knowledge and/or abilities second.

There has been a growth in serious games development specifically designed to be educational first and entertaining second. While these games have been successful within the classroom, they are seldom played in other contexts. A possible reason for this phenomenon may be due to an imbalance between language input and gameplay (de Haan 2005; Chen and Yang 2013). COTS games are primarily designed for fun but may present learning opportunities by proxy. There is both anecdotal and research evidence that RPGs and other socially interactive games have clearly demonstrated improvements in TL production and intercultural communication (Romero, Usart and Ott 2015). Game-based learning follows constructivist principles in that the kinaesthetic methods of 'learning by doing' or 'active learning' often form the basis of gameplay (Yang 2012). While it could be stated that the linguistic content and cultural knowledge offered by COTS games have the potential to be the equal of second language learning textbooks and curriculum, it should be noted that the primary function of CALL is to enhance and complement traditional language learning (Alyaz, Spaniel-Weise and Gursoy 2017). The research of Sung, Hwang and Yen (2015) demonstrated that by combining digital and traditional language learning methods, player flow is increased leading to improved motivation, which in turn enhances the ability to problem-solve and increases learning potential. Flow is the careful balance of task difficulty and player ability which gives enough challenge to make the game enticing but not so much that the player becomes frustrated and quits (Nylund and Landfors 2015). One genre of game that has shown benefits for education within the realm of CALL is RPGs. The discussion in the next section examines research findings that highlight several of the potential benefits of engaging learners in RPG-based gameplay.

Utilizing RPGs to facilitate second language learning: Hypothesized benefits

The potential causal relationship between RPGs and language acquisition is one that is of great interest to researchers and educators (Peterson 2013). As Table 7.1 shows, a number of features of RPGs are hypothesized as facilitating language learning. RPG-based gameplay often focuses on making meaning from riddles and quests as well as remembering information for use later, creating the experience of not only increasing vocabulary but also understanding the context of the language used. Previously, in-game communication was limited to text chat. However, now players are able to interact verbally with players from all around the world. This is coupled with real-time exchanges where the player must respond in a timely manner and has the ability to replay situations where the outcome was not satisfactory (Cornillie, Thorne and Desmet 2012). Being able to self-study at one's own pace and the ability to replay any situation with the option to use subtitles mean that RPGs appear well suited to language learning (de Haan, Reeed and Kuwada 2010). Subtitles serve to consolidate and confirm information heard, enhancing the comprehension of the language via multimodal input (Bird and Williams 2002). Furthermore, with in-game text second language learners can observe their speech pattern which in itself can help identify errors and allows focus on speech (Peterson 2010; Ellis 2019). The discussion in the remainder of this section provides an overview of key findings reported in the literature.

Research findings: Interactional context

Researchers who have investigated the use of RPGs in CALL argue that a major advantage of RPGs is the interactional context provided (Peterson 2011, 2012;

Table 7.1 Hypothesized advantages of using RPGs in language education

Features of RPGs	Hypothesized advantages	Author(s)
Individual gameplay	Learner-centred interaction	de Haan et al. (2010)
The use of avatars	Anonymity, reduction of social cues, reduced perceived threats to face and anxiety	Rankin et al. (2008)
	Opportunities for cross-cultural interaction	
Immersive gameplay	Reduction of inhibitions	McCreery et al. (2012)
Problem-solving	Provides deeper learning, inductive reasoning	Felicia (2011)
In-game tutorials	Provide a scaffolding system with which the player can learn the mechanics/language needed at their own pace; repetition helps the player to become familiar with the TL	de Haan (2005)
Social aspects	Team quests and guilds require need for interaction, provide community bases and social bonds	Alyaz, Spaniel-Weise and Gursoy (2017); Peterson (2011); Peterson (2006)
Game and peer feedback	Real-time modification of TL utterances	de Haan (2005)
Motivation	Learning efficacy, autonomy increased by gameplay and social interaction	Warschauer (2005)
Realistic situations/tasks	Authentic experiences to practice TL	Gee (2005)
Interaction with native speakers	Scaffolded language forum	Zhang et al. (2017)
Exposure to RPGs	Enhanced L2 vocabulary	Sylven and Sundqvist (2012)

Jabbari and Eslami 2018). As most RPGs are designed with a focus on the individual player, they provide opportunities for individualized immersion in a context that is feedback-rich, low-stress and that compels TL use (Kim 2018). Moreover, the online nature of these games provides opportunities for authentic collaborative interaction involving problem-solving in the TL with a wider range of interlocutors including native speakers, than may be found in many conventional language classrooms (Gee 2005). Moreover, game support features such as tutorials provide scaffolding and opportunities for L2 vocabulary learning (de Haan 2005). For the purposes of this research the lens has been narrowed to focus on text-based RPGs and textual language learning.

It is noted in the literature that while a relatively new area of research, there is strong evidence to support the value of implementing socially interactive games for language learning. RPGs provide an arena for deep learning through activities such as problem-solving and inductive reasoning (Felicia 2011). The social interaction aspect provides exposure to the TL culture enabling these games to benefit language learners (Alyaz, Spaniel-Weise and Gursoy 2017). Findings from research by Sylven and Sundqvist (2012) demonstrated that when compared to a non-gaming control group, the 11- to 12-year-old participants who played more than five hours of MMORPG games have significantly larger L2 vocabularies. RPG's stimulate the need for real-time interactions without the real-life consequences that may result from making mistakes. A fundamental feature of real-time game-based interactions is immediate feedback. By finding out instantly when a mistake has been made, a learner is able to amend their response as if in a real-time interaction. This increases the suspension of belief and immersion within the game world. In-game tutorials provide an inbuilt scaffolding system.

When a player first starts a game, they must progress through a series of basic levels in order to understand the specific controls and mechanics of the game. It is this repetition that helps the TL user become more familiar with the language through exposure and thereby facilitates gradual acquisition (de Haan 2005). Additionally, players form in-game communities which create social bonds and which may lead to support of language learning within the group (Peterson 2006). Peer-related teamwork and feedback can provide a positive atmosphere for language learning. These factors aid the development of communicative competence by providing access to a practice arena that may enhance learning.

Research findings: Affective factors, motivation

Within many classroom settings, language learning can be seen to be teacher-centric, where one teacher is in control of multiple students' learning progression (Topirceanu 2017). This can lead to disengagement within a class as students may feel that they are either ahead of the curve or being left behind. Both situations can lead to a lack of motivation to learn. A clear advantage of using RPGs to enhance the acquisition of a second language is that the learning is entirely in the hands of the student. Giving each student the ability to progress at their own pace increases engagement and motivation (Janebi and Haghighatpasand 2017). Furthermore, the student is free to use or ignore the learning scaffolding based on their own needs (Hanus and Fox 2015). One method employed by RPGs to enhance player motivation is the implementation of reward systems.

In-game reward systems encourage both informal and implicit learning as the learner is able to gain both knowledge through the tasks or quests and tangible rewards such as achievement badges, better weapons and new avatar skins. The motivation created by wanting to gain all of the tangible achievements or the latest collectibles in order to compare them with fellow players is a driving force in the sustained gameplay of RPGs. Research by Sailer et al. (2017) also supports the theory that in-game rewards help to create positive learning experiences and add meaning to the learning tasks. These rewards form visual representations of competence and success, thereby act not only as a personal motivator but also enhance competitive motivation and player autonomy.

Autonomy is present not only from the point of view of the learner but can also be witnessed in the cognitive processes behind the social collaborations and interactions (Warschauer 2005; Peterson 2008). The findings of such research into interactive CALL applications showed significant enhancements of not only the TL but also cross-cultural understanding. One of the reasons put forward for this is the anonymity created by use of player pseudonyms, meaning that it would not necessarily be easy to tell a native speaker from an L2 speaker. This aspect resonates strongly with Chinese native speakers, namely the concept of saving face (Wen and Clement 2003). As will be observed at a later stage of this discussion, this particular premise forms one of the cornerstones of the RPG and SLA project described later in this discussion and directly informs the avatar preference test.

Research findings: Affective factors, anxiety

As is noted in the literature, certain affective filters can interrupt SLA (de Haan 2005). These are the psychological factors which can inhibit language use and learning. Anxiety using the TL is a commonly reported feeling within the second language classroom, or indeed when faced with interactions with a native speaker (Ping et al. 2014; Tum 2015). Learner anxiety can exhibit itself through a reluctance to learn or progress, as well as reticence to use the language and a negative attitude within the classroom or take the form of mental blocks (Hashemi 2011). The feeling of being judged or that the level and correctness of the TL spoken is in some way an indicator of intelligence level can impact a learner's ability to learn effectively (Melchor-Couto 2017). This can display as reluctance to speak, utterances in low volume or freezing. The anxiety felt is closely related to how the language user feels they are being judged or viewed by others, native speakers or not.

Furthermore, a TL that has a significantly different culture may also exacerbate feelings of anxiety. The interactive, dynamic and fun aspects of RPGs are an intrinsic factor in reducing the anxiety a learner may feel interacting in the TL (Horowitz 2019). This resonates with Kolb's theory of experiential learning (Kolb 1981), in which the context of the situation and activity itself can lead to learning through a process of trial and reflection in order to achieve a goal. Experiential language learning may lead the user to recognize adaptability in their own TL use, feel personal growth and a greater contextual awareness of cultural differences. The findings of research by Sung, Hwang and Yen (2015) demonstrated that by utilizing experiential gaming methods, learners displayed deep learning strategies and higher motivation levels, both of which are essential for long-term learning. In research conducted by Tianjian (2010) into Chinese English language learners and anxiety, more than 50 per cent of the participants stated that they experienced moderate to high anxiety when using the TL. Feelings of enhanced anxiety can also be closely associated with the concept of face.

Research findings: Avatars

The utilization of avatars in RPGs alongside other communication media (in-game text and voice chat) further enhances the immersive experience and therefore flow for the player, as the avatar can show real-time physical reactions to actions. Additionally, feelings of 'telepresence' (being there) and 'co-presence' (being there with another person) are also enhanced (Peterson 2011) due to the immersive nature of games and feelings of ownership towards the avatar (McCreery et al. 2012). The avatar can be viewed as the channel for the emotional experience of play, supporting the view that an avatar can be an extension of the idealized self in the virtual world (Ratan and Sah 2015). The player/avatar relationship thus allows for higher levels of motivation.

The literature shows that avatars not only provide the opportunity for real-time interaction with native speakers but also create an arena for the development of cross-cultural competencies (Peterson 2011). While the interactions in many online games may take place all across the globe, the participants all exist as avatars on the same virtual plane providing a practice arena that would otherwise be unobtainable. Thereby, they potentially enhance not only TL acquisition but also intercultural competence and contribute to the creation of a more effective platform for communication within the online environment. This further increases the sense of immersion in games and in turn cognitive flow (Nylund and Landfors 2015). As noted previously, RPGs stimulate the need of real-time avatar interaction without real-life consequences for mistakes made.

The following section examines the importance of a key element in digital game-based language learning, namely the importance of face. The discussion then turns to providing an overview of an experiment into player avatar choice preferences in a purpose-built RPG designed specifically to facilitate language learning. In particular, how the avatar becomes the conduit for self-representation within the games space and how that is perceived by others.

The concept of face and relationship to learning in digital games

Face is a concept intrinsic to Chinese culture, which holds that the perception of a person and how they present themselves is potentially more important than the actual reality. The classic example of this is a Chinese student in a classroom who doesn't understand the lesson but is reluctant to ask for clarification. As this may be perceived as a clear indication of lack of knowledge which would be ascribed to a negative opinion. Asking for clarification online does not elicit the same issue; in essence online, a player is faceless. This allows a degree of freedom within the interactions as there can be no perceived loss of face (Wen and Clement 2003).

While the cultural concept of face may be rooted firmly in Chinese philosophy, the effects are also experienced by other second language users. Goffman (1967) produced one of the first definitions of face that is applicable to all nationalities. He asserted that a person's social face is a concept derived from that person's view of their own value and role within society. If their own interpretation of their social standing is in line with how others perceive them then it can be said that that person has face. He further states that while a person can assume that they have a certain level of face, it is actually how others view them that matters and that social value can easily be taken away should the person be found wanting or unworthy. This correlates directly to the Chinese concept of the fear of losing face. Within a language classroom how peers and native speakers view the learner has a strong influence on their anxiety, motivation and confidence to use the TL.

When relationships are formed and maintained entirely online via the medium of avatars, the player is likely to feel less anxiety due to the 'faceless' anonymity of the interaction. Additionally, the lack of visible social prompts based on context that may otherwise cause interference allows for a freer interaction without anxiety or inhibition (Rankin et al. 2008). This is particularly prevalent cross-linguistically between English and Mandarin. English language and social cues tend to be implicit with inference playing a large role in communication. The use of a racially neutral avatar may help to alleviate the anxiety that can be felt when communicating with a native speaker in the TL (Aymerich-Franch 2014).

The prevalence of online interactions has led to the state where social events and interactions take place solely online and with avatars acting as the conduit – being 'anti-socially social' (Harbord and Dempster 2019). These proxy exchanges allow less anxiety to be experienced as the user is 'faceless' and thereby no longer constrained by the social anxiety faced when using the TL. The limited visual stimuli as well as social prompts that can be connected to interference of TL production are negated by the lack of actual face-to-face interaction. When considering communication in a second language the use of a racially neutral avatar can help to alleviate the anxiety that can be felt when communicating with a native speaker (Melchor-Couto 2017). This also helps to override the Chinese societal concept of face (Wen and Clement 2003) and the related fear of losing it.

Feeding into the negation of face is a sense of impermanence and reduction of responsibility with online relationships. For example, should a major mistake or social faux pas occur, instead of trying to make amends, a new profile can be created and the cycle starts over (Nylund and Landfors 2015). This cycle can be described as 'trial and error' in which any mistakes made during the learning process can easily be amended without fear of recrimination (Hanus and Fox 2015). A contributing factor to the negation of face is the use of avatars. The following section outlines the pilot study on EFL learner avatar choice in the RPG noted previously.

Pilot project: Avatar preference test

A pregame test was carried out in order to tailor the RPG to the research needs and also make it more attractive to players. In order to fully assess the research hypotheses, sixteen avatars were created with a variety of cultural indicators to assess the influence that avatar choice might have over the likelihood of interaction in the TL within the RPG setting. The cultural indicators corresponded to the TLs as well as other races and fantasy styles. The research was directed at second language speakers and how willing or not they are to interact with avatars that represent the cultural and racial background of the TL. The choice of avatar of the TL speaker was investigated as the projection of an idealized perception. The participants were twenty Chinese students who had English as a second language and who took part in the Masters of Professional Practice Programme at Abertay University. They were given visual exposure only to a selection of avatars representing a potential TL interlocutor, with no other cues. They were then asked to express what their perception of the character was and what level of interaction they would likely take.

Second language learners reported that they experienced being more at ease when conversing with their peers within the 'safe' confines of the language classroom (Rublik 2018). However, if they are put in the position where a native speaker acts as the interlocutor, they feel anxious and unwilling to interact for fear of revealing their lower level of proficiency (Wen and Clement 2003). For these reasons it was expected that the choice of avatar for online interactions would follow the same pattern as a foreign language classroom.

One contributing factor is the comfort of anonymity (Roed 2010), which describes how players can interact without fear of being labelled a 'beginner' or being treated as interloper in the game. For example, it was hypothesized that Caucasian Mandarin learners would be more likely to feel comfortable interacting in the TL with a more Caucasian-looking avatar as opposed to an avatar that was more Asian. The reverse was also predicted for the Chinese

Figure 7.1 Avatar choices given to the participants. *Source*: Harbord (2018).

participants. When interacting in a TL environment, players may purposely choose a more racially neutral avatar in order to disassociate themselves from the stereotype of being a second language user (Kafai et al. 2007; Lee 2014).

The aim of the research was to test three hypotheses based on avatar perception and thereby inform the larger research project into RPGs and SLA. RPG maker MV (https://www.rpgmakerweb.com/products/programs/rpg-maker-mv) was used to create two identical RPGs (one in English and one in Mandarin) that could be used to test the larger hypothesis. In order to create a mutual platform with which the learners could interact, online text blogs were utilized – one for English and one for Mandarin. This meant that the correspondence between the two players could be kept track of and evaluated. Additionally, it was then easier to collect data regarding the balance between English and Mandarin. For the RPG to be fully personalized to the proposed players it became necessary to design custom avatars and for that purpose player preferences were tested. For the purposes of the study, avatars with Asian and Caucasian facial features and dress were used as well as those from other cultures and fantasy. This approach forms the basis of the future planned research into RPGs and their ability to enhance the SLA of both Mandarin and English. The resultant participant avatar preferences were then utilized to narrow the original sixteen avatars (see Figure 7.1) down to four choices which will be provided at the beginning of the RPG. The following sections discuss the methodology and results of the avatar preference research.

Methodology

The research was qualitative in nature, as the aim was to gain an awareness of the ethnographic knowledge and shared cultural preferences of each group of students. In order to achieve this goal, an online anonymous questionnaire was administered, focusing on the reasons why the participant may or may not have chosen a certain avatar to interact with.

Qualitative research does leave answers open to interpretation (Allwood 2012). However, the answers given were direct enough to avoid misrepresentation.

Once the sixteen avatars had been designed, an online questionnaire was created using Microsoft forms. The benefit of this format is that it was completely anonymous and thereby in line with current UK General Data Protection Regulation (GDPR) guidelines. Within the questionnaire participants were asked what their native language was, then they were asked to select one avatar for each of the three scenarios (the avatar they would choose for themselves, the avatar they would prefer to interact with and the avatar they would prefer not to interact with) and then state the reasons why they had made that choice. The participants were able to use as many or as few words as they desired to justify their responses. The questionnaire was open-ended, so they were able to take as much time as they felt necessary to complete it. The average response time was twenty-two minutes and fifteen seconds. The online questionnaire results were taken from the period 1–30 June 2019. The response was 100 per cent – a fact which may have been influenced by the researcher also being the participants' teacher.

Participants

All of the participants were given a research information sheet and consent forms and briefed about the project, and the research was carried out in line with Abertay University's code of ethics. Those who wished to take part were given access to an anonymous online questionnaire which presented sixteen avatars and four corresponding questions. The participants were asked to consider the scenario where they were imagined themselves as a player in an RPG played in the TL. They were then asked to choose which avatar they would prefer to represent themselves online, which they would be more likely to interact with and which they would not be likely to interact with.

Hypothesis 1: Participants are more likely to choose an avatar that resembles a native speaker to represent themselves.

The TL would serve as the instigator for the participant's choice. It was predicted that an avatar that corresponds to the TL would be chosen to represent themselves in the game.

Players will select an avatar to look more representative of the TL and be more comfortable interacting with avatars that present as less stereotypical.

Hypothesis 2: Participants are more likely to be comfortable interacting with an avatar that is more representative of the TLs and more uncomfortable when interacting with an avatar that is more representative of their own background.

Hypothesis 3: Through the above selection of preferred avatars, participants are likely to feel less anxiety and more motivation when interacting in the TL. Additionally, the converse is also true that when faced with an avatar that the participant does not feel is attractive, they will be negatively affected in terms of motivation and willingness to communicate.

Another aspect that increases the lack of inhibition is the anonymity of gameplay.

Players select an avatar which according to Peterson (2006) enhances not only the immersion and emotional investment but also the role play and communication between players. The use of an avatar can help negate the anxiety that a learner may feel within face-to-face conversation in the TL (Rankin et al. 2008). Peterson (2011) reported that in his research which utilized the RPG 'Allods Online' the second language learners stated that with the use of an avatar they were able to give themselves a new name which allowed a degree of anonymity and also a reduction in stress when speaking a second language, which meant that they felt less fear when conversing with a native speaker.

Findings

The findings of the preference test were analysed individually by each question and linked to the corresponding hypotheses. The results did follow the original hypotheses; however, they did not match the reasons expected. Figure 7.2 represents the three preferred choices from the questions given in the questionnaire.

Question 1 above shows the avatars that the Chinese participants were most likely to choose to represent themselves. The reasons given for these choices were: 'the Chinese boy looks most like me' and 'this avatar is the most neutral'. The results veered slightly from hypothesis 1 in that the more culturally similar and culturally opposite avatars were chosen along with the most neutral. With a larger participant sample size, a clearer picture could be garnered which would either help to prove or disprove the hypothesis.

Figure 7.2 The Avatar choices in order of popularity in response to the three questions given. *Source*: Harbord (2018).

Question 2 shows the avatars that the Chinese participants would choose to interact with in the TL. The reasons given for these selections were: 'She looks Scottish and I want to go to Scotland.' The results from question 2 support the hypothesis that participants will be more willing to interact with an avatar that is more identifiable as a TL user. This is backed up by the 'thin-slice' effect (Shin, Kim and Biocca, 2019), wherein the participant may be judging the veracity of the level of representation of the avatar they are interacting with based upon how well they have self-represented. Question 3 shows the avatars that the Chinese participants would not want to interact with. The reasons given for these selections were all based on personal senses of aesthetics. The results from question 3 showed the participant's motivation and willingness to interact is heavily influenced by avatar appearance.

Discussion

The following discussion will attach theoretical reasoning to the results of the findings. The results were unexpected due to the fact that online aesthetics played a much larger role in avatar selection than previously anticipated. However, this may lead back to the bias created by the selection of avatars that are more representative of the TL to interact with, with the supposition that the player may not be a native speaker.

Taylor (2002) demonstrated that for gaming, players tended to choose avatars that would either distract other players or be a close facsimile of the role that they wished to portray online. Societal norms of what is attractive can lead to the purposeful manipulation of avatars in order to present the player in a manner that elicits a far more positive response to first impressions from peers (Lin and Wang 2014; Fong and Mar 2015). Building on the premise that an avatar is a highly modified version of a person, it could then be assumed that during interactions there will be an element of dubiousness or distrust (Williams 2006). As can be seen by the results, 'identity tourism' (Taylor 2002) appears to have taken place as the participants chose to 'try out' a new personality, appearances or genders.

The degree of accuracy when interpreting an avatar can be predicted by the convergence between 'cue validity' (how close to reality the avatar is to the player) and 'cue utilization' (how the given cues are then used to create a perception of character/personality).

The higher the convergence, the more accurate the results. The Brunswick Lens Model of perception of personality (1956) is informed by both cue validity and utilization. The theory states that visual clues from exposure to a stimulus (in this case an avatar) can provide a 'lens' through which non-visual conclusions can be drawn. Through this lens, predictions about the real person can be drawn from their avatar's appearance and character traits leading to thin-slice judgments that are usually accurate (Shin, Kim and Biocca 2019).

Additionally, when dealing with NPCs the player may also find it easier to interact with an avatar that is a closer representation of the TL as they will feel safer from judgement for mistakes made. This will allow the player a forum in which they could practice production of language in use while seeming to interact with a native speaker. In order to bypass feelings of anxiety caused by interacting with a native interlocutor (Wen and Clement 2003; Roed 2010; Rublik 2018), participants are more likely to select avatars that are less racially representative of the TL.

Conclusion

As the prior discussion on the research involving RPGs in CALL has shown, the contributory factors to learning such as motivation, autonomy and real-time interaction appear ripe for further investigation (Peterson 2008). Furthermore, research indicates the use of avatars appears to also play a significant role in learning with this type of digital game. The increasing research in the above areas may shed new light on these aspects of language learning with RPGs.

Regarding the pilot project described in this chapter, the results followed the original hypotheses. However, the justifications made for the participant choices did not match prior expectations. The Chinese participants almost all stated aesthetics to be the main influencer on their decision-making. The reasoning may not be so surprising when parallels can easily be drawn between face and beauty to success and prestige. Furthermore, China has a rapidly growing beauty economy known as '美女经济 *Meinü Jingji*' (Xu and Feiner 2007), which places greater importance on outward appearance as it strongly correlated with perceptions of character, prestige and value.

From the reasonings offered by the participants in the avatar research, the general common theme arose with regards to playing RPGs in a second language. The utilization of avatars enhances SLA by allowing for greater immersion and suspension of inhibitions. By embodying an idealized avatar, the player is free to interact with other players and NPCs without any fear of losing face. By choosing an avatar that closely represents the culture of the TL, the player is able to try out 'identity tourism' (Taylor 2002), thereby enabling them to feel less anxious when interacting with the perceived native speaker. Additionally, the anonymity afforded by the use of an avatar and screen name also appears to lower the inhibitions that might normally be faced when using the TL in front of people.

Limitations

The first limitation within the study was number of participants (n = 20). Second, the number of avatars provided to choose from. These needed to be sensitive but also representative of different cultures. Ideally, the research would have the ability to allow participants to create their own avatars from a stock set of facial features and cultural identifiers. This would allow for a far more personalized response to the three questions given in the questionnaire.

One interesting factor to consider is that while the online questionnaire was completely anonymous, the students who took part were aware that it was for research purposes. For this reason, the researcher being Scottish could potentially have influenced the results for preferred avatars, thereby creating a confounding variable effect.

Future directions

The results of the avatar preference test are being used to directly inform the design and development of an RPG which aims to enhance the SLA of both Mandarin and English. To that end, the game has been designed twice, once in English and once in Mandarin and will have a collaborative blog between the two players of both games. The reason that an RPG was chosen refers back to the hypothesized advantages shown in Table 7.1. Additionally, RPGs tend to have simpler game mechanics and fewer twitch reflexes, allowing the player to progress at their own pace through the game. This means they are more accessible to non-gaming players. They create immersive atmospheres where the players can lose themselves within the gameplay and not worry about the level of language produced.

Moreover, they provide players with the option to read and reread their chats outside of the game allowing for consolidation and review of language used.

Although the research is ongoing, it is anticipated that that the results gained from the fully completed project will demonstrate that the students who utilize the RPG to enhance their language learning will show an increase in the accuracy of understanding, production and recall of the TL. Moreover, perhaps more importantly, it is hoped that their motivation for learning and using the TL should also increase.

Based on the results from the avatar study, the NPCs that are encountered in the beginning of the game when the players are more nervous and less confident using the TL were replaced by the preferred choices for interaction (see Figure 7.3). As the player progresses through the game and the levels become harder the NPCs will be represented by the least favoured avatars. As players start to feel more confident interacting within the confines of the game environment it is hypothesized that they will begin to feel more comfortable with less preferred avatars.

The resultant game will help to justify the use of RPGs to enhance SLA. It is hoped that it will provide enough evidence to warrant further expansion.

Several areas have been identified for potential developments and expansion. One approach under consideration is the inclusion of a speech-to-text programme for players to communicate verbally and still be able to keep a record of what was said. This would allow for a freer interaction between the players in TL conversation. Developing the game so that it can be played by two people remotely at the same time is another option, as this would enable

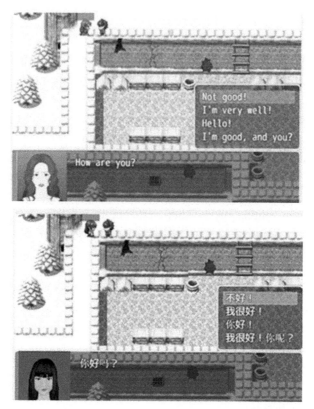

Figure 7.3 The preferred avatars in the context of the purpose-built RPG. *Source*: Harbord (2018).

players to combine speech or speech to text so that players would be able to experience genuine real-time TL interactions. A further promising area is the incorporation of augmented reality (AR) elements to the game, which can be used to overlay TL into the real world. An investment into the narrative of the game so that it can include deeper meaning and immersive gameplay that are culturally representative of the TLs as used. Once the game is completed it will be possible to swap the languages used. One proposition is to utilize Scots Gaelic and English as a way to encourage language use between peers in a motivational and diverting way. One advantage of tailoring the game to use Scots Gaelic is the cultural preservation of a language that is not in widespread use.

Further areas for future research within this field would allow for a greater understanding of cultural pedagogy and educational cultures, creating deeper contextual knowledge of how to approach SLA participants from different cultures.

Education should not be a one-size-fits-all approach, and through an awareness of how approaches can be adapted to specific cultural variables more efficient teaching practices may be developed.

This chapter is dedicated to Simon Harbord (1955–2019) – scientist, inventor and, best of all, father.

References

Allwood, C. M. (2012), 'The Distinction between Qualitative and Quantitative Research Methods Is Problematic', *Quality & Quantity* 46 (5): 1417–29.

Alyaz, Y., D. Spaniel-Weise and E. Gursoy (2017), 'A Study on Using Serious Games in Teaching German as a Foreign Language', *Journal of Education and Learning* [online] 6 (3): 250–64. http://dx.doi.org/10.5539/jel.v6n3p250.

Ames, M. G., and J. Burrell (2017), 'Connected Learning and the Equity Agenda: A Microsociology of Minecraft Play', in *Proceedings of the 2017 ACM Conference on Computer Supported Cooperative Work and Social Computing*, 446–57, New York: ACM.

Aymerich-Franch, L., R. F. Kizilcec and J. N. Bailenson (2014), 'The Relationship between Virtual Self Similarity and Social Anxiety', *Frontiers in Human Neuroscience* 8 (944).

Bird, S., and J. Williams (2002), 'The Effect of Bimodal Input on Implicit and Explicit Memory: An Investigation into the Benefits of Within-Language Subtitling', *Applied Psycholinguistics* 23 (4): 509–33. http://dx.doi.org/10.1017/s0142716402004022.

Blumberg, F., and E. Altschuler (2011), 'From the Playroom to the Classroom: Children's Views of Video Game Play and Academic Learning', *Child Development Perspectives* 5 (2): 99–103. http://dx.doi.org/10.1111/ j.1750- 8606.2011.00163.x.

Chen, H., and T. Yang (2013), 'The Impact of Adventure Video Games on Foreign Language Learning and the Perceptions of Learners', *Interactive Learning Environments* 21 (2): 129–41. http://dx.doi.org/10.1080/10494820.2012.705851.

Cheng, M.-T., Y.-W. Lin, H.-C. She and P.-C. Kuo (2017), 'Is Immersion of Any Value? Whether, and to What Extent, Game Immersion Experience during Serious Gaming Affects Science Learning', *British Journal of Educational Technology* 48 (2): 246–63.

Connolly, T., E. Boyle, E. MacArthur, T. Hainey and J. Boyle (2012), 'A Systematic Literature Review of Empirical Evidence on Computer Games and Serious Games', *Computers & Education* 59 (2): 661–86. http://dx.doi.org/10.1016/j.compedu.2012.03.004.

Cornillie, F., S. Thorne and P. Desmet (2012), 'ReCALL Special Issue: Digital Games for Language Learning: Challenges and Opportunities', *ReCALL* 24 (3): 243–56.

de Haan, J. (2005), 'Learning Language through Video Games: A Theoretical Framework, an Evaluation of Game Genres and Questions for Future Research', in S. Schaffer and M. Price (eds), *Interactive Convergence: Critical Issues in Multimedia*, 229–39, Oxford: Inter-Disciplinary Press.

de Haan, J. W., W. M. Reed and K. Kuwada (2010), 'The Effect of Interactivity with a Music Video Game on Second Language Vocabulary Recall', *Language Learning & Technology* 14 (2): 74–94. https://scholarspace.manoa.hawaii.edu/bitstream/10125/44215/1/14_02_dehaanreedkuwada.pdf.

Ellis, N. (2019), 'Essentials of a Theory of Language Cognition', *Modern Language Journal* 103: 39–60. http://dx.doi.org/10.1111/modl.12532.

Felicia, P., ed. (2011), *Handbook of Research on Improving Learning and Motivation through Educational Games: Multidisciplinary Approaches*, Hershey, PA: IGI Global.

Fong, K., and R. Mar (2015), 'What Does My Avatar Say about Me? Inferring Personality from Avatars', *Personality and Social Psychology Bulletin* 41 (2): 237–49. http://dx.doi.org/10.1177/0146167214562761.

Gee, J. P. (2005), 'Learning by Design: Good Video Games as Learning Machines', *E-Learning and Digital Media* 2 (1): 5–16.

Goffman, E. (1967), *Interaction Ritual*, New York: Doubleday.

Hadfield, J. (1984), *Elementary Communication Games*, Hong Kong: Thomas Nelson and Sons.

Hanus, M., and J. Fox. (2015), 'Assessing the Effects of Gamification in the Classroom: A Longitudinal Study on Intrinsic Motivation, Social Comparison, Satisfaction, Effort, and Academic Performance', *Computers and Education* 80: 152–61. http://dx.doi.org/10.1016/j.compedu.2014.08.019.

Harbord, C., and E. Dempster (2019), 'Avatars: The Other Side of Proteus's Mirror', in *Joint International Conference on Entertainment Computing and Serious Games*, 412–16, Cham: Springer.

Hashemi, M. (2011), 'Language Stress and Anxiety among the English Language Learners', *Procedia – Social and Behavioral Sciences* 30: 1811–16.

Horowitz, K. S. (2019), 'Video Games and English as a Second Language: The Effect of Massive Multiplayer Online Video Games on the Willingness to Communicate and Communicative Anxiety of College Students in Puerto Rico', *American Journal of Play* 11 (3): 379–410.

Jabbari, N., and Z. Eslami (2018), 'Second Language Learning in the Context of Massively Multiplayer Online Games: A Scoping Review', *ReCALL* 31 (1): 92–113. http://dx.doi.org/10.1017/s0958344018000058.

Janebi, E., and M. Haghighatpasand (2017), 'Exploiting Adventure Video Games for Second Language Vocabulary Recall: A Mixed-Methods Study', *Innovation in Language Learning and Teaching* 13 (1): 61–75. http://dx.doi.org/10.1080/17501229.2017.1359276.

Kafai, Y., D. Fields and M. Cook (2007), 'Your Second Selves: Avatar Designs and Identity Play in a Teen World', in *Situated Play*, Los Angeles: DiGRA. http://www.

digra.org/digital-library/publications/your-second-selves- resources-agency-and-constraints-in-avatar-designs-andidentity-play-in-a- tween-virtual-world/ (accessed 18 March 2019).

Kim, Y. (2018), 'Analysis of Research Trends Focusing on Outcomes in Language Learning using MMORPGs', *Multimedia-Assisted Language Learning* 21 (4): 111–42.

Kolb, D. A. (1981), 'Learning Styles and Disciplinary Differences', *Modern American College* 1: 232–55.

Krashen, S. (1989), *Language Acquisition and Language Education*, Hemel Hempstead: Prentice Hall International.

Lee, J. (2014), 'Does Virtual Diversity Matter?: Effects of Avatar-Based Diversity Representation on Willingness to Express Offline Racial Identity and Avatar Customization', *Computers in Human Behavior* 36: 190–7. http://dx.doi.org/10.1016/j.chb.2014.03.040.

Lee, J., and J. Pass (2014), 'Massively Multiplayer Online Gaming and English Language Learning', in H. R. Gerber and S. Schamroth Abrams (eds), *Bridging Literacies with Videogames*, 91–101, Rotterdam: Sense.

Lin, H., and H. Wang (2014), 'Avatar Creation in Virtual Worlds: Behaviors and Motivations', *Computers in Human Behavior* 34: 213–18. http://dx.doi.org/10.1016/j.chb.2013.10.005.

McCreery, M., K. S. Krach, P. Schrader and R. Boone (2012), 'Defining the Virtual Self: Personality, Behavior, and the Psychology of Embodiment', *Computers in Human Behavior* 28 (3): 976–83. http://dx.doi.org/10.1016/j.chb.2011.12.019.

Melchor-Couto, S. (2017), 'Foreign Language Anxiety Levels in Second Life Oral Interaction', *ReCALL* 29 (1): 99–119.

Mokhtar, A. A., R. M. Rawian, M. F. Yahaya, A. Abdullah and A. R. Mohamed (2017), 'Vocabulary Learning Strategies of Adult ESL Learners', *The English Teacher* 38: 133–45.

Nylund, A., and O. Landfors (2015), 'Frustration and Its Effect on Immersion in Games', MA diss., Umea: Umea University.

Peterson, M. (2006), 'Learner Interaction Management in an Avatar and Chat-Based Virtual World', *Computer Assisted Language Learning* 19 (1): 79–103.

Peterson, M. (2008), 'Virtual Worlds in Language Education', *JALT CALL Journal* 4 (3): 29–37.

Peterson, M. (2010), 'Massively Multiplayer Online Role-Playing Games as Arenas for Second Language Learning', *Computer Assisted Language Learning* 23 (5): 429–39.

Peterson, M. (2011), 'Towards a Research Agenda for the Use of Three-Dimensional Virtual Worlds in Language Learning', *Calico Journal* 29 (1): 67.

Peterson, M. (2012), 'Learner Interaction in a Massively Multiplayer Online Role Playing Game (MMORPG): A Sociocultural Discourse Analysis', *ReCALL* 24 (3): 361–80.

Peterson, M. (2013), *Computer Games and Language Learning*, New York: Palgrave Macmillan.

Ping, A., D. Baranovich, M. Manueli and S. Siraj (2014), 'Promoting Self-Regulation in Vocabulary Learning among Chinese EFL Learners: A Needs Analysis', *Asia-Pacific Education Researcher* 24 (1): 137–46. http://dx.doi.org/10.1007/s40299-013-0166-x.

Rankin, Y. A., M. McNeal, M. W. Shute and B. Gooch (2008), 'User Centered Game Design: Evaluating Massive Multiplayer Online Role Playing Games for Second Language Acquisition', in *Proceedings of the 2008 ACM SIGGRAPH Symposium on Video Games*, 43–9, Los Angeles: ACM.

Ratan, R., and Y. Sah (2015), 'Leveling Up on Stereotype Threat: The Role of Avatar Customization and Avatar Embodiment', *Computers in Human Behavior* 50: 367–74. http://dx.doi.org/10.1016/j.chb.2015.04.010.

Reinhardt, J. (2019), *Gameful Second and Foreign Language Teaching and Learning: Theory, Research, and Practice*, Basingstoke: Palgrave Macmillan.

Roed, J. (2010), 'Language Learner Behaviour in a Virtual Environment', *Computer Assisted Language Learning* 16 (2–3): 155–72. http://dx.doi.org/10.1076/call.16.2.155.15880.

Romero, M., M. Usart and M. Ott (2015), 'Can Serious Games Contribute to Developing and Sustaining 21st Century Skills?', *Games and Culture* 10 (2): 148–77.

Rublik, N. (2018), 'Chinese Cultural Beliefs: Implications for the Chinese Learner of English', *Sino-US English Teaching* 15 (4): 173–84. http://dx.doi.org/10.17265/1539-8072/2018.04.001.

Sailer, M., J. Hense, S. Mayr and H. Mandl (2017), 'How Gamification Motivates: An Experimental Study of the Effects of Specific Game Design Elements on Psychological Need Satisfaction', *Computers in Human Behavior* 69: 371–80. http://dx.doi.org/10.1016/j.chb.2016.12.033.

Shin, M., S. Kim and F. Biocca (2019), 'The Uncanny Valley: No Need for Any Further Judgments When an Avatar Looks Eerie', *Computers in Human Behavior* 94: 100–9. http://dx.doi.org/10.1016/j.chb.2019.01.016.

Sorensen, B., and B. Meyer (2007), 'Serious Games in Language Learning and Teaching – a Theoretical Perspective', in *DiGRA International Conference: Situated Play*, Tokyo: DiGRA.

Sung, H., G. Hwang and Y. Yen (2015), 'Development of a Contextual Decision-Making Game for Improving Students' Learning Performance in a Health Education Course', *Computers & Education* 82: 179–90. http://dx.doi.org/10.1016/j.compedu.2014.11.012.

Suzuki, Y., T. Nakata and R. Dekeyser (2019), 'Optimizing Second Language Practice in the Classroom: Perspectives from Cognitive Psychology', *Modern Language Journal* 103 (3): 551–61. http://dx.doi.org/10.1111/modl.12582.

Sylvén, L. K., and P. Sundqvist (2012), 'Gaming as Extramural English L2 Learning and L2 Proficiency among Young Learners', *ReCALL* 24 (3): 302–21.

Taylor, T. (2002), 'Living Digitally: Embodiment in Virtual Worlds', in R. Schroeder (ed.), *The Social Life of Avatars: Presence and Interaction in Shared Virtual Environments*, 40–62, London: Springer-Verlag.

Tianjian, W. (2010), 'Speaking Anxiety: More of a Function of Personality than Language Achievement', *Chinese Journal of Applied Linguistics* 33 (5): 95–109.

Topirceanu, A. (2017), 'Gamified Learning: A Role-Playing Approach to Increase Student In-Class Motivation', *Procedia Computer Science* 112: 41–50. http://dx.doi. org/10.1016/j.procs.2017.08.017.

Tum, D. O. (2015), 'Foreign Language Anxiety's Forgotten Study: The Case of the Anxious Preservice Teacher', *Tesol Quarterly* 49 (4): 627–58.

Warschauer, M. (2005), 'Socio-Cultural perspectives on CALL', in J. Egbert and G. Petrie (eds), *CALL Research Perspectives*, 41–51. Mahwah, NJ: Lawrence Erlbaum.

Wen, W., and R. Clement. (2003), 'A Chinese Conceptualisation of Willingness to Communicate in ESL', *Language, Culture and Curriculum* 16 (1): 18–38. http:// dx.doi.org/10.1080/07908310308666654.

Williams, D. (2006), 'Virtual Cultivation: Online Worlds, Offline Perceptions', *Journal of Communication* 56 (1): 69–87. http://dx.doi.org/10.1111/j.1460- 2466.2006.00004.x.

Xu, G., and S. Feiner (2007), 'Meinu Jingji/China's Beauty Economy: Buying Looks, Shifting Value, and Changing Place', *Feminist Economics* 13 (3–4): 307–23. http:// dx.doi.org/10.1080/13545700701439499.

Yang, Y. (2012), 'Building Virtual Cities, Inspiring Intelligent Citizens: Digital Games for Developing Students' Problem Solving and Learning Motivation', *Computers & Education* 59 (2): 65–377. http://dx.doi.org/10.1016/j.compedu.2012.01.012.

Zhang, Q. M. (2009), 'Affecting Factors of Native-Like Pronunciation: A Literature Review', unpublished dissertation, Seoul: Chung-Ang University.

Zhang, Y., H. Song, X. Liu, D. Tang, Y. Chen and X. Zhang (2017), 'Language Learning Enhanced by Massive Multiple Online Role-Playing Games (MMORPGs) and the Underlying Behavioral and Neural Mechanisms', *Frontiers in Human Neuroscience* 11. http://dx.doi.org/10.3389/fnhum.2017.00095.

8

Reinforcing international students' language skills for disaster preparedness: A case study of gamification that utilizes augmented reality technology

Kazuhiro Yonemoto

Introduction

Many immense natural disasters occurred in various regions of Japan in 2018. The Osaka/Kyoto area and Hokkaido were hit by earthquakes with a magnitude of 6.1 and 6.7 in June and September 2018, respectively, which caused significant damage and casualties. In addition, the eruption of a volcano near a ski resort in central Japan killed one person in January, torrential rains caused the deaths of more than two hundred people in western Japan in July and a powerful typhoon tore through southwest Japan in September, leaving eleven people dead. These events reminded us of the need for disaster preparedness, especially for foreign residents in Japan including international students.

Since much of the information related to natural disasters in Japan is only available in Japanese, disaster preparedness is inextricably linked with Japanese language competency. Especially since the Great East Japan Earthquake in 2011, several Japanese language educators have conducted learning enhancements for disaster preparedness (e.g. Matsumoto 2015; Miyagi, Hanazono and Nakai 2014; Kondo and Kawasaki 2015, 2016). However, presumably due to insufficient language skills, such implementations have rarely occurred at the beginner level.

To fill this gap, this paper explores the use of augmented reality (AR) technology in accordance with gamification principles (Kim et al. 2018), which indicates advantages in providing language learning experiences interconnected with location as in previous studies. In fact, the incorporation of such technology could potentially enable the reinforcement of beginner-level Japanese language skills for disaster preparedness. This paper reports on a case conducted at a university in Japan in which the author, as an instructor, and learners perceived the effectiveness of implementing gamification in disaster education for beginner-level learners of Japanese as a second language.

Background

Disaster preparedness

Information on natural disasters and disaster preparedness is increasingly provided in foreign languages throughout Japan. Furthermore, the use of the textbook *Yasashī Nihongo* (Plain Japanese, Iori 2019) is becoming more common in the case of natural disasters. Despite the provision of such linguistic supports, there is a marked difference in the information that can be obtained depending on whether one can understand the Japanese language or not (Shah and Murao 2013; Leleito et al. 2015). In the field of Japanese language education, opportunities to learn about disaster preparedness have been provided for international students (e.g. Miyagi, Hanazono and Nakai 2014; Matsumoto 2015; Kondo and Kawasaki 2015, 2016). Such cases stemmed from independent fieldwork promoting awareness of *jijo* (self-help), with the understanding that international students would be vulnerable due to lack of information in times of disaster (Kondo and Kawasaki 2015; Leleito et al. 2015).

As Kondo and Kawasaki (2016) and Matsumoto (2015) describe, due to a lack of experience, geographical and psychological distance from disaster-stricken areas, and fading of memories of disasters, international students are less likely to believe that natural disasters could happen to them. Consequently, it is more difficult to motivate them to participate actively in disaster preparedness learning. In this respect, it is necessary to examine how we can engage learners as active participants. In other words, we need to think about how we can implement disaster preparedness learning and in what way we can make it effective and meaningful for students. With regards to active participation, the concept of gamification is useful and advantageous in implementation.

Gamification and AR

Gamification is defined as 'the use of game elements and game design techniques in non-game contexts' (Werbach and Hunter 2012: 26). Various researchers' definitions of gamification differ according to necessary elements (Kim et al. 2018). As our primary purpose of implementing gamification is to improve learning for disaster preparedness, this paper adopts Kim et al's (2018: 29) definition: 'Gamification in learning and education is a set of activities and processes to solve problems related to learning and education by using or applying game mechanics.' Previous studies which have implemented gamification in second language learning have demonstrated its effectiveness, especially in providing an enjoyable learning experience while simultaneously motivating learners to participate in the learning process with enthusiasm (e.g. Hasegawa, Koshino and Ban 2015). This statement is also supported by Reinders and Wattana's (2014) study which found that digital gameplay can stimulate willingness to communicate in the target language, thereby lowering the affective filter for language learners.

This begs the question of how disaster preparedness learning can be gamified. Disaster preparedness learning is location specific in many ways; for example, it involves an understanding of the location of emergency facilities and equipment as well as evacuation routes and sites. Learners are necessarily engaging in these activities in a foreign language. In this respect, utilizing AR helps actualize gamification in disaster preparedness learning. AR, defined as an environment that is created by adding information to objects or places in the real world, has been gradually incorporated into second language education and showed positive effects on language teaching and learning (Godwin-Jones 2016; Kessler 2018).

Drawing on Klopfer, Squire and Jenkins's (2002; as cited in Klopfer and Squire 2008) discussion on affordances that mobile technology, including AR, could potentially benefit educational experiences (namely, portability, social interactivity, context sensitivity, connectivity and individuality), Reinders and Pegrum (2016) consider the potential of incorporating mobile technology into second language learning. With these perspectives, Reinders and Pegrum (2016) focus on how mobile technology can enrich learning experiences rather than how it can make learning more efficient. They also stress the importance of considering levels of mobility so as to maximize the affordances of mobile technology in learning. In the field of second language education, practices that support the affordances of AR technology have been accumulating.

Hatasa (2018), who reports on several cases of implementation in Japanese language learning, points out that utilizing AR can encourage learners to engage in communication even outside of the classroom in a foreign language learning context. Holden and Sykes (2011), stressing the importance of the interconnectedness between language learning and location, conclude that incorporating AR into Spanish language learning could result in learners' active participation in learning. Yonemoto (2019), who organized fieldwork activities for beginner-level Japanese language learners with AR games, observes that interactions with games and immediate responsiveness in the activities strongly motivated learners, producing a synergistic effect in their language learning. As such, AR has strengths and advantages, especially in language learning, indicating its potential for reinforcing learners' language skills for disaster preparedness.

This study answers the following research questions: (1) how does AR technology, incorporating gamification principles, impact beginner-level Japanese learners' language skills for disaster preparedness? and (2) how can such implementation of AR technology into a beginning-level course be successfully realized?

Methodology

Participants and setting

The author incorporated AR activities into a Japanese language course at a university in Tokyo, Japan. Since this study examines the perceived effectiveness of implementing gamification and AR in disaster preparedness education based on learners' reactions and the author's observations, this study was conducted in the form of a case study. This choice of research method was made due to the nature of disaster preparedness learning, which is usually location specific. Nevertheless, by making modifications that are appropriate to each site, findings and insights from the current study can be applied to various other learning situations.

The setting was a sixteen-week intensive beginner Japanese course which met for twenty-one class hours per week and included two sessions, one with fourteen students and the other with four. The students' backgrounds are described below (Table 8.1). Some learners already possessed knowledge about natural disasters such as earthquakes due to their personal experience. On the

Table 8.1 Student background

Session 1			Session 2		
	First language	Gender		First language	Gender
A	Chinese	Female	O	Mongolian	Female
B	Chinese	Male	P	Thai	Female
C	English	Male	Q	Thai	Male
D	English	Male	R	Uyghur	Female
E	English	Male			
F	Burmese	Male			
G	Thai	Female			
H	Thai	Female			
I	Thai	Female			
J	Thai	Male			
K	Vietnamese	Male			
L	Vietnamese	Male			
M	Vietnamese	Male			
N	Vietnamese	Male			

other hand, all were in their mid-twenties to early thirties and came to Japan not to study Japanese, but to pursue graduate degrees in different fields, most of which could be completed in English. As a result, the course objectives were to support the students' transition to life in Japan and their progress towards academic, personal and social success. With the exception of Learner R, who came to Japan five months before the course started, these students came to Japan about two weeks before the course started.

It was also common that the learners had never studied Japanese before and that they planned to live in Japan for at least four years. At the time of this activity, about ten weeks after the course started, students were able to produce not only single sentences but also compound ones and were becoming able to have short, coherent conversations.

Disaster preparedness learning

In light of the need to learn about natural disasters in Japan, the university provides information on preparing during orientation, soon after international students arrive. In addition, the Japanese language course incorporates a visit to the Life Safety Learning Center, a facility where visitors can learn about and practice how to handle emergency situations such as fires and earthquakes. Such activities are meaningful, especially because they raise students' awareness of the need to prepare for natural disasters; however, they seem to be insufficient in terms of enhancing students' self-help ability. This interpretation is based on the fact that (1) the activities at the centre are conducted mostly in Japanese, meaning students need to understand the information presented via translation into English, and (2) as these activities use general situations of natural disasters distinct from a particular place, the students may not perceive them as realistic. This may have led to passive participation in the activity, without achieving the development of self-help ability.

Thus, the purposes of the implementation of AR gamification are (1) enabling beginner-level learners of Japanese as a second language to deepen their understanding of natural disasters and preparation for them and (2) having learners actively learn how to help themselves in the event of a natural disaster by impressing upon them the belief that such disasters could happen to them. About three months after the students began learning Japanese, disaster preparedness learning was carried out, lasting approximately one week (Table 8.2).

First, a documentary film was screened to provide students with background knowledge about natural disasters and raise awareness of the importance of disaster preparedness learning. Then, reading activities were used to provide more information and to introduce new Japanese vocabulary and expressions related to natural disasters and disaster preparedness. This was done to ensure that the learners would not encounter words and phrases that were completely new to them in the fieldwork activities. These terms were also scaffolded into learning materials to continue students' exposure to them during this section of the course.

Table 8.2 Procedures of disaster preparedness learning

1. Watched a documentary film (with English subtitles) based on interviews conducted after the Great East Japan Earthquake
2. Read texts about the film as well as other natural disasters in Japan
3. Conducted fieldwork in groups on campus to learn about emergency facilities and equipment and shared the findings in class
4. Conducted off-campus fieldwork in groups to create an evacuation map and shared the information in class
5. Visited the Life Safety Learning Center to learn about and practice how to handle emergency situations
6. Reflected on the activities and wrote a report

Game implementation

Among the activities listed in Table 8.2, gamification was realized using AR technology in preparation for the reading activity (2), on-campus fieldwork (3) and off-campus fieldwork (4). These activities used ARIS (https://fielddaylab. org/make/aris/), an AR game editor developed at the University of Wisconsin–Madison in the United States. ARIS makes it possible to make AR games using location information and things that exist in the real world (Hatasa 2018; Yonemoto 2019). For example, one can create AR games on computers and play them on mobile devices such as smartphones and tablets. Creating, managing and playing games requires a personal account, which is free to set up.

The games were developed using the ARIS's function for identifying a player's current location information obtained through GPS. Players walk around holding a mobile device. Once a player enters a certain area set by a game developer, an event or message is shown on the device's screen. A specific task or a multiple-choice question can then be given to the player. A sound or a movie could be also incorporated into a task. Another function of ARIS used in the reading activity was to permit users to move around on the map on the screen without physically moving, and similarly engaging in the activity via their mobile devices.

Preparation for reading activity

The reading activity used two texts written by the author: one is about the documentary film based on interviews conducted after the Great East Japan Earthquake and another about natural disasters learners might experience while in Japan. Before reading the second text, learners were asked to play a game to learn about the damage and impact of natural disasters in Japan in 2018.

The game considered three natural disasters: earthquakes, heavy rains and volcanic eruptions. The on-screen map of Japan included four marked areas affected by such natural disasters. When a player chooses one of these areas, a short video clip is played to allow players to visually understand what happened in the area. Next, the player is provided with an explanation of what happened and what impact the disaster had with some photos (Figure 8.1).

The following images show the areas affected by the natural disasters in 2018 and the impact of the earthquake in Hokkaido.

At the end, players are asked to answer one question related to a natural disaster connected to their surrounding environment. These questions helped

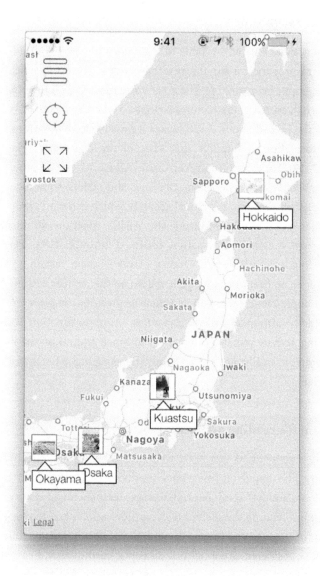

Figure 8.1 Screenshots of the game for the reading activity.

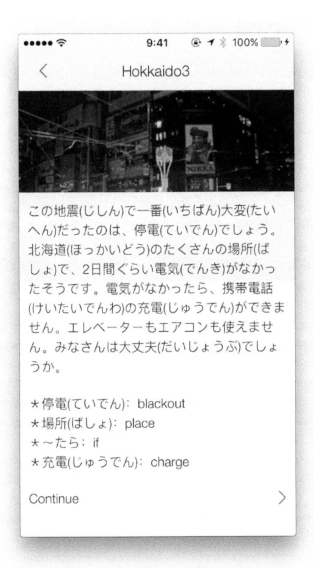

Figure 8.1 *Continued*

players feel closer to the natural disasters. For example, the question about earthquakes asked players to determine the most recent earthquake that had occurred in the area in which they live. Learners were asked to play the game at home and to share their answers and talk freely about how they felt about natural disasters.

On-campus fieldwork

The on-campus fieldwork aimed to familiarize learners with the signs, equipment and facilities related to natural disasters, such as campus public safety, automated external defibrillators (AEDs) and public phones. Learners were divided into groups and instructed to go to specific places using the campus map on their screens. Once they arrived at the correct destinations, ARIS provided additional instructions on the screens of their mobile devices (Figure 8.2). For example, when in front of a 'rescue vendor', a special vending machine that works without electricity during emergency situations, learners were asked to find another rescue vendor on campus. When they were near a public phone, an important means of communication in the event of a disaster, they were asked to call the author. In this way, ARIS could realize portability and connectivity while learners conducted fieldwork (Klopfer, Squire and Jenkins 2002; Reinders and Pegrum 2016). This meant that learners could engage in learning with the support of the instructor through games even while outside of the classroom.

The image on the left shows where to go on campus while the image on the right shows explanations and instructions about rescue vending machines.

While students were playing the game, they were also asked to take photos of and write memos about the signs, equipment and facilities related to natural disasters in addition to the ones that were provided in the game. For this purpose, one of ARIS's functions that can save and share photos and memos with other players was used.

After returning to the classroom, learners were asked to share what they had learned, as each group could have received different information. Based on the information, they created one campus map for disaster preparedness. At the end of the activity, the author provided further information on these facilities and equipment.

Off-campus fieldwork

The goal of the off-campus fieldwork was to travel to one of the evacuation sites from the campus. There are three evacuation sites within walking distance (fifteen to twenty minutes) of the campus, and each group of learners was asked to choose a different site. After choosing the destination, learners considered the best way to get there by using the *Tōkyō Bōsai* (Disaster Preparedness Tokyo) application. They were asked to imagine that an earthquake had occurred and they were to go to the evacuation site.

Figure 8.2 Screenshots of the game for the on-campus fieldwork.

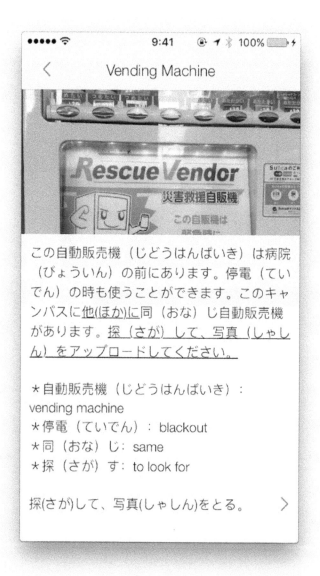

Figure 8.2 *Continued*

While evacuating, learners were instructed to keep the author-developed ARIS game on. In this game, as a player reached a certain area, an event occurred, requiring the player to manage the situation and/or to reconsider the initial evacuation plan (Figure 8.3). For example, when a player was walking past a building with glass walls, text would appear saying, '*ガラスが落ちてきました*. (The glass fell from above.)', along with a photo of scattered glass on the street. Another example was the text, '*100mぐらい前で何かが爆発しました*.

Figure 8.3 Screenshot of the game for the off-campus fieldwork.

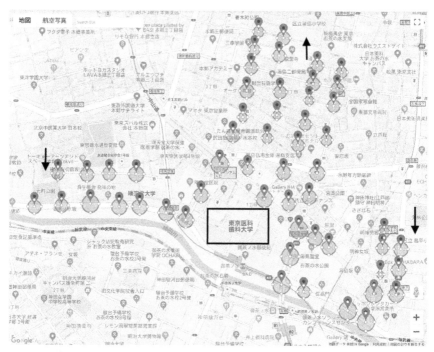

Figure 8.4 Screenshot of the game setting map.

(Something exploded 100 meters away.)', which was created by the sound of an explosion when a player came to an intersection.

Figure 8.3 contains a screenshot of the game for the off-campus fieldwork. The image shows where glass fell from above.

These events were randomly included in the ARIS game along possible routes to the evacuation sites (Figure 8.4). Learners were instructed to manage these events appropriately to arrive successfully at the evacuation sites.

In the setting map which was not shown to players, the campus is indicated by a rectangle and evacuation sites with arrows. Other markers indicate where events occur.

At each evacuation site, learners reviewed the routes they had chosen and discussed reasons for the choice. On the way back to campus, they were asked to carefully observe what the routes were like, such as whether the street was narrow or steep. In addition, they took memos about features along the route, such as vending machines and fire hydrants. Based on the information collected, they created an evacuation map and shared the information in class (Figure 8.5).

Figure 8.5 Evacuation map created by learners.

Analysis

Data collection

In this study, data were collected through (1) a questionnaire conducted with learners after all disaster preparedness learning activities were completed, (2) field notes written by the author during class hours and (3) the author's reflective accounts produced outside of the class. Before collecting data, the author obtained consent from the learners.

The questionnaire asked learners to rate each activity (Table 8.2) on a five-point Likert scale (very useless, useless, neutral, useful, very useful) and explain the reason for their perceived level of usefulness. This questionnaire was anonymous, and no individually identifiable data were retained. During the fieldwork sessions, the author recorded observations of the activities, focusing on learners' reactions and the author's thoughts while accompanying the learners. The author cited learners' opinions collected from the questionnaire to triangulate and further understand their personal perspectives and experiences.

When extrapolating information from the questionnaire, the author did not edit anything unless supplementary information was needed, which was indicated by square brackets. Also, when students gave their answers in Japanese, the author added an English translation which followed the original Japanese sentences.

Data analysis

In conducting data analysis, the author reviewed the field notes and reflective notes, as well as the students' questionnaire results, marking passages that raised issues regarding the research questions. The author used the constant comparative method (Glaser and Strauss 1967) to group passages into meaningful categories through comparison.

Results

This implementation was designed to provide international students with a beginner level of Japanese language with opportunities to reinforce their language skills for natural disasters and to learn about preparation while exploring their surrounding environment. Thus, in addition to a visit to the Life Safety Learning Center, learners used various resources and tools for learning. As a result, the data obtained indicate that it had positive influences on learning Japanese for disaster preparedness while students deepened their understanding about what possible natural disasters were like and how they could manage in different situations.

Overall, the implementation of gamification into disaster preparedness learning in a course for beginners was rated favourably by the learners. In sum, it could result in (1) meaningful communication and learning activities in the real world by expanding learning beyond the classroom and (2) a rapid consolidation of vocabulary and expressions through the use of actual signs and facilities. Also, one important factor that can successfully realize such learning is a more realistic understanding of natural disasters, as these exercises clearly indicated that such disasters could happen to learners.

Communication activities in the real world

Previous studies (e.g. Miyagi, Hanazono and Nakai 2014) have suggested that one of the challenges of implementing disaster preparedness learning into beginning-level courses is the insufficient language skills of learners. However, the current case shows that it actually encourages communication in Japanese as Reinders and Wattana's (2014) study illustrates. The following conversation occurred during the on-campus fieldwork between one of the learners and a university security guard. The task that they were doing at that time was to find as many public phones as possible near the campus. While they were walking, they saw a security guard nearby and asked if he knew where public phones were.

Learner R: 近くで他に公衆電話がありますか. (Are there other public phones nearby?)

Guard A: 公衆電話、近くは、あと、反対側になっちゃう. (Public phone, nearby, it is on the opposite side.)

Learner R: 反対側. (On the opposite side.)

Guard A: 通りになっちゃう。構内にはない、大学の中にはない. (It's on the street. There's none on campus. No public phones inside campus.)

Learner R: あ一、ない. (Ah, none.)

Before asking the guard for help, Learner R practiced the question sentence '近くで他に公衆電話がありますか. (Are there other public phones nearby?)' with other learners in group. After the conversation with the guard, they also asked questions about where the AED and campus public safety were, which they were looking for as part of the fieldwork. Thus, this activity naturally created a situation in which they could help each other and use Japanese in their everyday environment. In this respect, social interactivity (Klopfer, Squire and Jenkins 2002; Reinders and Pegrum 2016) was embodied in the activity, meaning that learners were able to interact and collaborate with others. Importantly, regarding this conversation, after returning to the classroom, the students communicated with the author:

Author: How did you know [the location]?

Learner O: We asked the security guard.

Author: 英語で? (In English?)

Learner O & P: 日本語で. (In Japanese.)

Author: 本当に. (Great.)

Through this experience, the learners seemed to recognize that they could communicate with other people in Japanese when necessary and that people would try to understand and help them.

Communication is not just about words or expressions. Another example of learning about communication in the real world occurred during one of the on-campus fieldwork tasks. The task was to find a public phone and make a phone call to the author (Figure 8.6). One group of students found a phone and

Figure 8.6 A scene of the on-campus fieldwork.

tried to make a phone call, but they failed twice and gave up. They talked about this experience during the review session in class and it turned out that they attempted to make the phone call using ten-yen coins.

Thanks to this episode, the author could explain that, in addition to the usefulness of public phones at times of natural disaster, ten yen is not enough to make a long-distance call, including on mobile phones, although these coins can be used with public phones.

As such, any instance of language use is embedded within a certain context, which is what Klopfer, Squire and Jenkins (2002) and Reinders and Pegrum (2016) call context sensitivity. Utilizing AR allowed students to expand their learning beyond the four walls of the classroom by relocating the place of learning to the real world. For example, it incorporated the real life surrounding the learners, such as the campus or their neighbourhoods, and provided information or set tasks related to specific real-world objects and locations (Figure 8.7). Furthermore, applications such as ARIS combined with the concept of gamification made it possible to create situations in which learners were actively participating in learning.

During off-campus fieldwork, the learners occasionally ignored the event even though they understood that something had happened in the game. For example,

Figure 8.7 A scene of the off-campus fieldwork.

in the event where '*たくさんの人がこちらに向かって歩いてきます*. (A lot of people are walking towards us)' on the way to the evacuation site, one group of students stopped and talked about the situation, but eventually continued walking, flowing back into the crowd. In the review of the activity after arriving at the evacuation site, they said that even though they could understand what the sentence meant, they did not know what they should do. During discussion, the learners explored possible reasons why many people would be walking in a certain direction and reconfirmed the importance of flexibility, meaning not only the route but also the chosen evacuation site need not be bound by the initial plan. As such, they appeared to realize the necessity of understanding language in the context of real life.

Consolidation of words and expressions

In addition to understanding communication outside the classroom, these activities helped beginner-level learners and contributed to the acquisition of relevant words and expressions. Generally speaking, most of the vocabulary related to natural disasters such as *jishin* (earthquake), *shōkaki* (fire extinguisher) and *hinanjo* (evacuation site) are rarely seen in beginner-level Japanese.

- Learning the words which are associated to natural disaster [was useful].
- マグニチュードと震度の違いを知っています. (I know the difference between magnitude and earthquake intensity.)

Aside from simply visiting the Life Safety Learning Center, through a variety of activities, learners were repeatedly exposed to the same words and expressions, most of which were embedded in a specific context. For instance, students were exposed to the word *shōkaki* (fire extinguisher) for the first time during on- and off-campus fieldwork assignments and then learned how to use it, actually using a fire extinguisher at the centre. Also, one student took a memo during the on-campus fieldwork regarding the altitude of a nearby subway station exit as follows: ここで*海抜は15.2メートル*です. (The altitude here is 15.2 metres.)

It seems students could consolidate their knowledge of vocabulary, which were, more critically, words that they considered important. The assertion that these activities helped students learn words better is based on the observation that these learners used more Japanese words related to natural disasters than previous learners when asked to reflect upon the activities. For example, the author noticed that the learners used *shōkaki* (fire extinguisher) even while speaking in English. Also, one student wrote in their reflection, 'Sometimes I didn't notice these facilities, ex. しょうかき, でんわボックス. (fire extinguisher, phone box).'

It was also observed that learners used new words repeatedly within an activity, such as *bōsai sentā* (disaster prevention centre). The on-campus fieldwork involves a task to find as many disaster prevention centres as possible, as several exist on campus. When one group asked a security guard the first time, they used Google Translate to figure out how to say *disaster prevention centre* in Japanese. When they subsequently asked another person the same question, they could successfully use *bōsai sentā* (disaster prevention centre) without checking the dictionary.

> Learner K: 防災センターは他にがありますか. (Are there other disaster prevention centers?)
> Guard B: スロープをのぼって. あ、今、案内しますね. (Go up the slope. Ah, I will show you now.)
> Learner K: はい、ありがとうございます. ありがとうございます.
> (Yes, thank you. Thank you.)

Likewise, by making meaningful use of games, it became possible to introduce certain forms of Japanese to learners under realistic and natural circumstances.

Figure 8.8 Photos that the learners took during the on-campus fieldwork. From left to right, Fire extinguisher, water hose and sea level sign.

Examples include the imperative and prohibitive forms, neither of which learners commonly have a chance to use in daily life as these forms could convey disrespect and impoliteness to interlocutors. However, as these forms were shorter than other forms and could send a strong message to listeners, they

Figure 8.8 *Continued*

were often used in emergency situations. During off-campus fieldwork, learners heard 'にげろ！ (Run away!)' and 'くるな！ (Don't come!)' in the AR game on the way to the evacuation site. When they heard these instructions in the game, they did not understand them at the time. Thus, when subsequently reviewing the activity, the author introduced and explained the forms.

Figure 8.8 *Continued*

Still, words related to natural disasters remained difficult for the beginner-level students, as the following questionnaire response indicates:

- We had a chance to learn vocabulary related to disasters. It is better to move the class slowly because the vocabulary is quite difficult.

Vocabulary challenges seemed more prominent in the reading activity. Although learners played a game before the reading activity, the focus of the game involved familiarizing them with natural disasters by providing information as well as asking questions. All information was given in Japanese, with English translations added to words that had not yet been learned. Nonetheless, as learners' attention was largely drawn to what happened during the disasters, they put less effort towards remembering the vocabulary. As this was a course for beginners, in future, it would be necessary to consider what can be done to ensure better understanding and reinforcement of vocabulary by drawing on the strength of games.

Awareness of natural disasters

The perceived effectiveness of these activities, especially in learning Japanese for disaster preparedness, is closely related to the fact that the learners could regard natural disasters as realistic and important. Previous cases of disaster preparedness learning (Matsumoto 2015; Kondo and Kawasaki 2016) point out the difficulty of having learners consider natural disasters a reality. This is partly because learners may have never experienced such disasters and, therefore, tend to think of the activities as training. Of course, this does not mean that the meaning of disaster drills can be denied. As the following survey responses indicate, knowledge about disaster preparedness is valuable for international students.

- It helped us to know for the first time where to access emergency response items and where to converge during emergency situations.
- I wasn't familiar with the on-campus things we could use during a disaster, so I really liked this activity.
- If in the future, earthquake happens, we have an experience of finding a shelter and it could be easier.

In addition, using AR games developed with gamification could transform this view on disaster preparedness learning from a simple exercise on learning about disaster preparedness through first-hand experience to an activity where students think on their own about what they need to do when natural disasters occur. One student wrote,

> This activity was fun and interesting because we had the opportunity to confront with the imitative accidental situations which may occur when disaster happens.

Figure 8.9 A scene of the off-campus fieldwork.

During the off-campus fieldwork, learners discussed ideas with each other and changed original routes to the evacuation site when they heard an explosion from the front. They also crossed to the other side of the road when they found scattered glass on the street (Figure 8.9).

In the above figure, the learners were trying to understand what happened in the game and discussing what to do.

Thus, AR games can help learners believe that these natural disasters could happen to them. This interpretation is based on the aforementioned observations and the following learners' excerpts.

- My attention was drawn to reality of experiencing a natural disaster while in Japan.
- 僕は前よりじしんがこわくなりました。僕はじしんのじゅんびは じゅうようだと思います. (I am more afraid of earthquakes than before. I think preparation for earthquakes is important.)

What is critical here is that learners' understanding transcended being familiar with disasters to reach the importance of preparing for them. Such an understanding of the significance of learning entails a positive and proactive attitude towards learning and, ultimately, effective language learning.

Conclusions

Utilizing Kim et al.'s (2018) definition, this paper has examined the effectiveness of implementing gamification in disaster education for beginner-level learners of Japanese as a second language. The study design resulted in several positive outcomes which are applicable for other learning topics in the second language classroom, namely providing learners with opportunities to actually use and practice language in a meaningful context while actively participating in disaster preparedness. As a consequence, in this case, during fieldwork the learners perceived that they could learn the necessary natural disaster vocabulary and expressions as well as communicate with others in Japanese. What made this possible was the learners' realistic understanding of natural disasters, especially by situating them in their natural environment. When it comes to enhancing learners' self-help ability (Kitagawa 2014; Kondo and Kawasaki 2015; Leleito et al. 2015), it seems to have become an opportunity to search for and consider information from the surrounding environment based on what they have learned. One student noted, '今，私の家と学校に近い防災施設のところと避難所と避難経路を知っています. (Now I know the location of the closest disaster prevention facility and evacuation site to my place and school as well as the routes there.)'

Having said that, for the future, it is necessary to examine how this learning can be extended beyond the exercise itself. In other words, developing ways to encourage learners to explore what is needed and to learn for themselves in terms of disaster preparedness. The following two pictures are an indication of continued individual engagement with course learning (Klopfer, Squire and Jenkins 2002; Reinders and Pegrum 2016) even after the activities ended (Figure 8.10). Throughout the semester, learners were asked to introduce Japanese words or phrases that they had seen or were curious about in turn. Usually, the students chose phrases that they often heard in everyday life. However, during these disaster preparedness activities, two learners chose and introduced phrases related to disaster preparedness.

The above figures show phrases chosen by the learners: 'Get under the desk! The shake seems to have subsided' on the left and 'This is the earthquake early warning. Watch out for strong tremors' on the right.

In this implementation, there are only a limited number of examples of successful realization of individualizing learning. Consequently, more consideration needs to be given to how language learning activities can be further connected to student lives outside the classroom.

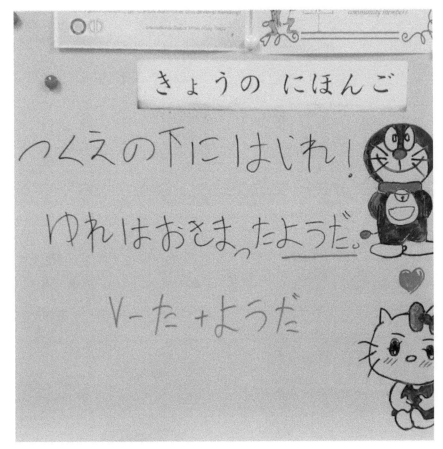

Figure 8.10 Photos of Japanese phrases that the learners introduced.

The focus of this implementation was to learn about the impact of natural disasters and preparations for them. As described herein, such implementation could contribute to the development of learners' self-help ability to some extent regardless of language proficiency level. As challenges in communication can also be attributed to listeners' perceptions of and attitudes towards foreign residents, including international students (Kondo and Kawasaki 2015), some difficulties that foreign residents might encounter during natural disasters cannot be solved by their efforts. However, this situation could not be dealt with in the current activity. Therefore, it is necessary to incorporate the situation of natural disasters into activities more comprehensively, involving those people who might come into contact with foreign residents in Japan such as Japanese students and university staff.

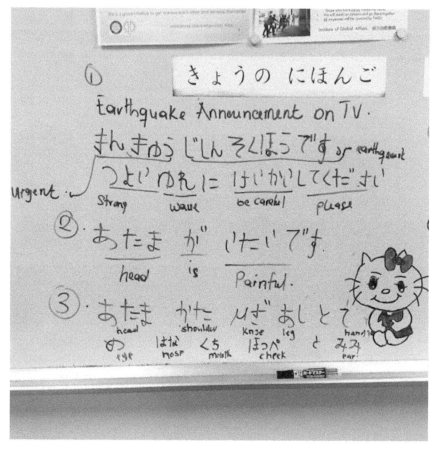

Figure 8.10 *Continued*

References

Glaser, B. G., and A. L. Strauss (1967), *The Discovery of Grounded Theory: Strategies for Qualitative Research*, New York: Aldine De Gruyter.

Godwin-Jones, R. (2016), 'Augmented Reality and Language Learning: From Annotated Vocabulary to Place-Based Mobile Games', *Language Learning & Technology* 20 (3): 9–19.

Hasegawa, T., M. Koshino and H. Ban (2015), 'An English Vocabulary Learning Support System for the Learner's Sustainable Motivation', *SpringerPlus* 4 (99): 1–9.

Hatasa, K. (2018), 'ARIS Kontentsu no Jissen to Hyōka: Shokyū, Chūkyū, Jōkyū Kara [Implementation and Evaluation of ARIS Contents for Language Instruction]', *The 24th Princeton Japanese Pedagogy Forum Proceedings*, 393–417.

Holden, C., and J. Sykes (2011), 'Leveraging Mobile Games for Place-Based Language Learning', *International Journal of Game-Based Learning* 1 (2): 1–18.

Iori, I. (2019), 'Immigrant Acceptance and "Plain Japanese"', *English Speaking Union of Japan*. Available online: http://www.esuj.gr.jp/jitow/558_index_detail.php (accessed 15 September 2019).

Kessler, G. (2018), 'Technology and the Future of Language Teaching', *Foreign Language Annals* 51 (1): 205–18.

Kim, S., K. Song, B. Lockee and J. Burton (2018), *Gamification in Learning and Education: Enjoy Learning Like Gaming*, New York: Springer.

Kitagawa, K. (2014), 'Continuity and Change in Disaster Education in Japan', *Journal of the History of Education Society* 44 (3): 371–90.

Klopfer, E., and K. Squire (2008), 'Environmental Detectives: The Development of an Augmented Reality Platform for Environmental Simulations', *Educational Technology Research and Development* 56 (2): 203–28.

Klopfer, E., K. Squire and H. Jenkins (2002), 'Environmental Detectives: PDAs as a Window into a Virtual Simulated World', Paper presented at the International Workshop on Wireless and Mobile Technologies in Education, Växjö, Sweden.

Kondo, Y., and K. Kawasaki (2015), 'Ryūgakusē o Jōhō Jakusha Tarashimeru Mono no Jittai: Ryūgakusē Niyoru Bōsai Jōhō Shūshū Katsudō Deno Jirē Kenkyū [The Causes of Inadequate Access to Disaster Prevention Education among Foreign Exchange Students: A Case Analysis of Disaster Prevention Information Gathering by Foreign Exchange Students]', *Studies of Language and Cultural Education* 13: 118–33.

Kondo, Y., and K. Kawasaki (2016), 'Gaikokujin Ryūgakusē ni Yoru "Bōsai Manyuaru" Dukuri: Bōsai Jijoryoku Ikusē no Tameno Kyōiku Jissen [A Disaster Prevention Manual by and for Foreign Exchange Students: An Educational Practice in Cultivating Self-Help Ability for Disaster Prevention]', *Ryūgaku Kōryu* 64: 10–19.

Leleito, E., K. Shimasaki, R. Watanabe and H. Kawabata (2015), 'Disaster Risk Reduction Education for International Students through Inter-University Collaboration', *Journal of the International Education & Exchange Center (IEEC), Nagoya University* 2: 37–47.

Matsumoto, H. (2015), ' "Bōsai o Kangaeyō" no Jissenhōkoku: Nihonjijō Kurasu de Okonaru igi to Kanōsē [A Report on "Let's Think about Disaster Prevention": Meanings and Possibilities of Japanese Culture and Society Class]', *Academic Japanese Journal* 6: 39–47.

Miyagi, T., S. Hanazono and Y. Nakai (2014), 'Kyōdō ni Yoru Bōsai Gakushū: Ryūgakusē ni Taisuru 4-tsu no Jissen Kara no Kōsatsu [Collaborative Learning of Disaster Prevention: Discussion Based on Four Practical Cases for International Students]', *Bulletin of Japanese Language Center for International Students, Tokyo University of Foreign Studies* 40: 201–17.

Reinders, H., and M. Pegrum (2016), 'Supporting Language Learning on the Move: An Evaluative Framework for Mobile Language Learning Resources', in B. Tomlinson (ed.), *Second Language Acquisition Research and Materials Development for Language Learning*, 116–41, London: Routledge.

Reinders, H., and S. Wattana (2014), 'Can I Say Something? The Effects of Digital Game Play on Willingness to Communicate', *Language Learning & Technology* 18 (2): 101–23.

Shah, M. F., and O. Murao (2013), 'Foreigners' Evacuation Behavior in the Great East Japan Earthquake: A Case of Iwaki City in Fukushima Prefecture', *Journal of Disaster Research* 8: 802–13.

Werbach, K., and D. Hunter (2012), *For the Win: How Game Thinking Can Revolutionize Your Business*, Philadelphia: Wharton Digital Press.

Yonemoto, K. (2019), '"To Combine Knowledge and the Real World" Kakuchō genjitsu o riyōshita nihongo gakushū no kokoromi [Incorporating Augmented Reality into Japanese Language Learning]', in Y. Tohsaku and J. Lee (eds), *ICT x Nihongo kyōiku: Jōhō tsūshin gijutsu o riyōshita nihongo kyōiku no riron to jissen [ICT x Japanese Language Education]*, 138–47, Tokyo: Hituzi Syobo.

9

The relationship between extramural digital gameplay and twenty-first-century skills in the language classroom

Daniel J. Mills and Benjamin Thanyawatpokin

Introduction

Recently, the acquisition of twenty-first-century skills has become an increasingly important part of the curriculum in the Japanese educational context, especially competencies and literacies related to digital technology. However, the way that language learning students interact with technologies is richer and more varied than the research portrays. Nowadays, students are exposed to various digital technologies before seeing them in the classroom. By primary school, students are using cell phones, social networking sites and digital games. Research has suggested that extramural digital technology usage has often played a part in facilitating the development of twenty-first-century literacies (Black 2009). Similarly, research has hinted that in-class gameplay could lead to twenty-first-century skill acquisition (Thomas, Ge and Greene 2011). Technology usage inside the classroom has also been investigated in regard to how it facilitates twenty-first-century skills (Bell 2010). Nonetheless, there has always been a divide between how students learn from technology inside and outside the classroom. It is here that we have identified a gap in the research. There is a paucity of studies that look at how out-of-classroom digital game playing can influence twenty-first-century skills inside the classroom. The purpose of this chapter is to investigate the link between out-of-classroom digital gameplay and twenty-first-century skill development.

In order to accomplish this goal, 377 university students at two Japanese universities were surveyed. The survey instrument consisted of four sections: (1) twenty-first-century skills, (2) digital game perceptions, (3) digital game usage and (4) demographics. The results of this research study were that the participants' assessment of their twenty-first-century skills was positive overall ($M = 3.20$); the subscale, collaboration, received the highest mean score ($M = 3.44$). Smartphones ($M = 3.13$) and portable game consoles ($M = 2.34$) were the most frequently used devices for the participants to engage in digital gameplay and they most often played adventure games ($M = 2.43$) as well as puzzle and sports games ($M = 2.42$). The digital game perceptions, device usage and genre usage scales were all positively correlated with the total twenty-first-century skill scale. This signified that games could be beneficial in promoting twenty-first-century skills outside of the classroom. Secondary conclusions also indicate that students who have gained a basis in twenty-first-century skills outside of the classroom would benefit from in-class training and solidification of those skills.

In the current pedagogical landscape in Japan, many educators, administrators and faculties have taken it upon themselves to develop twenty-first-century literacies among their English language students. This is mainly for the purpose of creating more globally minded graduates who can compete in the current international job market and bring much-needed skills to companies which are looking to expand beyond their borders. However, it is not understood the extent to which technology, that is omnipresent in our daily lives, affects the development of these skills and their application in the classroom. Twenty-first-century literacies in general comprise an extremely broad array of competencies; from critical thinking to technology literacy, life and career skills to leadership and responsibility, there are quite a large number of proficiencies that teachers must keep in mind (The Partnership for 21st Century Skills 2019). Currently, in the field of education, 'digital natives' are often viewed as having more exposure to technology than those of previous generations (Van Eck 2006). However, to what extent digital natives benefit from this increased exposure is not yet fully understood. Moreover, there are opportunities outside of the classroom that can impact the above-mentioned twenty-first-century skills before or in tandem with classroom instruction. This becomes more important when observing how these out-of-school technologies can impact English as a Foreign Language (EFL) education. The current research will focus upon the role that games specifically play in the formation of these twenty-first-century skills and how these skills correlate with digital games usage outside of the classroom.

Literature review

Twenty-first-century skills and new literacies

Modern pedagogies and frameworks which deal with fostering literacies and skills needed for the ever-changing landscape of business and international society have recently confronted a change in the conceptualization of what to teach students. This has led researchers to investigate the interplay between skills such as language, socioeconomics, culture, politics, technology and how this knowledge can be utilized to create more globally and professionally minded students (Cope and Kalantzis 2009). Originally, from this impetus to change the way we approach education, the concept of multiliteracies was created by the New London Group (1996). They conceived of this term in order to provide new ways of looking at how meaning was made in discourse. In essence, this term conceptualizes how meaning arises from many different modes, influences and cultural considerations. An important point in this conversation was the emphasis on multimodality, or what the scholars argued was the power that digital literacies and technology had on learners in the modern world. This led to a different approach to teaching known as situated learning, which was the philosophy to teach students based on the skills they had, and then what they needed. An attempt to catalogue these skills arose in the form of twenty-first-century skills (The Partnership for 21st Century Skills 2019). A brief conceptualization of what these skills involve is shown below:

Learning skills

- Critical thinking
- Creativity
- Collaboration
- Communication

Literacy skills

- Information literacy
- Media literacy
- Technology literacy

Life skills

- Flexibility
- Initiative

- Social skills
- Productivity
- Leadership

The cataloguing of these skills gave teachers a reference for what they may encounter when approaching their classrooms with a multiliteracies or a twenty-first-century skills style. A point of interest is the emphasis in this field of study on digital technologies and multimodalities. New affordances for learning and methodology have cropped up due to the increased proliferation of technology in today's educational landscape. Due to this, there is a need for more research concerning how these technologies fully impact students outside the classroom, and how those skills translate into classroom contexts so that teachers can work towards properly building them up.

Digital game-based language learning (DGBLL)

Research in the past decade has paved the way for digital and non-digital games to be recognized as tools that could support learning. Gee (2007) remarked that games can impart linguistic knowledge on those who played them to build literacy skills. deHaan (2019) also echoed this sentiment observing that games, if used correctly, provide substantiations of language that can, with pedagogical assistance, be viable as language learning materials. Examples of this include online games and their impact on online and classroom communication (Chik 2015), single-player games and linguistic gains (Miller and Hegelheimer 2006; Ranalli 2008; deHaan 2013), teacher roles in the game-based language learning classroom (Suh, Kim and Kim 2010; Molin 2017), in-class use of multiplayer game contexts in order to facilitate better scores on standardized tests (Suh, Kim and Kim 2010) and surveys which investigate the feasibility of learning from games inside and outside the classroom (Wiklund and Love 2009; Sundqvist and Wikstrom 2015; Sundqvist 2019). Meta-analyses of games in educational settings both inside and outside the classroom are also prevalent (Ke 2011; Connolly et al. 2012; Hung et al. 2018). However, there is evidence that some of the literature surrounding games may have been mistakenly reporting gamification or gamified activities. This is evident when looking into research designs such as Young and Wang (2014) and Allen et al. (2014).

As mentioned above, a new and emerging element of research in DGBLL has been the extramural (or outside-the-classroom) side of the field. Most students get their first exposure to games outside of school and this arena in which learning occurs cannot be ignored. There are connections that can be made between exposure to language outside of the classroom and real language-learning benefits (Sylven and Sundqvist 2012; Chik 2015; Sundqvist and Wikstrom 2015; Scholz and Schulze 2017; Sundqvist 2019). Sylven and Sundqvist (2012) reported that elementary students who played games outside of the classroom were more likely to exhibit higher scores on English tests. This suggests that gameplay outside of the classroom context can have an influence on what happens inside the class. Chik (2015) also indicated that if there is an underlying motivation to play games in a different language (there could be a variety of reasons such as there not being a native-language version of the game), games can promote learning of language acquisition strategies, facilitate autonomy and help players communicate with people whom they would normally not communicate with in order to get help to play the game. Sundqvist and Wikstrom (2015) also proved a positive relation of language skills when learned in out-of-classroom contexts and performance in language classrooms. Thus, it can be seen that extramural gameplay is important to understanding the full profile of language learners when considering the entire ecology of language learning.

Games and twenty-first-century skills

In terms of literacies and competencies outside of pure language learning, there has also been much research done in this area that suggests games can promote learning on a deeper level. Hung et al. (2018) mentioned a current paucity of empirical studies which include the development of twenty-first-century skills and other literacies in the language classroom. However, there are many researchers in the field of game-based learning who do work related to or touching upon skills that are directly relatable to twenty-first-century skills. Hourdequin, York and deHaan (2017) mentioned that games may vary in content and affordances for learning in the classroom, but that does not take away the fact that as a whole there are affordances for learning various skills and competencies such as twenty-first-century skills. Projects that forego gameplay but rather focus on the design and activities which go into creating a game have also found that engaging with these types of problems may, in fact, also improve critical thinking, the ability to incorporate feedback into personal projects and creativity (Thomas, Ge and Greene 2011). Squire et al. (2004) reported that digital simulation games could aid in mastery of abstract concepts through active play, visual representations of those concepts on screen and goal-based activities which promote understanding. In their case, it was teaching concepts in the subject of physics. Steinkuehler and Duncan (2008) also observed players in online digital worlds as participating in sharing knowledge, constructing knowledge with other players, and processes involving argument, evaluation and synthesizing knowledge. Taken in total, it can be seen that from the studies mentioned above, games played both in and outside the classroom do have the potential to facilitate growth in competencies normally associated with twenty-first-century skills. There may not be much research at the current time of studies investigating their impact on the language classroom, but this study will seek to delve deeper in this area.

Research questions

As the field currently has a lack of studies which investigate the link between extramural DGBLL and their effect on twenty-first-century skills, the current study will investigate the following research questions:

1. What are Japanese university students' overall self-assessment of their twenty-first-century skills in terms of creativity, critical thinking, communication and collaboration?
2. What are Japanese university students' actual usage of digital games outside of the classroom?
3. What is the relationship between Japanese university students' extramural digital gameplay and twenty-first-century skills?

Methodology

Setting and sample

The research took place at two Japanese universities located in Western Japan. One was a public university and the other was private. The public university had a student population of 16,256 Japanese students and 1,303 international students as of 2018. The private university was larger with a total student enrolment of 32,600 in the same year.

A sample of students were drawn from seven academic departments including economics, sociology, business, education, gastronomy management, medicine and Law. Four-hundred and twenty students enrolled in fifteen classes were asked to participate in this research project. The response rate was 84 per cent; 377 students completed the survey.

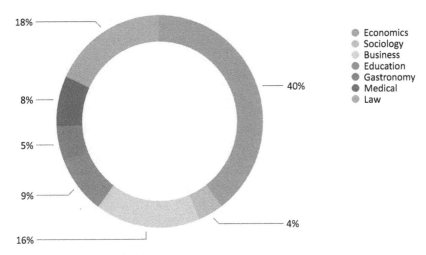

18%

8%

5%

9%

16%

40%

4%

- Economics
- Sociology
- Business
- Education
- Gastronomy
- Medical
- Law

Figure 9.1 Participants' majors.

Participants

A small majority of participants were male (54.9 per cent); females made up 42.7 per cent of the sample and 2.4 per cent of students declined to answer. The participants ranged in age from 17 to 33 ($M = 18.8$). The majority of participants attended the private university (66.6 per cent) rather than the public university (33.3 per cent) and were studying a variety of subjects (see Figure 9.1).

Survey instrument

The survey instrument consisted of four sections: (1) twenty-first-century skills, (2) digital game perceptions, (3) digital game usage and (4) demographics. Section 1 was influenced by several studies and instruments (Dawson and Siemens 2014; Ravitz 2014; The Partnership for 21st Century Skills 2019) and was divided into four subscales: (1) creativity, (2) critical thinking, (3) communication and (4) collaboration. A five-point Likert scale was utilized with the responses of 1 (*strongly disagree*), 2 (*disagree*), 3 (*neutral*), 4 (*agree*) and 5 (*strongly agree*). Section 2 of the survey contained several items related to participants' perceptions towards the use of digital games. These items were based on the researchers' experiences as well as previous informal categorizations (Hurst 2015). The five-point Likert scale identified in section 1 was used for the items in this section.

Data collection and analysis

The data were collected during the spring semester of 2019 (April–July). The researchers created a Google Forms document that was provided to students at the two locations through the universities' learning management systems. The survey and cover letter were in Japanese. The cover letter gave potential participants information regarding the study and their rights as research subjects. It was made clear to the students that participation was voluntary and would not affect their course evaluation.

After the data collection phase was completed, the researchers transcribed the data into an Excel spreadsheet, which was later transferred to Statistical Package for the Social Sciences (SPSS) for further data analysis. Frequencies and descriptive statistics were calculated for all of the twenty-first-century and digital game scales and subscales. In addition, a Pearson's product-moment correlation test was conducted to ascertain the relationship between digital game perceptions and usage and twenty-first-century skills.

Results and discussion

Research question one: Twenty-first-century skills

Creativity

Creativity for this survey centred around not only the traditional sense of making and creating media but also the ability to synthesize knowledge and solve problems in novel ways. Nevertheless, the participants in this study did not see themselves as very creative. Less than half of participants agreed or strongly agreed with items 1 (42.7 per cent) and 3 (40.9 per cent). Items 2 and 4, which referred to the inception and completion of creative endeavours, received some of the lowest mean values (Table 9.1). Furthermore, participants were not confident in their ability to create media, with only 27.3 per cent agreeing or strongly agreeing with item 5. As most students at the school use smartphones and normally access materials in class on these devices, it was surprising that more of them were not involved in the creation of media. Item 2 is notable due to the very wide implication of what it means to do 'creative projects'. This low score suggests another dimension to students' collaborative and critical thinking skills, as there is less confidence when a project is thought to be something 'creative'.

Table 9.1 Means and standard deviations of creativity

Item	M	SD
1. I am a creative person.	3.14	1.15
2. I can think of and finish creative projects.	2.88	1.12
3. I know how to use knowledge from many different subjects to solve problems.	3.13	1.06
4. I'm not good at thinking of new creative projects. [R]	2.67	1.10
5. I can make media (YouTube videos, music, paintings, photographs, etc.).	2.65	1.31

Note: Scale ranging from 1 – *strongly disagree* to 5 – *strongly agree*. [R] = reversed item.

Table 9.2 Means and standard deviations of critical thinking

Item	M	SD
6. I can reason effectively.	3.13	1.11
7. I can't analyse complex problems or systems. [R]	2.89	1.20
8. I am able to make judgements and decisions in a group.	3.52	1.12
9. I am skilled at solving problems I am not familiar with.	2.73	1.08
10. I can evaluate information I find when researching online/at the library to understand if it is valuable/truthful/related to my work.	3.56	1.01

Note: Scale ranging from 1 – *strongly disagree* to 5 – *strongly agree*. [R] = reversed item.

Critical thinking

Regarding critical thinking, the participants' responses varied depending on the task. The highest mean values were associated with items 8 and 10 (Table 9.2). More than half of the students agreed or strongly agreed that they were skilled at making decisions in a group (60.2 per cent) and that they could evaluate information to ensure its veracity (59.7 per cent). In contrast, the lowest mean was associated with question 9, with almost half of respondents disagreeing or strongly disagreeing that they could solve problems with which they were unfamiliar. Due to a Japanese cultural propensity to favour group actions and to avoid uncertainty (Gudykunst and Kim 2003), these responses were not surprising.

Communication

Responses to the items in the communication subscale were varied. As Table 9.3 shows, more than half of the students agreed or strongly agreed with statements

Table 9.3 Means and standard deviations of communication

Item	M	SD
11. I can communicate in a variety of ways (speaking, writing, etc.).	3.68	1.08
12. I can communicate in a variety of formats (presentation, discussion, online communication, etc.).	3.37	1.09
13. I can use communication for many purposes (persuasion, explanation, motivation).	3.49	1.06
14. I try to meet and communicate with people outside my own culture.	3.09	1.34
15. I don't view myself as a good communicator. [R]	2.70	1.23

Note: Scale ranging from 1 – *strongly disagree* to 5 – *strongly agree*. [R] = reversed item.

pertaining to their ability to communicate in a variety of ways (63.1 per cent), formats (51.2 per cent) and for many purposes (57.9 per cent). However, less than half of the respondents (42.4 per cent) indicated that they made an effort to meet and communicate with individuals who are not of the same culture. Even more surprising, almost half of the participants (49.6 per cent) agreed or strongly agreed that they were not good communicators.

Collaboration

A majority of the participants agreed or strongly agreed that they worked well with others in a group (Table 9.4). In addition, more than half of respondents (53.5 per cent) agreed or strongly agreed that they could work in group settings on creative projects. However, they were slightly less confident in their ability to plan and manage projects in a group (item 20). Only 29 per cent of participants agreed or strongly agreed that they couldn't use digital technology for group collaboration. The lowest mean value in this subscale was associated with working in diverse groups (item 19). This may suggest that students do not believe they work as well with 'out-of-group' individuals.

Overall, the students' assessment of their twenty-first-century skills was positive. As Table 9.5 shows, the lowest mean value was associated with the subscale of creativity, while collaboration received the highest. Taken on their own, it seems that many students think they were relatively well-rounded in twenty-first-century skills; however, the extent to which the students who reported themselves to play games coloured this data will be further investigated in research question 3.

Table 9.4 Means and standard deviations of collaboration

Item	M	SD
16. In groups, I can work well with other people.	3.75	1.02
17. I can work together with people to do a creative task.	3.40	1.01
18. I cannot use digital technology to collaborate with others. [R]	3.23	1.15
19. I can work in diverse groups of people (different cultures, languages, etc.).	3.06	1.14
20. I'm good at planning and managing projects with others.	3.21	1.09
21. I don't respond well to feedback from teachers/senpai to improve how I work. [R]	4.01	0.97

Note: Scale ranging from 1 – *strongly disagree* to 5 – *strongly agree*. [R] = reversed item.

Table 9.5 Means and standard deviations of twenty-first-century skills scales and subscales

Scale	M	SD
Total	3.20	0.56
Creativity	2.89	0.80
Critical thinking	3.17	0.72
Communication	3.26	0.80
Collaboration	3.44	0.63

Research question 2: Digital games

Perceptions

The mean values associated with the first three items (22, 23 and 24) of this scale (Table 9.6) seem to indicate a slightly negative perception towards digital games among the participants. In particular, only 22.8 per cent of respondents agreed or strongly agreed that they were gamers. However, participants seemed to believe that digital games could help them learn new things (70.3 per cent agree or strongly agree) and interact with people (70.8 per cent agree or strongly agree). Participants were slightly less positive about the ability of digital games to help think deeply about world issues and to experiment with what they had learned in the classroom with 44.3 per cent and 45.9 per cent agreeing with those statements, respectively. As a whole, the data indicate how students viewed games and learning. Interestingly, most students did not report they play games; however, they seem to recognize the potential of them to learn. This signifies a willingness to experiment with games to help support learning materials, but

Table 9.6 Means and standard deviations of digital games perceptions

Item	M	SD
22. Compared to people of my age, I play a lot of digital games.	2.67	1.43
23. I look forward to time when I can play games.	2.81	1.51
24. I would describe myself as a gamer.	2.20	1.43
When you play games, you can:		
25. learn about new things.	3.85	1.04
26. control what I see and experience.	3.59	1.03
27. experience things I learn about.	3.53	1.01
28. use my language skills in the real world.	3.39	1.14
29. interact with other people.	3.85	1.04
30. think deeply about issues in the world.	3.16	1.17
31. become motivated to learn more.	3.53	1.17
32. experiment with things I learned in the classroom.	3.18	1.13
33. interact with others in a foreign language.	2.96	1.26

Note: Scale ranging from 1 – *strongly disagree* to 5 – *strongly agree*. [R] = reversed item.

Table 9.7 Digital game usage: Device

	Response (per cent)				
Item	N	R	O	F	V
34. Smartphone	22.5	18.3	9.3	23.3	26.5
35. Personal computer	67.4	13.8	5.6	7.4	5.8
36. Game console	48.3	14.6	8.8	14.9	13.5
37. Tablet	67.6	11.4	6.6	7.4	6.9
38. Portable game console	47.2	14.9	9.0	14.9	14.1

Note: Scale items: N = *Never*, R = *Rarely*, O = *Occasionally*, F = *Frequently*, V = *Very Frequently*.

there is still an unwillingness to take part. Low scores and high standard deviation on item 30 signify perceptions in relation to what kinds of messages students believe games can impart. In other words, the depth of playing games. Students seem to believe that games cannot facilitate critical thinking of important issues.

Usage

As Table 9.7 shows, the device used most frequently to engage in digital gameplay was the smartphone (M = 3.13) followed by portable game console (M = 2.34). Personal computers (M = 1.71) and tablets (M = 1.75) were used the least.

Table 9.8 Digital game usage: Genre

Item	Response (per cent)				
	N	R	O	F	V
39. MMORPG	62.9	12.2	5.3	12.7	6.9
40. Simulation	50.4	15.4	7.2	18.3	8.8
41. Adventure	43.0	15.6	9.3	19.9	12.2
42. Real-time strategy	56.2	11.1	8.8	11.4	12.5
43. Puzzle	45.1	14.3	7.7	19.4	13.5
44. Action	58.1	12.2	7.7	12.7	9.3
45. Augmented reality	62.9	12.5	6.6	10.6	7.4
46. Fighting	61.3	12.7	10.3	8.5	7.2
47. First-person shooter	61.0	10.1	6.9	11.9	10.1
48. Sports	48.5	12.7	7.7	10.1	21.0
49. Role playing	52.8	11.9	6.9	13.5	14.9
50. Educational	53.3	18.3	12.2	10.6	5.6

Note: Scale items: N = *Never*, R = *Rarely*, O = *Occasionally*, F = *Frequently*, V = *Very Frequently*.

Table 9.9 Means and standard deviations of usage scales

Scale	*M*	*SD*
Perceptions	3.23	0.69
Device	2.24	1.08
Genre	2.12	1.00

As Table 9.8 shows, the type of game most frequently played by respondents was adventure games ($M = 2.43$). In second place were puzzle and sports games ($M = 2.42$). The least frequently played game was augmented reality (AR) ($M = 1.87$), followed by massive multiplayer online role-playing games (MMORPGs) ($M = 1.89$) and fighting games ($M = 1.88$).

Overall, perceptions towards digital games were slightly below the median value (Table 9.9). Actual usage of digital games among the Japanese university students surveyed in this study seems to indicate that they are not frequent users of the technology, based on the means of the device and genre scales. However, according to the participants' self-reported data, they engage in digital gameplay an average of 5.81 hours a week for 7.46 years.

Research question 3: The relationship between
digital games and twenty-first-century skills

Correlation coefficients were computed for the three digital game measures (perceptions, device usage and genre usage) and the total twenty-first-century skill scale as well as its four subscales (creativity, critical thinking, collaboration and communication). In order to control for type I errors across the eight correlations, a Bonferroni approach was utilized. Therefore, a p value of less than 0.005 (0.05/10 = 0.005) was a requirement for significance. Table 9.10 shows that eleven of the fifteen correlations were statistically significant. However, while all the correlation coefficients between digital game perceptions and the twenty-first-century skills total and subscales were greater than 0.35, the correlations associated with device usage and genre usage and twenty-first-century skills were lower.

Data in this section describe the relationship between digital games and self-perceived twenty-first-century skills. While the link is tenuous, the data suggest that students who have a more favourable view of digital games (or possibly secondary sources of information outside of school that have a close link with technology) also exhibit higher confidence in twenty-first-century skills. This falls in line with findings by Sylven and Sundqvist (2012) and Sundqvist (2019) and also slightly deepens the argument. In their study, elementary school children who played games extramurally had higher rates of English literacy. While the findings of this study take data from a completely different culture and set of circumstances, presumably students who continued playing games throughout childhood and into their university years would begin to build other literacies as well. This is an area which requires more research in the future.

Table 9.10 Correlations between twenty-first-century skills and digital games perceptions and usage

Twenty-first-century skills	Digital game perceptions	Device usage	Genre usage
Creativity	0.391*	0.240*	0.258*
Critical thinking	0.444*	0.150*	0.133*
Communication	0.397*	0.050	0.063
Collaboration	0.440*	0.053	0.083
Total	0.539*	0.160*	0.175*

Note: *p < 0.005.

Finally, extramural digital game usage and overall twenty-first-century skill reporting showed a statistically significant correlation; however, it was not so high as to suggest a definitive link between the two. This could have been due to the low amount of self-reported game players in the study; thus, the data were more skewed towards non-users and what they reported. However, extrapolating conclusions from the current data, it suggests the actual playing of games outside the classroom weakly benefits twenty-first-century digital skills. This set of data is quite different from the above-mentioned digital game perception data. In addition, there was no significance found regarding how much students played games and increases in communication and ability to collaborate with other people. This was the same for sorting out games by genre as well. Gameplay, especially in Japan, is not normally something done to communicate with others; it is more of an individual pursuit. Findings appear to support that notion as players who play more games seem to exhibit less inclination to rate themselves as good communicators. In conclusion to the above remarks, it could be said that gameplay does contribute to the formation of twenty-first-century skills; however, simply understanding or adopting a more accepting attitude towards digital games signifies a student who has higher proficiency or (at the least) confidence in their abilities.

Implications and limitations

In a country with many 'false beginners', the university level of English learning in Japan must take into account much more than simply English proficiency level. There are many latent skills that facilitators and students themselves do not consider when designing a curriculum. Each group of students will inevitably be composed of many individuals, all with varied backgrounds and proficiencies. Understanding to what extent certain activities, technologies or literacies are already built up in the students is paramount to making English tasks 'fit' better. This culminates in the recommendation for more instances of needs analysis. It is true that the field has long suffered from a lack of established methodology regarding *how* to do NA (Long 2005), but the research that was presented in this chapter supports carrying out NA with students to some degree. This is especially true if the context in question contains administrative or curriculum-based goals that involve the training of twenty-first-century skills. Sundqvist (2019) suggested that teachers learn how their students think about games when coming up with pedagogical interventions which involve them. It becomes apparent now more than ever that with the increased proliferation of technologies (and games) in the classroom, teachers should be focusing on understanding their students' beliefs and needs. This is especially true when universities in countries such as Japan are pushing students into the international realm and incorporating twenty-first-century skills into language classes. On the subject of NA, the tools that were used in this study were quite unwieldy if used in a normal classroom. Some students remarked it was quite lengthy. Thus, further research into creating a shorter, more succinct way of analysing student needs and beliefs about games and twenty-first-century skills will need to be carried out.

Games as a learning tool should be more seriously considered as a tool for recommended extramural learning. It has been shown through this research that there is a chance games could contribute to the growth of twenty-first-century skills. With sufficient consideration, a list of games can be created that help students visualize and analyse topics that are studied in class. The out-of-class link to twenty-first-century skills may need more research, but with support from in-class time and teacher intervention through appropriate tasks and activities, the bridge towards acquisition can be more readily built. Gee (2007) reported that affinity spaces in games could promote literacy learning. Thus, the usage of MMORPGs or other online-based platforms which incorporate gaming elements could help students gain linguistic skills while concurrently also training literacies that could help students later in life. The shape this will take when connecting it to a pedagogical context is an area that requires more investigation in the future. What steps can teachers take in order to properly ensure gameplay extramurally? How can progress be tracked? What does a curriculum which takes advantage of online games look like? These are questions which require more time to be answered.

Finally, implications for the usage of games in the classroom can also be drawn from the data. Positive perceptions of game usage show that students have a relatively high opinion of the learning benefits games have to offer. However, this brings up the question of pedagogical utilization of games and how activities and tasks can be devised to take advantage of them and further train twenty-first-century skills. As Miller and Hegelheimer (2006) and Ranalli (2008) stated, more consideration into pedagogical intervention is necessary for in-class usage of games. In addition, teacher roles in game-based interventions must also be considered (Molin 2017). Placing games into the classroom context is not enough to support meaningful acquisition of language or learning goals. The data showed students did not believe games were suitable carriers of critical thinking content, but that they could impart knowledge and linguistic content. This again underscores the fact that teachers must devise suitable activities and tasks in order to have students look at games in a different light if they are to use them in ways outside of pure grammar and vocabulary drilling tools. Outside of the above-mentioned studies and efforts by Lombardi (2015), York and deHaan (2018) and Molin (2017), there is not enough research into teacher intervention and practical use of games or gamification in the classroom to facilitate learning. With this research, we know that students feel they are learning things outside the classroom when they play games; the challenge for educators is to find ways in which to utilize those skills inside the classroom. This could range from the use of games to promote cooperation between students in English lessons, or the gradual integration of games as a meaningful message content for content and language integrated learning (CLIL) or task-based language teaching (TBLT) in the language classroom.

Conclusion

In order to provide more relevant insight into how out-of-class technology usage can impact in-class teaching, this study explored the link between extramural gameplay and student self-reported twenty-first-century literacy skills. Data were gathered through a questionnaire completed by 377 students across two different universities and seven different departments. Several findings were reported. Namely, Japanese students tend to rate most of their twenty-first-century skills highly and extramural gameplay is low. However, many students (even those who do not play games) appear to highly regard games as a learning tool. Finally, there is only a low correlation with extramural gameplay and twenty-first-century skills. However, from analysing correlations between each set of data, it was found that twenty-first-century skill reportage correlated higher with simply perceiving that games were beneficial for learning. This led to several significant conclusions. First, in the changing landscape of education and demands placed on graduates from university, it is important to perform some kind of needs analysis in order to match technology and game usage among different groups of students. Second, due to students in this study believing that games were beneficial for learning, games can be an effective method in promoting extramural language learning outside of schools. How this is achieved and connected to an in-class setting is still an area which requires more research. Finally, there is support for the notion that if students can gain some competency in twenty-first-century skills outside the class by playing games, then the in-class context could also prove more beneficial for solidifying those skills.

As mentioned above, the effectiveness of the in-class context in promoting twenty-first-century skills would be determined through a needs analysis. However, as mentioned above, more research is needed into teacher roles, pedagogical tasks and frameworks which can be utilized to take advantage of games in the classroom.

References

Allen, L. K., S. A. Crossley, E. L. Snow and D. S. McNamara (2014), 'L2 Writing Practice: Game Enjoyment as a Key to Engagement', *Language Learning and Technology* 18 (2): 124–50.

Bell, S. (2010), 'Project-Based Learning for the 21st Century: Skills for the Future', *The Clearing House* 83: 39–43.

Black, R. W. (2009), 'English-Language Learners, Fan Communities, and 21st Century Skills', *Journal of Adolescent and Adult Literacy* 52 (8): 688–97.

Chik, A. (2015), 'Using Digital Games for Out-of-Class Language Learning', in D. Nunan and J. C. Richards (eds), *Language Learning beyond the Classroom*, 75–84, New York: Routledge.

Connolly, T. M., E. A. Boyle, E. MacArthur, T. Hainey and J. M. Boyle (2012), 'A Systematic Literature Review of Empirical Evidence on Computer Games and Serious Games', *Computers and Education* 59 (2): 681–6.

Cope, B., and M. Kalantzis (2009), 'Multiliteracies: New Literacies, New Learning', *Pedagogies: An International Journal* 4 (3): 164–95.

Dawson, S., and G. Siemens (2014), 'Analytics to Literacies: The Development of a Learning Analytics Framework for Multiliteracies Assessment', *International Review of Research in Open and Distance Learning* 15: 284–305. 10.19173/irrodl.v15i4.1878.

deHaan, J. (2013), *Video Game and Second Language Acquisition*. Champaign, IL: Common Ground.

deHaan, J. (2019), 'Teaching Language and Literacy with Games: What? How? Why?', *Ludic Language Pedagogy* 1: 1–57.

Gee, J. P. (2007), *What Video Games Have to Teach Us about Learning and Literacy*, New York: Palgrave Macmillan.

Gudykunst, W. B., and Y. Y. Kim (2003), *Communicating with Strangers*, New York: McGraw-Hill.

Hourdequin, P., J. York and J. deHaan (2017), 'Learning English and Other 21st Century Skills through Games: Lessons for Japanese Higher Education from Learning Spaces in New York City', *Tokoha University Research Review Faculty of Foreign Studies* 33: 41–59.

Hung, H., J. C. Yang, G. Hwang, H. Chu and C. Wang (2018), 'A Scoping Review of Research on Digital Game-Based Language Learning', *Computers and Education* 126: 89–104. https://doi.org/10.1016/j.compedu.2018.07.001.

Hurst, J. (2015, February 18), '12 Types of Computer Games Every Gamer
Should Know About'. Available online from https://thoughtcatalog.com/
jane-hurst/2015/02/12-types-of-computer-games-every-gamer-should-know-about/.

Ke, F. (2011), 'A Qualitative Meta-Analysis of Computer Games as Learning Tools',
in R. E. Ferdig (ed.), *Gaming and Simulations: Concepts, Methodologies, Tools and Applications*, 1619–65, Hershey, PA: IGI Global.

Lankshear, C., and M. Knobel (2006), *New Literacies: Changing Knowledge and Classroom Learning*, Philadelphia, PA: Open University Press.

Lombardi, I. (2015), 'Fukudai Hero: A Video Game-Like English Class in a Japanese
National University', *EL.LE: Educazione Linguistica. Language Education* 3 (4): 483–
99. https//doi.org/10.14277/2280–6792/ELLE-4-3-15-7.

Long, M. (2005), 'Methodological Issues in Learner Needs Analysis', in M. Long (ed.),
Second Language Needs Analysis, 19–76, Cambridge: Cambridge University Press.

Miller, M., and V. Hegelheimer (2006), 'The SIMs Meet ESL Incorporating Authentic
Computer Simulation Games into the Language Classroom', *Interactive Technology and Smart Education* 3(4): 311–28. https://doi.org/10.1108/17415650680000070.

Molin, G. (2017), 'The Role of the Teacher in Game-Based Learning: A Review and
Outlook', *Serious Games and Edutainment Applications* 2: 649–74. https://doi.org/10.1007/978-3-319-51645-5_28.

Peterson, M. (2012), 'Language Learner Interaction in a Massively Multiplayer Online
Role-Playing Game', in H. Reinders (ed.), *Digital Games in Language Learning and Teaching*, 70–92, Basingstoke: Palgrave Macmillan.

Rama, P. S., R. Black, E. van Es and M. Warschauer (2012), 'Affordances for Second
Language Learning in World of Warcraft', *ReCALL* 24 (3): 322–38.

Ranalli, J. (2008), 'Learning English with The Sims: Exploiting Authentic Computer
Simulation Games for L2 Learning', *Computer Assisted Language Learning* 21
(5): 441–55.

Ravitz, J. (2014), 'A Survey for Measuring 21st Century Teaching and Learning: West
Virginia 21st Century Teaching and Learning Survey' [WVDE-CIS-28]. https//doi.org/10.13140/RG.2.1.2246.6647.

Reinders, H., and S. Wattana (2015), 'Affect and Willingness to Communicate in Digital
Game-Based Learning', *ReCALL* 27 (1): 38–57.

Rowsell, J., and M. Walsh (2011), 'Rethinking Literacy Education in New
Times: Multimodality, Multiliteracies, and New Literacies', *Brock Education: A Journal of Educational Research and Practice* 21 (1): 53–62.

Scholz, K. W., and M. Schulze (2017), 'Digital-Gaming Trajectories and Second
Language Development', *Language Learning and Technology* 21 (1): 100–20.

Squire, K., M. Barnett, J. M. Grant and T. Higginbotham (2004), 'Electromagnetism
Supercharged! Learning Physics with Digital Simulation Games', *ICLS '04 Proceedings of the 6th International Conference on Learning Sciences*, 513–20.

Steinkuehler, C., and S. Duncan (2008), 'Scientific Habits of Mind in Virtual Worlds',
Journal of Science Education and Technology 17: 530–43.

Suh, S., S. Kim and N. Kim (2010), 'Effectiveness of MMORPG-Based Instruction in Elementary English Education in Korea', *Journal of Computer Assisted Learning* 26 (5): 370–8. https//doi.org/10.1111/j.1365-2729.2010.00353.x.

Sundqvist, P. (2019), 'COTS Games in the Digital Wild and L2 Learner Vocabulary', *Language Learning and Technology* 23 (1): 87–113.

Sundqvist, P., and P. Wikstrom (2015), 'Out-of-School Digital Gameplay and In-School L2 English Vocabulary Outcomes', *System* 51: 65–76.

Sylven, K. L., and P. Sundqvist (2012), 'Gaming as Extramural English L2 Learning and L2 Proficiency among Young Learners', *ReCALL* 24 (3): 302–21. https//doi.org/10.1017/S095834401200016x.

The New London Group (1996), 'A Pedagogy of Multiliteracies: Designing Social Futures', *Harvard Educational Review* 66 (1): 60–92.

The Partnership for 21st Century Skills (2019), 'Framework for 21st Century Learning'. Available online from http://static.battelleforkids.org/documents/p21/P21_Framework_DefinitionsBFK.pdf (accessed 16 July 2019).

Thomas, M. K., X. Ge and B. A. Greene (2011), 'Fostering 21st Century Skill Development by Engaging Students in Authentic Game Design Projects in a High School Computer Programming Class', *Journal of Educational Computing Research* 44 (4): 391–408.

Van Eck, R. (2006), 'Digital Game-Based Learning: It's Not Just the Digital Natives Who Are Restless', *Educause Review* 41 (2): 16–30.

Wiklund, M., and E. Love (2009), 'Going to School in World of Warcraft: Observations from a Trial Programme Using Off-the-Shelf Computer Games as Learning Tools in Secondary Education', *Designs for Learning* 2 (1): 36–55.

York, J., and J. deHaan (2018), 'A Constructivist Approach to Game-Based Language Learning: Student Perceptions in a Beginner-Level EFL Context', *International Journal of Game-Based Learning* 8 (1): 19–40. https://doi.org/10.4018/IJGBL.2018010102.

Young, S., and Y. Wang (2014), 'The Game Embedded CALL System to Facilitate English Vocabulary Acquisition and Pronunciation', *Educational Technology and Society* 17 (3): 239–51.

10

Gaming as a gateway to L2 English learning: A case study of a young L1 Swedish boy

Liss Kerstin Sylven

Introduction

In recent years, there has been an abundance of studies indicating the potential for second/foreign language (L2) learning inherent in digital games (e.g. Gee 2007; Ranalli 2008; Peterson 2012; Reinders 2012). Studies from the Nordic countries, which are relatively small with limited use for their respective first languages (L1) and with a large presence of English in everyday society, have shown effects of digital gaming on young learners' proficiency in English (Sylvén and Sundqvist 2012; Sundqvist and Sylvén 2014; Olsson and Sylvén 2015; Sundqvist and Wikström 2015; Brevik 2016; Hannibal Jensen 2017). The present chapter is aimed at providing a case study of an L1 Swedish boy, Jimmy, who has acquired a relatively high level of L2/FL English proficiency mainly through playing digital games and watching YouTube clips.

Jimmy's extramural exposure to L2 English started when he was about 4 years old. At the time, he started to play a number of digital games. Since then, he has continued gaming, but YouTube clips, illustrating other gamers at play, have successively become another important source of exposure to English. The data forming the basis for this chapter consist of interviews and language tests carried out over a period of three years, starting when Jimmy was 8 years old. The interviews cover aspects such as his views on gaming, what distinguishes extramural exposure to English and formal English education in school and his future as a language user. Language tests of various kinds (receptive and productive vocabulary and reading comprehension) have been administered on several occasions. The study is longitudinal and ongoing, starting when Jimmy was 8 years old and with the latest data collection when he had just turned 11. The chapter will account for Jimmy's exposure to L2 English through gaming and other digital sources, the results obtained on the tests administered as well as discussing possible pedagogical implications of the role of digital gaming as a gateway paving the way for L2 learning.

An abundance of evidence for the language learning potential inherent in digital games has been gathered in recent years (e.g. Forsman 2004; Rankin, Gold and Gooch 2006; Gee 2007; Ranalli 2008; Piirainen-Marsh and Tainio 2009; Benson and Reinders 2011; Cornillie, Thorne and Desmet 2012; Peterson 2012; Reinders 2012; Sykes and Reinhardt 2012; Sylvén and Sundqvist 2012; Sundqvist and Wikström 2015; Brevik 2016; Olsson 2016; Hannibal Jensen 2017; Vosburg 2017; Reinhardt 2019). Most studies into the effects of digital gaming on L2 learning have been conducted among young adults in higher education. There are several reasons for this, for instance, many individuals in that age group take an interest in digital gaming, large groups are available for researchers at universities and the administration of consent is facilitated when informants are adults. However, there is emerging evidence for L2 learning taking place through gameplay and other extramural activities involving an L2 also among learners at primary and secondary levels (Piirainen-Marsh and Tainio 2009; Sylvén and Sundqvist 2012; Sundqvist and Sylvén 2014; Hannibal Jensen 2018). This chapter provides a case study of Jimmy, who is taking part in an ongoing, longitudinal study, which started when he was 8 years old.

Theoretical assumptions

Within second language acquisition (SLA), some of the basic theoretical concepts are input, output and interaction (Krashen 1985; Swain 2000; Gass and Selinker 2008), all three of which are available in abundance in digital gaming. Within sociocultural theory, a core assumption is that learning in the zone of proximal development takes place in a social context and with the help of more knowledgeable peers, who often come in the form of a teacher, parent or friend (Lantolf and Poehner 2008). With respect to L2 learning in combination with technology, the term *affordance* is often used (Gibson 1979; Van Lier 2004). In the present study, games and YouTube clips are viewed as affordances for L2 learning.

In addition, motivation is theoretically known to be of importance with regard to any type of learning and perhaps mostly so in connection with L2 learning (Dörnyei 2005, 2009). It can indeed be argued that much of what is happening in the digital world in general and in digital games in particular is optimal for L2 learning to take place (Gee 2007).

In fact, Gee (2007) lists as many as thirty-six learning principles applicable in connection with gaming and learning. In Sundqvist and Sylvén (2016), the principles specifically relevant for L2 learning were focused on at some length. Here, the three principles of greatest interest will be discussed, namely the psychosocial moratorium principle, the practice principle and the transfer principle. The psychosocial moratorium principle means that learners can take risks in a space where the consequences are of minimal concern as compared with a real-life situation. Being able to try various ways of expressing oneself in an L2, without the risk of being corrected or made fun of, is an efficient way of becoming more and more secure in one's own role as an L2 user. The practice principle stipulates that the player/learner practices a great deal to complete tasks. What makes such practice in a gaming environment special is that it rarely gets boring (as the case may be for repetitive classroom activities), as the player is in control and can monitor the ongoing success in the game (or L2 learning process). Finally, the transfer principle concerns the transferability of gained knowledge in one domain into others. The ability to use words or phrases learned in one environment (for instance, in gameplay) in completely different contexts (such as when encountering a stranger in the street) is an important skill to master in any L2 learning process. The fact that the automatization of an acquisition procedure that may have started in one context may be facilitated by its practice in another has been pointed out by, among others, DeKeyser (2007). All of Gee's (2007) principles, including the three discussed here, depict an ideal, theoretical gaming situation. In practice, there are obstacles to overcome. Regarding the psychosocial moratorium, for instance, it is not always the case that beginners feel secure enough to express themselves freely when gaming. They may indeed feel intimidated by knowing that there are more experienced players online at the same time. The same critique can be voiced against the practice principle, which takes its point of departure in the fact that language is being practiced while gaming. The transfer principle does not always work automatically. In other words, for the transfer principle to be effective, learners may need the help of, for instance, teachers.

Previous literature

Today, studies abound on the effectiveness of extramural exposure to an L2, in particular regarding engagement in digital gaming. As this chapter is concerned with such effects among young learners, this section deals specifically with the literature focusing on digital gaming and aspects of L2 learning among young learners in various parts of the world.

Set in Turkey, the study by Turgut and Irgin (2009) targets 10- to 14-year-olds. Empirical data consisted of interviews and observations of individuals engaged in digital gaming at internet cafes and were analysed using a phenomenological theoretical framework. The findings indicate that participants perceive their engagement in gaming as beneficial both for L2 vocabulary acquisition and increased motivation for L2 learning. In addition, gaming seemed to raise gamers' awareness about positive and negative aspects of gameplay.

The study by Piirainen-Marsh and Tainio (2009) included video recordings of two 13-year-old Finnish boys engaged in the science-fantasy multiplayer role-playing game *Final Fantasy X*. In this game, lexical and prosodic repetitions are an integral part. Findings suggested that the gamers developed both their linguistic and interactional competence in English. During the game, the players reproduced, practiced, performed and played with different characters' styles and accents of English. Specifically, the frequent repetition of language used in the game was found to be linked to the L2 learning of these boys (see also Piirainen-Marsh 2011).

Focusing on vocabulary and spoken language, Sundqvist (2009) studied 15- to 16-year-old L1 Swedish students (N = 80). Data from language diaries and questionnaires investigating students' exposure to English outside of school were correlated with learning outcomes as measured by written vocabulary tests and interactional, dyadic speaking tests. The findings indicated clear correlations between amount of exposure to L2 English and vocabulary and speaking proficiency. However, the strongest correlation was found between productive use of L2 English in activities such as digital gaming and oral proficiency. A gender difference was also noticed in the data; as more boys engaged in extramural activities in English, they were also the ones who performed best on the tests.

Also set in Sweden, Sylvén and Sundqvist (2012) looked into exposure to L2 English among children in 5th grade (age 11–12) and whether such exposure correlated with some aspects of L2 proficiency. Just like in the study by Sundqvist (2009) described above, analyses were based on empirical data consisting of language diaries and vocabulary tests. In addition, results on national tests in English (reading and listening) and final grades were included in the database. The findings clearly revealed an advantage for those who had reported large amounts of exposure to English. In particular, those with a high degree of engagement in digital games scored significantly higher than those who had lower levels of exposure to L2 English in their spare time. In a related study, even younger learners were involved, namely students in the 4th grade (age 10–11) (Sundqvist and Sylvén 2014). Also in this age group, the amount of exposure to English outside of school was measured through language diaries, and findings showed that boys were exposed to English to a larger degree than the girls. This gender difference applied both to the amount of time and type of exposure. The boys were significantly more engaged in, for instance, digital gaming than the girls. It was found that the frequent gamers were those who were most motivated to study English, and they also reported the lowest amount of speaking anxiety. The results are seen as indicative of the positive influence of exposure to L2 English outside of school, not only with regard L2 learning but also for lowering affective factors of importance in the L2 learning process.

Another Scandinavian study (Sletten, Strandbu and Gilje 2015) identified a link between L1 Norwegian students' (age 13–16) in- and out-of-school activities. It was found that there was a correlation between the amount of gaming (more than three hours several times a week) and final grade in English, but lower grades in the subject L1 Norwegian and mathematics.

Looking into extramural English gameplay and its correlation with English vocabulary proficiency, Sundqvist and Wikström (2015) investigated Swedish learners in 9th grade (aged 15–16) and found similar links as Sletten et al. (2015). Based on questionnaires, language diary data, essays, vocabulary tests and final grades in English, analyses showed a positive correlation between the usage of advanced words, essay grades and final grades. It was also concluded that boys engaged to a significantly larger degree in gameplay than girls (Sundqvist and Wikström 2015). These findings are similar to those established by Carr and Pauwels (2006), who came to the conclusion that boys seem to prefer to learn languages through games rather than in more traditional ways.

Having identified a number of outliers in regard to reading proficiency in L2 English compared to their L1 Norwegian, Brevik (2016) interviewed five of these, all males, aged 16–17. The results suggested that the out-of-school contacts with English, among them digital gaming, were decisive for these boys' reading skills. All of them claimed that they felt more at ease reading in English, as most of their input during out-of-school activities was, and had been for a long time, in English.

This brief overview of some of the most relevant studies into extramural exposure to English, in particular gameplay, and L2 English proficiency among young learners, strongly supports the potential of a positive and causal link between the two. However, as research in this area on learners younger than teenagers is scarce, there is little empirical evidence that such a link indeed exists also among very young learners. We will therefore now turn to the study in focus in this chapter, which concerns an individual in that age group.

The study

Context

The context of this study is Sweden, and it is imperative that the reader understands the role of English in Swedish society. Swedish is the official language, and in addition, there are five minority languages, Finnish, Meänkeäli, Sami, Jiddish and Romani Chib. English is considered as a foreign language, but holds a very special position in comparison to other foreign languages. English is introduced as a school subject in 3rd grade (age 9–10) of primary school at the latest. Often, it is introduced much earlier than that, and sometimes even in preschool. In grade 6, another foreign language can be selected, but English is the only mandatory foreign language in the Swedish educational system. In nationwide surveys, English is considered as the most important and valuable subject in school by a majority of students. Also, Sweden scores high in international comparisons of L2 English proficiency (Bonnet 2004). In fact, Sweden came in first place in Education First's English Proficiency Index 2018 and second in the same index for 2019 (http://www.ef.com/epi). School is not the only place where English is encountered in Sweden. Rather, Swedes are exposed to English on an everyday basis through the media and commercial ads. In addition, many larger corporations use English as the medium of communication (Bel Habib 2013).

Method and material

In this section, the methods of compiling data and the types of material used will be presented. First, however, Jimmy will be introduced in some more detail and my role as a researcher described. Jimmy and I first met when he was 8 years old. When his parents, acquaintances of mine, learned of my interest in effects of extramural English (Sylvén 2006; Sundqvist and Sylvén 2016), they suggested that their son might be an interesting individual to include in my studies. Since then, Jimmy and I have met over a period of several years with approximately one meeting per year. Our meetings have been filled with talks about his extramural

English activities and Jimmy illustrating several of the games he presently engages in. At some of these occasions, certain tests have also been administered (see below for details). The method, thus, is ethnographically inspired, with an emic perspective, focusing on Jimmy's own accounts of his activities, thoughts and feelings in connection with extramural English.

Jimmy started playing digital games when he was about 4 years old, and has continued ever since. To start with, he played on a console, then on a computer, some time later on an Xbox and more recently he has returned to playing on a computer. The types of game he plays include first-person shooter games and games such as *Heartstone* and *Overwatch*. In recent years, he has watched YouTube clips of others playing the games he has taken an interest in. In school, Jimmy has studied English as a separate subject since 2nd grade (when he was 8 years old).

All the interviews and tests have been carried out by myself in my role as a researcher into young learners of English and their exposure to English out of school. As an acquaintance of Jimmy's parents, I have had the opportunity to meet with Jimmy in his own home. This means that all data collection has taken place in an environment where Jimmy has felt secure. Every time we have met, I have made sure that Jimmy wants to talk to me, and is interested in doing the tests I have brought with me. He has been informed that he can stop at any time, and that his participation is voluntary. This is completely in line with the ethical guidelines set out by the Swedish Research Agency (Vetenskapsrådet n.d.), which have been adhered to.

The empirical material on which the study is based is in the form of audio-recorded and transcribed interviews, as well as vocabulary and reading comprehension tests. The two types of vocabulary tests accounted for here are the yes/no test (Meara 1992) and the Young Learners' Vocabulary Assessment Test (YLVAT) (Sylvén and Sundqvist 2016). Both of them are described below. All tests were administered using pen and paper.

Reliability, validity, generalizability and ethics

In this case study, all the empirical data were collected by myself in meetings with Jimmy. Jimmy did not have access to any sources that could have affected his responses to the various tasks administered. Thus, the results obtained are reliable in the sense that he has not used any external help. However, test fatigue may have skewed the results on at least one of the tests, leaving those results somewhat unreliable. All tests that were used have been previously validated in other studies, albeit with older learners. The validity of the tests for such a young learner can therefore be questioned.

As a case study involving one learner, the results are in no way generalizable. However, it is yet another study adding to our knowledge and understanding of the relationship between extramural exposure to English and English proficiency. As touched upon above, the study has been conducted in accordance with the ethical principles set out by the Swedish Research Agency (Vetenskapsrådet n.d.). In addition, care has been taken to create a safe environment and a rapport between the informant and the researcher that is based on trust.

The YLVAT

While vocabulary tests aimed for older learners abound, tests designed for younger learners are rare. The YLVAT (see Appendix 1) was designed specifically to test young learners' vocabulary proficiency (Sylvén and Sundqvist 2014, 2016) and to tap into learners' general lexical proficiency rather than proficiency in the more academic, school-related domains. It consists of three parts: the first is word recognition, the second receptive vocabulary and the third productive vocabulary. The items included in the test were selected from existing versions of the vocabulary levels test (VLT) (Laufer and Nation 1999; Nation 2001) as well as from the productive levels test (PLT) (Laufer and Nation 1999), both of them found on the Lextutor web page (http://www.lextutor.ca). In the selection process, a number of principles were applied. First, items were selected from the 1,000 and 2,000 levels, in order to keep the test at an acceptable level of difficulty for young learners. Second, the majority of words selected were nouns, some were verbs and the minority were adjectives. Finally, it was decided to include a number of cognates (Rogers, Webb and Nakata 2015). This principle was applied as an affective measure to ensure that the self-confidence of young learners was not crushed, an important aspect to take into account when dealing with young learners (McKay 2006). It was anticipated that most learners would be able to solve these items.

Another factor to bear in mind when designing the YLVAT is test fatigue. Dealing with young learners, fatigue is always a risk. For this reason, together with other reasons, such as test validity, three different parts were decided on. The first part, Part A, consists of thirteen statements to which the test taker has to indicate whether they are (a) true (T), (b) not true (N) or (c) not known (X). An example from this part is:

1.	All the world is under water.	☐	T
		☐	N
		☐	X

As is clear, Part A tests word recognition. All items are taken from the 1,000 level.

The second part of YLVAT, Part B, consists of twelve items from the VLT. An example from this part is:

Question 1	1.	Apply		
	2.	Elect	–	Choose by voting
	3.	Jump	–	Become like water
	4.	Manufacture	–	Make
	5.	Melt		
	6.	Threaten		

The items in Part B are taken from the 2,000 level, with six nouns and six verbs.

Finally, the third part, Part C, consists of twelve sentences chosen from the PLT. In each sentence, one word is left out, but the initial two or three letters are given, as in the following example:

1.   Plants receive water from the soil through their ro_____.

Thus, Part C taps into students' productive vocabulary knowledge, as opposed to Parts A and B, where receptive knowledge is in focus. The target items are from the 2,000 level and consist of five nouns, four verbs and three adjectives.

In sum, YLVAT represents widely recognized test types. It taps into receptive knowledge of the meanings of words in Parts A and B, as well as productive knowledge, certain syntactic and collocational patterns and knowledge of spelling in Part C.

The yes/no test

Another type of vocabulary test is the so-called yes/no test, developed by Paul Meara and his team in the early 1980s (Meara and Jones 1990). It is a test with a large number of words, where the test taker is asked to indicate whether s/he knows the word or not (yes or no). In order to check the reliability of the test takers responses, so-called nonsense words are included among the words tested. Examples of such nonsense words are nonagrate, lannery and aistrope. This test is also divided into various levels of frequency and is available on Lextutor's web page (http://www.lextutor.ca). An advantage of the yes/no test is that it is quick and easily administered, along with the fact that a large number of words are being tested in a very limited time. A problem with the test, however, is that the calculation of results needs to correctly control for the presence of the nonsense words and how each individual test taker has responded to them by implementing relevant calculation formulae (Mochida and Harrington 2006). Due to the problems related to the yes/no test, it has been viewed as somewhat controversial, but studies have shown significant correlations with other types of vocabulary tests (e.g. Mochida and Harrington 2006). The yes/no test is limited to testing receptive vocabulary proficiency.

The English reading comprehension test

In order to test Jimmy's English reading comprehension proficiency, a cloze test from the Swedish Scholastic Assessment Test (SSAT) was used. The SSAT is an entrance test into Swedish higher education and consists of two basic parts: one quantitative and one verbal. The verbal part consists of various tests of Swedish and the English reading comprehension test. The English reading comprehension part consists of two long texts with five multiple-choice questions each, five short texts with one multiple-choice question each and the cloze test with five gaps with multiple-choice alternatives. Each multiple choice consists of three distractors and one correct answer. The cloze test, in particular, has been shown to be a very valid and reliable test of L2 English proficiency (Reuterberg and Ohlander 1999), and for that reason along with the fact that it is an easily administered test, it was decided to use that specific format to test Jimmy's English reading comprehension skills.

The specific tests administered to Jimmy were chosen based on their respective level of difficulty. As all tests included in the SSAT are first pretested in connection with the administration of the high-stakes test twice a year, statistics are available on various factors such as level of difficulty, gender differences and r-bis values from large cohorts of test takers (ranging from $N = 800$ to $N = 2,000$). It was thus possible to choose four different cloze tests whose values were distributed to represent both fairly easy and fairly difficult texts, as illustrated in Table 10.1.

Table 10.1 Average scores (in percentages), in total and per gender, from adult SSAT test takers on the four reading comprehension tests

	Total solution rate	Males	Females	R-bis
RC1: Bigfoot	68	74	63	61
RC2: Birds	63	67	59	62
RC3: Wings	57	63	51	58
RC4: Mountains	54	59	49	59

Table 10.2 Type of data collection and at what age

Test	Age (years)
YLVAT	9
Yes/no	9
Reading comprehension 1	10
Reading comprehension 2	11
Reading comprehension 3	11
Reading comprehension 4	11

The first cloze test was administered to Jimmy in the fall of 2018, the three others in the spring of 2019. In Table 10.2, all the tests performed by Jimmy, and at what age, are shown.

Results

From the talks with Jimmy, it emerged that he has been engaged in activities involving L2 English since the age of approximately 4. In the early meetings, Jimmy described how he engaged himself predominantly in digital gaming. While continuing playing a number of games online, later he also has developed an interest in watching video clips on YouTube. These clips are typically of other gamers filming themselves while playing. He spends between one and six hours every day playing games and/or watching YouTube. In school, Jimmy started with English as a subject in grade 2 (when he was 8 years old), totalling approximately two classes of forty-five minutes each per week. Thus, the exposure to and use of English in his spare time vastly exceeds the time spent on English in school. Jimmy explained at one point that he does not like the subject of English in school, as he finds it rather boring. His favourite school subject is arts and crafts.

Table 10.3 Jimmy's results on the yes/no test (in percentages of total)

	Jimmy's results
Level 1	95
Level 2	48
Level 3	73
Level 4	38

Table 10.4 Jimmy's and the average results among 5th graders on the YLVAT test (raw scores)

	Jimmy's results	Average results among 5th graders
Part 1 (word recognition), max 12	12	9.7
Part 2 (receptive vocabulary), max 13	12	5.3
Part 3 (productive vocabulary), max 12	9	4.4
Total (max 37)	33	19.3

As accounted for above, three different kinds of vocabulary tests were administered to Jimmy. The yes/no test was performed when he was 9 years old. On this particular test, which tests a large number of words, Jimmy showed great test fatigue resulting in him not performing to the best of his ability in all four parts of the test. This was evidenced by the fact that he skipped a large number of items in levels two and four. Thus, the results, illustrated in Table 10.3, on this test need to be interpreted with caution.

The results from the YLVAT, which also was administered when Jimmy was 9 years old and in 3rd grade, are shown in Table 10.4. For comparison, results obtained on the same test previously performed by informants in 5th grade (see Sundqvist and Sylvén 2014 for full details) are included.

The reading comprehension tests were administered on two different occasions. The first, Bigfoot, was administered in the fall when Jimmy was 10, and the three others in the spring when he turned 11. Jimmy's performance on the reading comprehension tests is illustrated in Table 10.5.

The results illustrated here will be discussed in the next section.

Table 10.5 Jimmy's and the average results (in per cent) among adult SSAT test takers on English reading comprehension

	Jimmy's results	Average results among adult SSAT test takers
RC1: Bigfoot	100	67
RC2: Birds	100	65
RC3: Wings	80	54
RC4: Mountains	60	54

Discussion

This chapter has accounted for Jimmy's contacts with and use of English in his spare time and attempted to measure his L2 English proficiency by means of a variety of valid and reliable instruments. Both vocabulary proficiency and reading comprehension were tested.

As regards the results on the vocabulary tests, they all indicated that Jimmy had achieved an impressive level of L2 English knowledge. When asked how he had learnt so much English, Jimmy said that it is all thanks to his own engagement in digital gaming where English is used as the medium of communication and watching YouTube videos of others playing similar games.

From the results accounted for above concerning L2 English reading comprehension, it is clear that the full score obtained on the first test was not an accident, but that he indeed performed overall very well on these advanced cloze tests. In all four tests, sentence connectors such as however and although were among the target items. Such items are typical for the academic genre in focus in the English reading comprehension part of the SSAT and are usually quite difficult for the high-stakes test takers, with scores ranging from 60 to 83 per cent. Yet, Jimmy answered correctly on these in every one of the four tests. In addition, Jimmy mastered items such as descendant (which only 43 per cent of the SSAT test takers did), something like (19 per cent) and talent (31 per cent).

Turning back to Gee (2007) and the principles set out to illustrate why digital gaming is beneficial for language learning, it is evident that they apply also for as young a learner as Jimmy. In particular, the principles referred to above will be discussed in relation to Jimmy's learning path. First, the psychosocial moratorium principle, which focuses in on the fact that digital games are not judgemental. Language can be practiced without fear of being punished for making mistakes, and mistakes that are made can be corrected by, for instance, starting all over again. In such cases, learning has taken place. From a sociocultural point of view, the mistakes are made within the zone of proximal development, and then knowledge is gained about the correct language form, not necessarily through the help of 'more knowledgeable peers', but often from the computer and the game itself. In other words, the game takes on the role of the more knowledgeable peer in the interactivity in a certain community of practice, in this case gaming, and pushes the individual learner forward in his/her L2 learning process.

The second principle I would like to focus on is the practice principle. Jimmy has been playing various games since the age of 4. Over the years, he has been able to practice a large number of skills in connection with his gaming activities. Among other things, he related how he used to play games on a computer some time ago, but since then has played more on an Xbox, which resulted in him losing some advanced skills using the computer keyboard. However, after having returned to the computer and playing a couple of games, his skills returned. This is one example of how much of the repetitiveness inherent in gaming results in gaining the skills necessary to excel at the game. The same is true for the language used in the games. One of the affordances offered in games is the possibility for a gamer to start over, stop the game, slow it down and repeat until s/he has understood what is needed for advancement (Reinhardt 2019).

Finally, turning to the transfer principle, it is clear that digital games offer a unique framing of the language used in each individual game, and the vocabulary used is often contextual. Nevertheless, and not least as evidenced by the performance of Jimmy in the various tests, what is being learned while gaming can be transferred to other contexts. Above, it has, among other things, been shown that Jimmy scored better than the average adult test taker of the SSAT on English reading comprehension, which not only contains different types of text than what is encountered in gaming but is also specifically designed to test academic language proficiency.

As touched upon previously, motivation seems to be of decisive importance as regards L2 learning (Dörnyei 2009). It is difficult to fathom a more motivational context for an individual than trying to understand what is communicated in a game that is played voluntarily and in which success depends on such understanding. Judging from the literature review above, this type of context is indeed conducive for L2 learning. What is perhaps surprising with the case of Jimmy is that an individual of such a young age is able to, first, learn as much L2 English merely through gameplay and watching YouTube videos and, second, transfer that knowledge into a completely different domain. This has pedagogical implications of some magnitude, which is touched on in the following section.

Pedagogical implications

This chapter has shown that Jimmy has obtained a relatively high level of L2 English proficiency considering his age. Previous studies are in line with the findings here, and it can be concluded that he is not the only one who seems to benefit from exposure to English in his spare time. Evidence now abounds on the beneficial impact of such exposure on learners' proficiency in a large number of skills in L2 English. However, as a school subject, English is still taught as a foreign language, and in many cases as though students come into school with no previous knowledge in the language at all. While this may still be true for some individuals, for others, Jimmy being one example, the design of the English subject poses an imminent risk of students becoming bored and losing interest. The heterogeneity found in many L2 English classrooms today must somehow be dealt with. It is close to an impossible task for a teacher to successfully cater both to students with virtually no prior knowledge and to those who are practically fluent in the same classroom.

A question that begs an answer, of course, is whether games should be introduced as a teaching tool in school. Reinhardt (2019), for instance, promotes the use of games for L2 teaching based on all the available positive insights into the inherent learning potential in such games. Future studies will hopefully shed light on whether or not games are a successful tool for in-school teaching and learning. There are indications that they indeed could be useful. There are also, however, suggestions that games are personal, with a preference of engaging in them at one's own initiative in spare time (see e.g. Brevik 2016).

Concluding remarks

This chapter has described a young Swedish L1 individual, his contacts with and his proficiency in L2 English. It is a case study adding to other studies with a similar focus. Nonetheless, the need for further research in this area is abundantly clear. As pointed out, there are many studies on older learners, but studies targeting such young learners as the one in focus here are rare (but cf. Hannibal Jensen 2017). Therefore, more studies into very young learners would

PART A (*Del A*) – WORD RECOGNITION (*Att känna igen ord*)

Instructions / *Instruktioner*

There are 13 questions in Part A. Check "T" if a sentence is **true**. Check "N" if a sentence is **not true**. Check "X" if you **do not understand** the sentence. Follow the example!

Del A består av 13 frågor. Kryssa för "T" om meningen är sann (True). Kryssa för "N" om meningen inte är sann (Not true). Kryssa för "X" om du inte förstår meningen. Följ exemplet!

Example) We can stop time.

☐ T (This is **True**)
☒ N (This is **Not true**)
☐ X (I **do not understand** the question)

1)

Two of these are little.

☐ T
☐ N
☐ X

2) When someone says 'What are you called?', you should say your name.

☐ T
☐ N
☐ X

3) There are many ways to get money.

☐ T
☐ N
☐ X

4) All the world is under water.

☐ T
☐ N
☐ X

5) When you keep asking, you ask once.

☐ T
☐ N
☐ X

6) Sometimes people die when they fall off a building.

☐ T
☐ N
☐ X

7) Day follows night and night follows day.

☐ T
☐ N
☐ X

Appendix 1 The young learner vocabulary assessment test.

8)   *Remain here* means 'stay'.   ☐ T
                                                                ☐ N
                                                                ☐ X

9)   When there is a change of scene, we see a different   ☐ T
       place.   ☐ N
                                                                ☐ X

10)   Dirty hands cannot make marks on glass.   ☐ T
                                                                ☐ N
                                                                ☐ X

11)   Each society has the same rules.   ☐ T
                                                                ☐ N
                                                                ☐ X

12)   Three examples of food are: shops, homes and markets.   ☐ T
                                                                ☐ N
                                                                ☐ X

13)   It is a short way from one side to the other side of a   ☐ T
       wide river.   ☐ N
                                                                ☐ X

                                          PART A TOTAL SCORE: ☐

Appendix 1 *Continued*

PART B (*Del B*) – MAKE THE RIGHT COMBINATIONS (*Gör rätt kombinationer*)

Instructions / *Instruktioner*

There are 4 questions in Part B. Make the right combinations by writing the number next to the synonym or meaning of the word. Follow the example!

Del B består av 4 frågor. Gör rätt kombinationer genom att skriva siffran bredvid ordets synonym eller betydelse. Följ exemplet!

Example)   1.   original
              2.   private   __6__   complete
              3.   royal   __1__   first
              4.   slow   __2__   not public
              5.   sorry
              6.   total

Question 1)   1.   apply
              2.   elect   _____   choose by voting
              3.   jump   _____   become like water
              4.   manufacture   _____   make
              5.   melt
              6.   threaten

Question 2)   1.   blame
              2.   hide   _____   keep away from sight
              3.   hit   _____   have a bad effect on something
              4.   invite   _____   ask
              5.   pour
              6.   spoil

Question 3)   1.   accident
              2.   choice   _____   having a high opinion of yourself
              3.   debt   _____   something you must pay
              4.   fortune   _____   loud, deep sound
              5.   pride
              6.   roar

Question 4)   1.   basket
              2.   crop   _____   money paid for doing a job
              3.   flesh   _____   heat
              4.   salary   _____   meat
              5.   temperature
              6.   thread

              PART B TOTAL SCORE: [   ]

Appendix 1 *Continued*

PART C (*Del C*) – PRODUCTIVE VOCABULARY (*Produktivt ordförråd*)

Instructions / *Instruktioner*

Complete the underlined words as has been done in the example!

Skriv färdigt de understrukna orden på det sätt som exemplet visar!

Example)   He was riding a bi*cycle*_____.

1)   Plants receive water from the soil through their ro_____.

2)   The nu_____was helping the doctor in the operation room.

3)   He is walking on the ti_____ of his toes.

4)   The mechanic had to replace the mo_____of the car.

5)   There is a co_____ of the original report in the file.

6)   They had to cl_____ a steep mountain to reach the cabin.

7)   The railway con_____ London with its suburbs.

8)   The house was su_____ by a garden.

9)   This work is not up to your us_____standard.

10)   She wan_____ aimlessly in the streets.

11)   They sat down to eat even though they were not hu_____.

12)   The doctor ex_____ the patient thoroughly.

PART C TOTAL SCORE:

TOTAL SCORE ON THE WHOLE TEST (Max: 37)

Appendix 1 *Continued*

add to our understanding of the potential of, for instance, gameplay on L2 English learning. Ideally, such studies should include all four skills – reading, writing, speaking and listening. Such detailed studies would help delineate between what is and can be learned outside of the educational context, and what school needs to focus on.

In the present study, all extramural English activities engaged in by Jimmy, which were all directly or indirectly related to digital gaming, have been collapsed and viewed as a single source of L2 English input. Further studies are needed to probe deeper into effects of the specific types of activities. Studies on games used as a teaching and learning tool in school would be of great interest. Based on the solid evidence of the positive impact of extramural exposure to English on L2 English learning, and considering the easy availability of English in many parts of the world, we may be witnessing a shift in how to best model early L2 English teaching and learning.

References

Bel Habib, I. (2013), *Språkets Ekonomiska Värde För Individer, Företag Och Nationer – En Introduktion Till Språkekonomi*, Stockholm: Stockholm University.

Benson, P., and H. Reinders, eds (2011), *Beyond the Language Classroom: The Theory and Practice of Informal Language Learning and Teaching*, Basingstoke: Palgrave Macmillan.

Bonnet, G. (2004), *The Assessment of Pupils' Skills in English in Eight European Countries 2002*, Groningen: University of Groningen.

Brevik, L. (2016), 'The Gaming Outliers: Does Out-of-School Gaming Improve Boys' Reading Skills in English as a Second Language?', in E. Elstad (ed.), *Educational Technology and Polycontextual Bridging*, 39–61, Rotterdam: Sense.

Carr, J., and A. Pauwels (2006), *Boys and Foreign Language Learning: Real Boys Don't Do Languages*, Basingstoke: Palgrave Macmillan.

Cornillie, F., S. Thorne and P. Desmet (2012), 'Digital Games for Language Learning: From Hype to Insight?', *ReCALL* 24 (3): 243–56. doi: 10.1017/S0958344012000134.

DeKeyser, R. (2007), 'Introduction: Situating the Concept of Practice', in R. DeKeyser (ed.), *Practice in Second Language: Perspectives from Applied Linguistics and Cognitive Psychology*, 1–18, Cambridge: Cambridge University Press.

Dörnyei, Z. (2005), *The Psychology of the Language Learner*, Mahway, NJ: Lawrence Erlbaum Associates.

Dörnyei, Z. (2009), 'The L2 Motivational Self System', in Z. Dörnyei and E. Ushioda (eds), *Motivation, Language Identity and the L2 Self*, 9–42, Clevedon: Multilingual Matters.

Forsman, L. (2004), 'Language, Culture and Context: Exploring Knowledge and Attitudes among Finland-Swedish EFL-Students with Particular Focus on Extracurricular Influence', Licentiate thesis, Åbo: Åbo Akademi.

Gass, S., and L. Selinker (2008), *Second Language Acquisition*, 3rd ed., New York: Routledge.

Gee, J. (2007), *What Video Games Have to Teach Us about Learning and Literacy*, revised and updated edn, New York: Palgrave Macmillan.

Gibson, J. (1979), *The Ecological Approach to Visual Perception*, New York: Psychology Press.

Hannibal Jensen, S. (2017), 'Gaming as an English Language Learning Resource among Young Children in Denmark', *CALICO Journal* 1 (34): 1–19. doi: 10.1558/cj.29519.

Hannibal Jensen, S. (2018), 'Extramural English Engagement in a Danish Context: A Young Learner Perspective', PhD thesis, Odense: University of Southern Denmark.

Krashen, S. (1985), *The Input Hypothesis: Issues and Implications*, London: Longman.

Lantolf, J. P., and M. E. Poehner, eds (2008), *Sociocultural Theory and the Teaching of Second Languages*, London: Equinox.

Laufer, B., and P. Nation (1999), 'A Vocabulary-Size Test of Controlled Productive Ability', *Language Testing* 16 (1): 33–51.

McKay, P. (2006), *Assessing Young Language Learners*, Cambridge: Cambridge University Press.

Meara, P. (1992), *EFL Vocabulary Tests*, Swansea: Centre for Applied Language Studies, University College Swansea.

Meara, P., and G. Jones (1990), *The Eurocentres 10K Vocabulary Size Test*, Zurich: Eurocentres.

Mochida, A., and M. Harrington (2006), 'The Yes/No Test as a Measure of Receptive Vocabulary Knowledge', *Language Testing* 23 (1): 73–98.

Nation, P. (2001), *Learning Vocabulary in Another Language*, Cambridge: Cambridge University Press.

Olsson, E. (2016), 'On the Impact of Extramural English and CLIL on Productive Vocabulary', PhD thesis, Gothenburg: University of Gothenburg.

Olsson, E., and L. K. Sylvén (2015), 'Extramural English and Academic Vocabulary. A Longitudinal Study of CLIL and Non-CLIL Students in Sweden', *Apples – Journal of Applied Language Studies* 9 (2): 77–103.

Peterson, M. (2012), 'Learner Interaction in a Massively Multiplayer Online Role Playing Game (MMORPG): A Sociocultural Discourse Analysis', *ReCALL* 24 (3): 361–80. https//doi.org/10.1017/S0958344012000195.

Piirainen-Marsh, A. (2011), 'Enacting Interactional Competence in Gaming Activities: Coproducing Talk with Virtual Others', in J. K. Hall, J. Hellerman and S. Pekarek Doehler (eds), *L2 Interactional Competence and Development*, 19–44, Bristol: Multilingual Matters.

Piirainen-Marsh, A., and L. Tainio (2009), 'Other-Repetition as a Resource for Participation in the Activity of Playing a Video Game', *Modern Language Journal* 93 (2): 153–69. https//doi.org/10.1111/j.1540-4781.2009.00853.x.

Ranalli, J. (2008), 'Learning English with The Sims: Exploiting Authentic Computer Simulation Games for L2 Learning', *Computer Assisted Language Learning* 21 (5): 441–55.

Rankin, Y., R. Gold and B. Gooch (2006), '3D Role-Playing Games as Language Learning Tools', EuroGraphics 2006, vol. 25, Vienna, Austria, 4–8 September 2006. Available from http://www.thegooch.org/ (accessed 27 December 2010).

Reinders, H., ed. (2012), *Digital Games in Language Learning and Teaching, New Language Learning & Teaching Environments*, Basingstoke: Palgrave Macmillan.

Reinhardt, J. (2019), *Gameful Second and Foreign Language Teaching and Learning: Theory, Research, and Practice*, Cham: Palgrave MacMillan.

Reuterberg, S.-E., and S. Ohlander (1999), *Engelsk Läsförståelse i Högskoleprovet*, Göteborg: Göteborgs universitet.

Rogers, J., S. Webb and T. Nakata (2015), 'Do the Cognacy Characteristics of Loanwords Make Them More Easily Learned Than Noncognates?', *Language Teaching Research* 19: 9–27. doi: 10.1177/1362168814541752.

Sletten, M. A., Å. Strandbu and O. Gilje (2015), 'Idrett, Dataspilling og Skole – Konkurrerende Eller «på lag»? [Sports, Gaming and School – Competing or "on the Same Team"?]', *Norsk Pedagogisk Tidsskrift* 5: 334–50.

Sundqvist, P. (2009), 'Extramural English Matters: Out-of-School English and Its Impact on Swedish Ninth Graders' Oral Proficiency and Vocabulary', PhD thesis, Karlstad: Karlstad University.

Sundqvist, P., and L. K. Sylvén (2014), 'Language-Related Computer Use: Focus on Young L2 English Learners in Sweden', *ReCALL* 26 (1): 3–20. https//doi.org/10.1017/S0958344013000232.

Sundqvist, P., and L. K. Sylvén (2016), *Extramural English in Teaching and Learning: From Theory and Research to Practice*, London: Palgrave Macmillan.

Sundqvist, P., and P. Wikström. (2015), 'Out-of-School Digital Gameplay and In-School L2 English Vocabulary Outcomes', *System* 51: 65–76. https//doi.org/10.1016/j.system.2015.04.001.

Swain, M. (2000), 'The Output Hypothesis and Beyond: Mediating Acquisition through Collaborative Dialogue', in J. Lantolf (ed.), *Sociocultural Theory and Second Language Learning*, 97–114, Oxford: Oxford University Press.

Sykes, J., and J. Reinhardt (2012), *Language at Play: Digital Games in Second and Foreign Language Teaching and Learning*, New York: Pearson.

Sylvén, L. K. (2006), 'How Is Extramural Exposure to English among Swedish School Students Used in the CLIL Classroom?', VIEWS – *Vienna English Working Papers* 15 (3): 47–53.

Sylvén, L. K., and P. Sundqvist (2012), 'Gaming as Extramural English L2 Learning and L2 Proficiency among Young Learners', *ReCALL* 24 (3): 302–21. https//doi.org/10.1017/S095834401200016X.

Sylvén, L. K., and P. Sundqvist (2014), '*Needed: A Vocabulary Test for Young Learners of English*', *Early Language Learning: Theory and Practice*, Umeå: Umeå University.

Sylvén, L. K., and P. Sundqvist (2016), 'Validation of a Test Measuring Young Learners' General L2 English Vocabulary Knowledge', *Novitas Royal* 10 (1): 1–23.

Turgut, Y., and P. Irgin (2009), 'Young Learners' Language Learning via Computer Games', *Procedia – Social and Behavioral Sciences* 1 (1): 760–4.

Van Lier, L., ed. (2004), *The Ecology and Semiotics of Language Learning: A Sociocultural Perspective*, Boston, MA: Kluwer Academic.

Vetenskapsrådet (n.d.), *Forskningsetiska Principer*, Stockholm: Swedish Research Agency.

Vosburg, D. (2017), 'The Effects of Group Dynamics on Language Learning and Use in an MMOG', *CALICO Journal* 34 (1): 58–74. doi: 10.1558/cj.29524.

Part Three

Towards the future of game-based language learning

11

Issues in the current state of teaching languages with games

Benjamin Thanyawatpokin and James York

Introduction

Implementing games in educational contexts is a highly active field of research inquiry, as evidenced by a growing literature on the topic (Becker 2017). The trend also exists in the field of applied linguistics, and more specifically computer-assisted language learning (CALL), known as (digital) game-based language learning ((D)GBLL) (Reinders 2012; Sykes and Reinhardt 2012; Peterson 2016; Reinhardt 2018). Research on games as a tool for learning has grown due to the potentially beneficial cognitive, meta-cognitive, affective and interactive affordances that games facilitate. Video game literacy is also considered a component of multiliteracy education which therefore legitimizes further examination of games in language classrooms (Jones 2018).

Some researchers explore the pedagogical implementation of games as part of well-established (e.g. task-based language teaching (TBLT)) or progressive (e.g. multiliteracies) approaches to second language acquisition (SLA) (York and deHaan 2018; Warner Richardson and Lange 2019; York 2020). Other research uses massively multiplayer online role-playing games (MMORPGs) in extramural language learning environments to connect learners to L2 speakers (Rama et al. 2012; Peterson 2013; Suh, Kim and Kim 2010; Sundqvist 2019). Thus, there is a great deal of variety in terms of theoretical approaches and assumptions to conducting GBLL. In addition to appropriating vernacular games, or teachers designing games for use in their language classrooms, activities may be modified to incorporate points, leader boards or badges in the hope of making things more appealing to learners. This approach is known as gamification (e.g. Lombardi 2015; Rachels and Rockinson-Szapkiw 2018) or 'game-informed' language learning (Reinhardt 2018).

Taking into account the wide variety of approaches to using games in language learning and teaching contexts, it is easy to see how the literature may be easily confounded. That is, practitioners confusing gamification for GBLL or using games as content without additional teacher mediation. In order to better position this chapter for prospective educators, we also make a distinction between GBLL and what we term 'game-based language teaching' (GBLT) which implies formal, pedagogically sound, teacher-mediated uses of games. We hope to start a dialogue with the research community and solidify the definitions of GBLL, GBLT and gamification in the field.

A taxonomy of games

There is a large variety in terms of game genres and the technology required to play them. In this paper, our definition of game is inspired by the definition of Salen and Zimmerman (2004: 80): 'A game is a system in which players engage in an artificial conflict, defined by rules, that results in a quantifiable outcome.' For a more nuanced comparison of game definitions, see Salen and Zimmerman (ibid.). Additionally, we distinguish between entertainment games (EGs) and games for learning (GL) based on works by Boyle et al. (2016) and Hainey et al. (2016). These definitions of *game* coincide with the concept of game-based (use of GLs) and game-enhanced (use of EGs) learning as considered by Sykes and Reinhardt (2012). Finally, we outline what we do not consider games: gamified activities or studies that utilize virtual worlds (VWs).

Here the most common types of games that appear in the literature on games and language learning are presented succinctly in Table 11.1.

The above taxonomy highlights the major game types that have been used in the literature on games and language learning and teaching. Of additional note is that for the most part the majority of MMORPG, commercial off-the-shelf (COTS) and casual games featured in the literature are classed as EGs, whereas serious games are an example of GL.

Additionally, we have deliberately left out game-*like* systems from our consideration of what constitutes a game. This term, which appears in the literature on games and language learning, generally refers to flashcard or quiz systems which award points for successful completion (Berns, Gonzalez-Pardo and Camacho 2013; Wichadee and Pattanapichet 2018). The term 'game-like' is a possible signifier that the authors or developers themselves do not consider their project a legitimate 'game', opting to include 'gamification' in their paper's

Table 11.1 A taxonomy of common game types in the literature on games and language learning

Category	Typical devices	Examples	Description	Relevant studies
MMORPG	PC	*World of Warcraft, Guild Wars, Everquest, The Elder Scrolls Online*	Large, simulated worlds primarily based on fantasy themes Massive numbers of players connect at any one time	Peterson (2012) Rama et al. (2012) Newgarden, Zheng and Liu (2015) Sholz and Schulze (2017)
COTS	PC, console mobile	*Zelda* series, *Pokemon, Life Is Strange, Fortnite, Minecraft, Her Story*	Covers a wide range of game genres from single-player action and adventure games to multiplayer online battle or sandbox games	Coleman (2002) Miller and Hegelheimer (2006) Ranalli (2008) Lee (2019)
Tabletop	N/a (some tablet PCs)	*Pandemic, One Night Ultimate Werewolf, Diplomacy*	Games played face-to-face. Typically use cards and dice	York and deHaan (2018) deHaan (2019)
Serious games	PC, console	*3rd World Farmer, 2030 SDGs Game, America's Army*	Games or simulations fundamentally designed with an educational intent (Ulicsak and Wright 2010)	Hitosugi, Schmidt and Hayashi (2014) Franciosi et al. (2015)

keywords section as well (Castañeda and Cho 2016). While these activities could technically be classed as games under Salen and Zimmerman's (2004) definition, and GL based on Boyle et al's classification (2016), they are relegated to 'gamified system' here due to their lack of ludic elements and explicit learning goals which have been dubbed 'chocolate-covered broccoli' like content (Bruckman 1999).

Finally, although the term 'VW' often appears in the literature on games and language learning, these domains are not classified as games in this paper. As Melchor-Couto writes (2019: 1), 'In contrast to computer games that require players to undertake pre-designed activities such as for example, engaging in trading, VWs are designed primarily to support communication.' One final point regarding VWs is that their classification as 'games' is not only done by researchers, but by participants themselves. In a study by Dalton and Devitt (2016), although the researchers firmly position the paper as an exploration into the use of a VW for promoting young learners' motivation to study Irish, participants were found to refer to their actions in the world as 'playing the game', which is something the authors had not predicted. They concluded that the addition of goal orientation to activities made them more game-like and that a 'fuzzy classification' exists around games and VWs (2016: 26). Therefore, even though a researcher may not categorize a VW as a game, participants themselves may make their own conclusions. We have elected to construct our critique of the field based on the taxonomy introduced above.

Research trends and issues

Meta-analyses

The first step in assessing the state of the field of GBLL is to refer to meta-analyses. This section focuses specifically on Hung et al.'s meta-analysis (2018) as it represents one of the most recent, scoping reviews of the field. Their criteria for inclusion were based on the date of publication (2007–16), Social Sciences Citation Index (SSCI), provision of empirical evidence and a focus on language learning *through* digital gameplay. The italic is added to outline a potential problem with the GBLL literature at the outset. Learning through digital gameplay excludes any learning that may occur *around* gameplay such as analysing gameplay texts, communities, transcriptions, communities and other tangential or peripheral activities connected to gameplay (see Reinhardt and Sykes 2011; deHaan 2019 for considerations of learning through gameplay versus learning around gameplay).

    Games included in the meta-analysis were categorized into simulation games, immersive games, tutorial games, exergames, board games, adventure games, music games and alternate reality games. The authors provide definitions for each of their classifications; however, there appears to be considerable leeway in terms of how games are classified. As a concrete example of the confusing classification system, the studies included in the largest category 'immersive games' (n = 21) range from the use of three-dimensional virtual worlds (3DVWs) (Berns et al. 2013; Dalton and Devitt 2016), interactive fiction (Neville et al. 2009), MMORPGs (Rama et al. 2012; Zheng et al. 2015), teacher-modified RPGs (Reinders and Wattana 2015) and finally studies which only tangentially assess the affordances of digital games for language learning (Ryu 2013). Additionally, it is unclear why the study by Yang and Zapata-Rivera (2010), which features an interactive sentence completion system, is kept separate from this categorization and placed into a small (n = 2) category: 'simulation games' with Ranalli (2008). Moreover, in terms of a breakdown of EG and GL, the 'immersive games' category features fifteen GL studies and seven EG studies. Of note is that the GL studies include non-games (VWs) based on our definition of games above.

The most frequently reported finding of the meta-analysis is the affective affordances of games (n = 38) followed closely by studies which reported on language acquisition from playing games (n = 37), of which vocabulary acquisition was the most reported outcome (n = 15). The trend in results is therefore skewed towards affective affordances of GL, including student perceptions of learning environments and tools, and the acquisition of vocabulary. These research findings may be considered low-hanging fruit of sorts compared to the potential benefits of games and language learning mentioned in the literature (see Sykes and Reinhardt 2012). The overall picture, based on this meta-analysis, is that as a field, we are still far from 'insight' and still very much caught up in the 'hype' (see Cornillie et al. 2012).

Peterson (2016) provides a detailed meta-analysis on the depth and breadth of research that is taking place around the use of MMOGs from both socially informed and cognitive perspectives. The meta-analysis introduces hypothesized benefits of using MMOGs for language learning, as well as exemplary studies which explore the validity of such hypotheses. As a concrete example, Lee and Gerber (2013) provide details of a year-long ethnographic study of a single player's language development as they played in the game *World of Warcraft* (Blizzard 2004). While Peterson's meta-analysis outlines the work being done on understanding how an L2 can be acquired through MMOG play, he recognizes that studies such as Lee and Gerber's year-long ethnography are the exception in the field, and calls for more longitudinal studies with a mixed-methods design to be conducted with students of varying proficiencies. What is missing, from a GBLT perspective however, is a call for more studies on the successful implementation of MMOGs in classroom contexts.

Massively multiplayer online games (MMOGs)

As stated above, the main draw for these platforms are psycholinguistic and sociocultural affordances such as communication with L2 speakers while simultaneously taking advantage of the positive affective aspects of games

(Peterson 2016). Suh, Kim and Kim (2010) used a teacher-created MMOG with younger learners and found higher achievement rates on standardized English tests. Additionally, some studies involving MMOGs have focused upon their affordances for communication. For example, Reinders and Wattana (2015) give evidence for MMOGs' lowering affective filters and increasing willingness to communicate during free play sessions. Peterson (2012) observed students using several communicative strategies when using MMOGs as a medium for communication including episodes of turn-taking, politeness, humour and small talk to build rapport with native-level players. Rama et al. (2012) propose three main characteristics that facilitate learning: the creation of safe spaces, promotion of communicative competence and that they promote goal-directed action. The paper also showed how game literacy was important in aiding learning in such domains.

As shown above, studies on MMOGs are numerous and provide valuable insight into their benefits for language learning. However, there is a lack of papers on how MMOGs may be used in formal classroom contexts. One interpretation is that MMOGs are only suited to extramural contexts and calls for this usage case exist in the literature (Peterson 2012; Scholz and Schulze 2017). How MMOGs can be used in teacher-mediated courses or for teaching specific skills remains to be explored.

Digital COTS games

The role of the teacher and non-gameplay activities in COTS studies has also received little attention. Exceptions do exist, such as in Miller and Hegelheimer (2006), who used teacher-designed worksheets and materials with *The Sims* to facilitate vocabulary acquisition. Findings of the study suggested that games could help with language learning in the classroom but also emphasized the need for supplementary materials. These findings were validated and further elaborated upon in a follow-up study by Ranalli (2008). Outside of these two studies however, research findings which investigate the use of games with pedagogical support are rare (see the tabletop games section below for examples of pedagogically sound implementations of games). Research by Marklund and Taylor (2015), Molin (2017), Sykes and Reinhardt (2012) and Reinhardt (2018) provides a wealth of suggestions and advice for practitioners in classroom contexts. However, there is a lack of practical, implementable reports or empirical studies based on their advice. A concrete example of the disconnect between theory and practice is with Reinhardt and Syke's Explore, Examine and Extend model (2011) which still has not been adopted in a single empirical study to date (theoretical articles do exist however: Kim 2016; Pearson 2016).

It has been noted that the incorporation of games into the classroom is difficult for a number of logistical, financial, contextual and curricular constraints (Wiklund and Mozelius 2013). There is therefore a gap in the literature for studies which feature pedagogical considerations, or, more simply how to *teach* with games.

Tabletop games

Currently, the term 'game' generally refers to digital or video games. Tabletop games however, while also being a type of COTS game, are receiving increased interest from practitioners and researchers over the past decade as the media gains popularity for game designers and players (Selinker 2011; Masuda and deHaan 2015). York (2019) explored the use of tabletop games in a TBLT-inspired framework to promote agency and productive language skills with Japanese university students. Observations of students' work over multiple gameplay sessions and extensive pre- and post-play activities suggested that gameplay supplemented with non-gameplay activities helped promote critical awareness of interlanguage errors and improve productive language skills. deHaan (2019) explored the use of games in a multiliteracies approach to language teaching in an extramural context and found that while games were core to the curriculum, the student learned more from teacher-mediated activities outside of playing games.

The two above studies represent examples of *GBLT* (as opposed to GBLL), where teacher mediation and roles, pedagogical underpinnings and classroom-based integrations are considered throughout. The strong classroom orientation of these exemplary studies may be due to the affordances and logistics of the medium used. For example, compared to MMOGs, tabletop games do not require individual PCs, network connections or game subscriptions. Jones (2019) also provides evidence that language teachers are more familiar with the application of non-digital games in their classrooms. One caveat is that tabletop gameplay does not afford a direct connection to L2 speakers as is possible with MMOGs or other networked games. However, other non-gameplay affordances for learning and participation exist such as participation in online gaming communities found on YouTube or boardgamegeek.com.

Gamification

Gamification is the incorporation of gaming elements into non-game applications or activities. For digital applications, this could be instantiated in the form of vocabulary flashcard systems, cooperative fast-paced review activities as seen in *Quizlet Live* or making tests a class-wide competition such as with *Kahoot*. In non-digital contexts, this could be as simple as providing points for participation in class (Raine 2014).

Lombardi's (2015) work with a gamified classroom revealed that gamification can produce significant affective benefits. He reported higher rates of participation and exhibited overall better attitudes towards learning English with a gamified system. However, the basic, behaviouristic foundation of Lombardi's context is as follows: 'Do an activity, get points', with no overarching narrative or ludic elements. That is, providing points for grades is likely to result in increased engagement without calling it a game. Conversely, Rachels and Rockinson-Szapkiw (2018) conducted research using *Duolingo* but found no significant correlation between a gamified treatment group and control group (traditional classroom instruction) in vocabulary and grammar scores in a pre/post-test design. The researchers (dangerously) argue that the lack of significant correlation means that the gamified app *Duolingo* was just as effective as standard teaching methods.

Dicheva and Dichev (2015) suggest that the literature on gamification in language learning contexts lacks rigorous empirical studies. This is attributed to the 'hype cycle', or in other words the intense popularity gamification has received in a very short amount of time leading to the production of theoretical, or exploratory, studies only. There is also a concern that there is little understanding of what design elements contribute to learning in gamification studies. They write, 'Gamification in education is still growing and the practice has outpaced researchers' understanding of its mechanisms' (1445).

Finally, as outlined in the meta-analyses section, some studies and meta-analyses exhibit tendencies to conflate the terms 'GBLL' and 'gamification'. This has led to, at best, less cohesion in naming conventions which leads to more difficulty in discovering relevant research, and at worse, a diluting of important, empirical findings from GBLL and teaching research as they are compounded with the results of gamification studies.

Problematic trends

This section will attempt to distil the issues we have presented in the above sections and give suggestions on how they may be alleviated.

An excess of exploratory studies

Continuing attention on games as language learning tools and mediating artefacts in L2 learning contexts has caused the number of studies to grow extensively in a relatively short period of time. However, upon investigating the literature and meta-analyses such as Hung et al. (2018), Connolly et al. (2012) and Peterson (2016), we find that there is a substantial lack of information for practitioners on how to implement games in their classrooms. Research findings are largely based on laboratory-based, experimental studies which suggest that GBLL can benefit language acquisition. However, the field is still bereft of findings which are immediately applicable to classrooms such as the inclusion of frameworks, taxonomies and detailed accounts of teacher interventions. That is, in our understanding of the field, practitioners are not using games in their classrooms (Jones 2019). Additionally, for classroom implementation, the predominant conceptualization is to fit games into a TBLT framework (Sykes 2014; York and deHaan 2018; Vegel 2019). More should be done on the intersection between pedagogy and games in language teaching.

Considering the efforts required to use games in classes may hold clues as to why there is no widespread adoption. Games require extensive pre-teaching, both in terms of how to play and the content. COTS games are not made expressly for the purpose of language learning, thus time is required to facilitate learners adaption to game scenarios and specialized discourse (Thorne, Fischer and Lu 2012). During playtime, class-length sessions of gameplay may be possible for some games, but not for others. This also calls attention to the teacher's understanding of the game and what they can teach with it during class time. The real-world application of in-game language may also require explicit instruction. Finally, games should be debriefed so that students may reflect upon their experience with a game and consider what they learned.

Some researchers have raised the issue and explored the topic of classroom application, namely Miller and Hegelheimer (2006), York and deHaan (2018), deHaan (2019) and York (2020); however, these papers do not do enough to serve an entire burgeoning field of GBLL and teaching. There is a need for more longitudinal, empirical research that explores the pedagogical application of games.

Confusing terminology around learning and teaching with games

As stated above, Salen and Zimmerman (2004) propose that games have three core components: rules, competition and a quantifiable outcome. However, stricter definitions are required when using games in educational contexts. The terms EG and GL were introduced to classify games into those that were designed for entertainment and learning, respectively. Three classifications regarding the use of games for language learning were introduced in Sykes and Reinhardt (2012):

- **Game-enhanced:** Use of EG for learning or teaching.
- **Game-based:** Use of GL for learning or teaching.
- **Game-informed:** Application of game and play principals to non-game contexts to teach a language (both digital and non-digital).

Currently, few researchers have used these definitions to describe the method with which they have applied games or game-like activities in their contexts (for an exception see Lombardi 2015). Reinhardt (2018) has brought in even more terms to refer to the above classifications: *gameful* as an umbrella term for any 'disposition or attitude toward language learning' which is playful or game-inspired (viii), and separates the term *gamification* from *game-informed* to create a subset of terms here.

A taxonomy for game use in language learning and teaching: Our proposal

In order to clear up some of the misconceptions and work towards a more succinct set of classifications that would more clearly illustrate the role of teachers in using games or gamification in the classroom, and in keeping with the dichotomy of informal versus formal learning, we propose the following terms:

- **GBLL:** The use of games to support learning informally or independently 'in the wild' (see Sauro and Zourou 2019).
- **GBLT:** Teacher-mediated uses of games in formal contexts. In other words, GBLT may be considered the pedagogical application of GBLL.
- **Gamification:** The application of game mechanics to activities or applications that are not games for the purpose of language learning or teaching.

This classification emphasizes a split between studies which focus on learning and teaching rather than being based on the kind of game used. This is a deliberate decision in response to a lack of empirical studies on the use of games in classroom contexts. As a result, we call for more GBLT studies (a term that is not currently used in the literature), which feature teacher mediation and theoretically informed implementation of games in classrooms. Of note is that neither GBLL nor GBLT in the above definitions mandate the use of EGs or GLs. However, as described at the outset of this paper, VWs or gamified activities are not considered games. Gamification refers to studies which implement such gamified activities or the application of game mechanics to non-game contexts.

Implications for the field

This section will be split into two subsections, addressing implications for both researchers and educators using, considering or interested in GBLT.

Research implications

First and foremost, the field as a whole requires more rigorous categorization of studies incorporating games. There are currently too many naming conventions for games and ambiguities in classifications for game-related studies that result in an unclear message regarding the state of the field. Were more researchers to adhere to strict naming conventions, results in the field would be more easily recognizable and, moreover, applicable to teaching contexts. The classifications provided above are a starting point (GBLL, GBLT and gamification). We invite criticisms and further considerations for suitable terms. Additionally, we emphasize that researchers in this field must begin to use more standardized terminology, in order not to obscure future findings in GBLL and GBLT research.

Second, we call for more explicit reference to any teacher mediation that is carried out in interventions. Simply stating that games were used is no longer a valid explanation, as this reinforces a techno-utopian conceptualization of learning with games (Selwyn 2011), or more specifically, that games are only suitable as informal learning tools or to provide content to learners. Researchers in the field must be more willing to share what they did within their classes, the underlying pedagogic and theoretical considerations and how gameplay was supported with pre-play or debriefing sessions as seen in the simulation and gaming literature (see Codita 2016 as an example). This should promote a more concrete legitimization of game use in language classrooms. Additionally, including *how* GBLT pedagogy is used in various contexts may ultimately help diversify and increase the number of educators who adopt GBLT into their classrooms.

Last, games are as varied as textbooks. Not every game has innate affordances for language learning or promoting communication between students. Thus, a need for defining pedagogical interventions in teaching with games. Some scholars have proposed that *any* game can work if focus is turned away from *game-as-content* and towards games as a starting point for theoretically sound implementation (deHaan 2019). Up to this point, many studies have focused efforts on the use of a few specific games (e.g. *World of Warcraft* and *The SIMs*) and studied their affordances for language learning. More research must be done into how a wider variety of games or game genres lend themselves to in-class application in order to provide practitioners with more information regarding which games can be used for the promotion of different skills.

Educator implications

Games are not 'one-off' activities. They should not be used without any scaffolding or supervision from the teacher. Research has shed light on possible teacher roles in the GBLT classroom (Miller and Hegelheimer 2006; Ranalli 2008; Marklund and Taylor 2015; Molin 2017; Wang 2019). As previously explained, much of the literature surrounding teacher roles is still exploratory; however, there is a general consensus that games require intervention by a teacher in order to be effective. Games require pre-play activities and constant scaffolding: priming to learn about the content of the game, priming to learn the controls of how to play the game and priming for the language that may occur during the game. They also require post-play interventions: debriefing the content seen or read during the course of the game and debriefing for the language. There are frameworks which utilize games in unique ways (deHaan 2019; York 2019); however, such research is nascent.

It is also imperative that teachers in the field understand the differences between GBLT, GBLL and gamification. By understanding the three main ways games or gamified activities can be used in the language classroom, educators can consider the learning outcomes attributed to each method and align themselves accordingly. Each of the three classifications emphasized by this chapter entail different pedagogies, approaches and styles of teacher mediation. Learning outcomes are also varied. Gamification may be extrinsically motivating for students to acquire simple rote skills (Lombardi 2015); on the other hand, GBLT can often expose students to a larger variety of skills with the caveat of increased need for teacher planning and mediation.

Conclusion

In this chapter we have outlined the current state of the literature regarding games in language learning and teaching contexts. Through our attempts at creating a taxonomy of games used in the literature, it is evident that more effort is required in defining the term 'game'. We have adopted the concept of EG and GL as a way to distinguish between two primary avenues of inquiry. This simple dichotomy, however, is blurred by increasingly sophisticated gamified applications, as well as learners' subjective experience of such systems. That is, as seen in Dalton and Devitt (2016), although the authors were conscious of their study utilizing a VW, participants in the study referred to it as a game. In addition to the issue mentioned above, the chapter also covered the overabundance of exploratory studies (Cornillie et al. 2012; Peterson 2016; Hung et al. 2018). We call for more studies which feature teacher mediation and teacher roles in order to make GBLT more accessible to the average teacher and not only to those working in specific contexts with numerous resources. In taking these two issues into account, we hope that the field will work towards restructuring itself in order to present more empirical and groundbreaking research. With the conceptualization proposed in this chapter, we hope to begin a dialogue with the community at large about how research on games and language learning and teaching can be categorized to best represent the underlying goal of the research. Ultimately, this is done in the hope that GBLL and teaching research will find more widespread use in classrooms.

References

Allen, L. K., S. A. Crossley, E. L. Snow and D. S. McNamara (2014), 'L2 Writing Practice: Game Enjoyment as a Key to Engagement', *Language Learning & Technology* 18 (2): 124–50.

Becker, K. (2017), *Choosing and Using Digital Games in the Classroom*, Heidelberg: Springer International. https://doi.org/10.1007/978-3-319-12223-6.

Berns, A., A. Gonzalez-Pardo and D. Camacho (2013), 'Game-Like Language Learning in 3-D Virtual Environments', *Computers and Education* 60 (1): 210–20. https://doi.org/10.1016/j.compedu.2012.07.001.

Blizzard Entertainment (2004), *World of Warcraft* [PC video game], Irvine, CA: Activision Blizzard.

Boyle, E. A., T. Hainey, T. M. Connolly, G. Gray, J. Earp and M. Ott (2016), 'An Update to the Systematic Literature Review of Empirical Evidence of the Impacts and Outcomes of Computer Games and Serious Games', *Computers & Education* 94: 178–92. https://doi.org/10.1016/j.compedu.2015.11.003.

Bruckman, A. (1999), 'Can Educational Be Fun?', *Game Developers Conference* 99: 75–9.

Castañeda, D. A., and M. H. Cho (2016), 'Use of a Game-Like Application on a Mobile Device to Improve Accuracy in Conjugating Spanish Verbs', *Computer Assisted Language Learning* 29 (7): 1195–204. https://doi.org/10.1080/09588221.2016.1197950.

Codita, A. M. (2016), 'Integrating an Immigration Law Simulation into EAP Courses: Instructors' and Students' Perceptions', *Simulation and Gaming* 47 (5): 684–700. https://doi.org/10.1177/1046878116659201.

Coleman, D. W. (2002), 'On Foot in SIM CITY: Using SIM COPTER as the Basis for an ESL Writing Assignment', *Simulation and Gaming* 33 (2): 217–30. https://doi.org/10.1177/1046878102332010.

Connolly, T. M., E. A. Boyle, E. MacArthur, T. Hainey and J. M. Boyle (2012), 'A Systematic Literature Review of Empirical Evidence on Computer Games and Serious Games', *Computers & Education* 59 (2): 681–6.

Cornillie, F., G. Clarebout and P. Desmet (2012), 'Between Learning and Playing? Exploring Learners' Perceptions of Corrective Feedback in an Immersive Game for English Pragmatics', *ReCALL* 24 (3): 257–78. doi: 10.1S017/S0958344012000146.

Dalton, G., and A. Devitt (2016), 'Irish in a 3D World: Engaging Primary School Children', *Language Learning and Technology* 20 (1): 21–33.

deHaan, J. (2019), 'Teaching Language and Literacy with Games: What? How? Why?', *Ludic Language Pedagogy* 1: 1–57.

Dicheva, D., and C. Dichev (2015), 'Gamification in Education: Where Are We in 2015?', E-Learn 2015, Kona, HI, 2015, 1445–54.

Franciosi. S., J. Yagi, Y. Tomoshige and S. Ye (2015), 'The Effect of a Simple Simulation Game on Long-Term Vocabulary Retention', *CALICO Journal* 33 (2): 355–79.

Hainey, T., T. M. Connolly, E. A. Boyle, A. Wilson and A. Razak (2016), 'A Systematic Literature Review of Empirical Evidence on Computer Games and Serious Games', *Computers & Education* 102: 202–23. https://doi.org/10.1016/j.compedu.2012.03.004.

Hitosugi, C. I., M. Schmidt and K. Hayashi (2014), 'Digital Game-Based Learning (DGBL) in the L2 classroom: The Impact of the UN's Off-the-Shelf Videogame, Food Force, on Learner Affect and Vocabulary Retention', *CALICO Journal* 31 (1): 19–39.

Hung, H. T., J. C. Yang, G. J. Hwang, H. C. Chu and C. C. Wang (2018), 'A Scoping Review of Research on Digital Game-Based Language Learning', *Computers and Education* 126: 89–104. https://doi.org/10.1016/j.compedu.2018.07.001.

Jones, D. M. (2019), 'Teacher Cognition Related to Tabletop Game Use in Language Learning Classrooms', MA diss., British Columbia: Trinity Western University.

Jones, R. D. (2018), *Developing Video Game Literacy in the EFL Classroom: A Qualitative Analysis of 10th Grade Classroom Game Discourse*, Giessener Beiträge zur Fremdsprachendidaktik, Tübingen: Narr Francke Attempto Verlag.

Kim, J. (2016), 'Bridging Activities Cycle: Design and Defense', *Issues in EFL* 12 (2): 56–60.

Lee, S. M. (2019), 'Her Story or Their Own Stories? Digital Game-Based Learning, Student Creativity, and Creative Writing', *ReCALL* 31 (3): 1–17. https://doi. org/10.1017/S0958344019000028.

Lee, Y., and H. Gerber (2013), 'It's a WoW World: Second Language Acquisition and Massively Multiplayer Online Gaming', *Multimedia-Assisted Language Learning* 16 (2): 53–70.

Lombardi, I. (2015), 'Fukudai Hero: A Video Game-Like English Class in a Japanese National University', *EL.LE: Educazione Linguistica. Language Education* 4 (3): 483–500. https//doi.org/10.14277/2280–6792/ELLE-4-3-15-7.

Marklund, B. B., and A. S. A. Taylor (2015), 'Teachers' Many Roles in Game-Based Learning Projects', *Proceedings of the European Conference on Games-Based Learning*, January 2015, 350–67.

Masuda, R., and J. deHaan (2015), 'Language in Game Rules and Game Play: A Study of Emergence in Pandemic', *International Journal of English Linguistics* 5 (6): 1–10. https://doi.org/10.5539/ijel.v5n6p1.

Melchor-Couto, S. (2019), 'Virtual Worlds and Language Learning', *Journal of Gaming and Virtual Worlds* 11 (1): 29–43. https://doi.org/10.1386/jgvw.11.1.29_1.

Miller, M., and V. Hegelheimer (2006), 'The SIMs Meet ESL Incorporating Authentic Computer Simulation Games into the Language Classroom', *Interactive Technology and Smart Education* 3 (4): 311–28. https://doi.org/10.1108/17415650680000070.

Molin, G. (2017), 'The Role of the Teacher in Game-Based Learning: A Review and Outlook', in *Serious Games and Edutainment Applications: Volume II*, 649–74, Cham: Springer. https://doi.org/10.1007/978-3-319-51645-5_28.

Neville, D. O., B. E. Shelton and B. McInnis (2009), 'Cybertext Redux: Using Digital Game-Based Learning to Teach L2 Vocabulary, Reading, and Culture', *Computer Assisted Language Learning* 22 (5): 409–24.

Newgarden, K., D. Zheng and M. Liu (2015), 'An Eco-Dialogical Study of Second Language Learners', World of Warcraft (WoW) Gameplay, *Language Sciences* 48: 22–41. https://doi.org/10.1016/j.langsci.2014.10.004.

Pearson, B. (2016), 'Using Analog Games to Improve Negotiation Skills in Upper Intermediate Level ESL Learners', MA diss., Eugene: University of Oregon.

Peterson, M. (2010), 'Computerized Games and Simulations in Computer-Assisted Language Learning: A Meta-Analysis of Research', *Simulation & Gaming* 41 (1): 72–93.

Peterson, M. (2012), 'Language Learner Interaction in a Massively Multiplayer Online Role-Playing Game', in H. Reinders (ed.), *Digital Games in Language Learning and Teaching*, 70–92, Basingstoke: Palgrave Macmillan.

Peterson, M. (2013), *Computer Games and Language Learning*, New York: Palgrave Macmillan.

Peterson, M. (2016), 'The Use of Massively Multiplayer Online Role-Playing Games in CALL: An Analysis of Research', *Computer Assisted Language Learning* 29 (7): 1181–94.

Rachels, J., and A. Rockinson-Szapkiw (2018), 'The Effects of a Mobile Gamification App on Elementary Students' Spanish Achievement and Self-Efficacy', *Computer Assisted Language Learning* 31 (1): 72–89. https//doi.org/10.1080/09588221.2017.13 82536.

Raine, P. (2014), 'The Use of a Participation Point System to Encourage More Proactive Learner Participation in Japanese University English Classes', *Obirin Today: In Search of a Learner-Centered Education* 14: 87–102.

Rama, P. S., R. Black, E. van Es and M. Warschauer (2012), 'Affordances for Second Language Learning in World of Warcraft', *ReCALL* 24 (3): 322–38.

Ranalli, J. (2008), 'Learning English with The Sims: Exploiting Authentic Computer Simulation Games for L2 Learning', *Computer Assisted Language Learning* 21 (5): 441–55.

Reinders, H. (2012), 'Introduction', in H. Reinders (ed.), *Digital Games in Language Learning and Teaching*, 1–8, Basingstoke: Palgrave Macmillan. https://doi. org/10.1057/9781137005267.

Reinders, H., and S. Wattana (2015), 'Affect and Willingness to Communicate in Digital Game-Based Learning', *ReCALL* 27 (1): 38–57. https://doi.org/10.1017/ S0948344014000226.

Reinhardt, J. (2018), *Gameful Second and Foreign Language Teaching and Learning: Theory, Research, and Practice*, Basingstoke: Palgrave Macmillan.

Reinhardt, J., and J. Sykes (2011), *Framework for Game-Enhanced Materials Development*, Tucson, AZ: Center for Educational Resources in Culture, Language, and Literacy.

Ryu, D. (2013), 'Play to Learn, Learn to Play: Language Learning through Gaming Culture', *ReCALL* 25 (2): 286–301.

Salen, S., and E. Zimmerman (2004), *Rules of Play: Game Design Fundamentals*, Cambridge: MIT Press.

Sauro, S., and K. Zourou (2019), 'What Are the Digital Wilds?', *Language Learning & Technology* 23(1): 1–7. https://doi.org/10125/44666.

Scholz, K. (2017), 'Encouraging Free Play: Extramural Digital Game-Based Language Learning as a Complex Adaptive System', *CALICO Journal* 34 (1): 39–57. https://doi. org/10.1558/cj.29527.

Scholz, K., and M. Schulze (2017), 'Digital-Gaming Trajectories and Second Language Development', *Language Learning and Technology* 21 (1): 100–20.

Selinker, M., ed. (2011), *The Kobold Guide to Board Game Design*, Kirkland, WA: Open Design LLC.

Selwyn, N. (2011), *Schools and Schooling in the Digital Age: A Critical Analysis*, London: Routledge.

Suh, S., S. Kim and N. Kim (2010), 'Effectiveness of MMORPG-Based Instruction in Elementary English Education in Korea', *Journal of Computer Assisted Learning* 26 (5): 370–8. https//doi.org/10.1111/j.1365-2729.2010.00353.x.

Sundqvist, P. (2019), 'COTS Games in the Digital Wild and L2 learner Vocabulary', *Language Learning and Technology* 23 (1): 87–113.

Sykes, J. (2013), 'Multi-User Virtual Environments: Learner Apologies in Spanish', in N. Taguchi and J. Sykes (eds), *Technology in Interlanguage Pragmatics Research and Teaching*, 71–100, Amsterdam: John Benjamins.

Sykes, J. (2014), 'TBLT and Synthetic Immersive Environments What Can In-Game Task Restarts Tell Us about Design and Implementation?', in M. González-Lloret and L. Ortega (eds), *Technology-Mediated TBLT Researching Technology and Tasks*, 149–82, Amsterdam: John Benjamins.

Sykes, J. E., and J. Reinhardt (2012), *Language at Play: Digital Games in Second and Foreign Language Teaching and Learning*, New York: Pearson.

Thorne, S. L., I. Fischer and X. Lu (2012), 'The Semiotic Ecology and Linguistic Complexity of an Online Game World', *ReCALL* 24 (3): 279–301.

Ulicsak, M., and M. Wright (2010), 'Games in Education: Serious Games. A FutureLab Literature Review', 139. Retrieved from http://www.futurelab.org.uk/projects/games-in-education (accessed 2 April 2019).

Vegel, A. (2019), 'Critical Perspective on Language Learning: TBLT and Digital Games', *Proceedings from the TBLT in Asia 2018 Conference*, Kyoto: Ryukoku University.

Wang, J. (2019), 'Classroom Intervention for Integrating Simulation Games into Language Classrooms: An Exploratory Study with the Sims 4', *CALL-EJ* 20 (2): 101–27.

Warner, C., D. Richardson and K. Lange (2019), 'Realizing Multiple Literacies through Game-Enhanced Pedagogies: Designing Learning across Discourse Levels', *Journal of Gaming and Virtual Worlds* 11 (1): 9–28. https://doi.org/10.1386/jgvw.11.1.9_1.

Wichadee, S., and F. Pattanapichet (2018), 'Enhancement of Performance and Motivation through Application of Digital Games in an English Language Class', *Teaching English with Technology* 18 (1): 77–92.

Wiklund, M., and P. Mozelius (2013), 'Learning Games or Learning Simulating Games: An Indirect Approach to Learning Stimulating Effects from Off-the-Shelf Games', *International Journal of Digital Information and Wireless Communications* 3 (3): 290–300.

Yang, H. C., and D. Zapata-Rivera (2010), Interlanguage Pragmatics with a Pedagogical Agent: The Request Game', *Computer Assisted Language Learning* 23 (5): 395–412. https://doi.org/10.1080/09588221.2010.520274.

York, J. (2019), 'Kotoba Rollers Walkthrough: Board games, TBLT and Player Progression in a University EFL Classroom', *Ludic Language Pedagogy* 1: 58–114.

York, J. (2020), 'Promoting Spoken Interaction and Student Engagement with Board Games in a Language Teaching Context', in *Global Perspectives on Gameful and Playful Teaching and Learning*, 1–26, Hershey, PA: IGI Global. https://doi. org/10.4018/978-1-7998-2015-4.ch001.

York, J., and J. DeHaan (2018), 'A Constructivist Approach to Game-Based Language Learning: Student Perceptions in a Beginner-Level EFL Context', *International Journal of Game-Based Learning* 8 (1): 19–40. https://doi.org/10.4018/ IJGBL.2018010102.

Zheng, D., M. Bischoff and B. Gilliland (2015), 'Vocabulary Learning in Massively Multiplayer Online Games: Context and Action before Words', *Educational Technology Research and Development* 63 (5): 771–90. https://doi.org/ 10.1007/ s11423-015-9387-4.

12

Is game-based language teaching 'vaporware'?

Jonathan deHaan

Introduction

Yes. ;)

Now loading …

I am a teacher, and I've used numerous games to teach language and literacy. I've cobbled together game-based teaching practices from activity books and lesson plans and many of the papers cited in this chapter. I am also a researcher of games and learning. When I started, I asked, 'Can students learn language *from* games?' Twenty years later, I ask, 'What can *I* do to help students learn and do more *around* games?' I've shifted from a technology-only focus to seeing what pedagogy and technology can do together. In this chapter, I examine the 'field' of game-based language teaching (GBLT) – what teachers (and researchers of teaching) report about language teaching with games. This chapter is an overview, and a critique, and (spoiler) concern about what the field may become. GBLT literature starts in the 1960s, but most inclusions here are post-2000. I included literature on various games. I included well-cited and recently published reports. I hoped to find a trend of teacher-researchers working to integrate and normalize GBLT theory, research and practice, either across the field or in one paper that integrated theory, research and practice all on its own. I was not looking for a 'magic bullet' but rather evidence of a mature field, and for models to guide my own teaching and research. I didn't find it. Have I missed 'the' normalized GBLT paper(s) in my literature review? Please let me know so I can (apologize and) improve my teaching and research. Also, my approach is just one; I encourage scholars to share others.

GBLT, not game-based language learning (GBLL) or gamification

I used initial criteria to sort GBLT from GBLL or gamification: *Did the project report actual practice of teaching with games? Was a teacher involved? Was a game used?* Dozens of papers offer theory and conjecture about games in language teaching, but teachers benefit more from practical implementation of those ideas, and verified learning outcomes. I looked for papers that described actions taken, for example, 'I did X' rather than hypothetical actions, for example, 'X can be done.' I looked for projects that were done in classes, not experiments in labs that overly isolated the learning with games. I stressed teaching over GBLL (student-gamers studying or using language independently). I treated GBLT as ideologically and practically distinct from GBLL. Thanyawatpokin and York (2021) explore this in depth. Games, role plays, simulations, virtual worlds, activities and flash card systems can overlap. I focused on games with 'endogenous' connections between form and content, not game-like systems with 'exogenous' form and content disconnections (Squire 2006). I set aside papers on *gamification* – teachers adding game elements (e.g. levels, points) to their classes. I treated GBLT as ideologically and practically distinct from gamification. Thanyawatpokin and York (2021) explore this distinction in depth.

The initial criteria (*Did the project report actual practice of teaching with games? Was a teacher involved? Was a game used?*) required that I set aside many papers. Approximately one-third of the papers were theoretical and did not include teaching practice or learning outcomes. The majority of the remainder were GBLL-focused (i.e. did not involve a school or class or teacher). I estimate that less than 10 per cent of all games and language education literature concerns GBLT; I included as many of these as possible.

Criteria for reports of GBLT

I used the following fourteen questions (dealing with theory, practice and research) to examine the field. In terms of theory:

1.   Was a specific *language teaching and learning theory* used to create or discuss the project?

How did the authors frame language learning – in behaviourist, interactionist, sociocultural or other terms? What underlaid the project? Did the project align or distance itself from other theories?

2. Were *other ideologies or purposes* identified as a rationale or base or discussion of the project?

Were there other reasons besides language learning, such as cultural connections, for conducting the project? Did the project address other ideological or practical issues? Why, or why not?

In terms of practice:

3. What was the *context*?

Was the context identified or described? Was it a classroom, an online space, a computer lab or a community space? Did the paper explore contextual constraints to give teachers practical advice?

4. What was the *structure*?

Was the structure identified or described? Was it a regular class, a comparison of a regular class to a special game-based class or a separate project?

5. Was the game *integrated*?

Were games integrated into the context, goals, textbook or curriculum? Were the games cordoned off for some reason? Did games change the teaching practices? Was the gameplay and related work graded?

6.1. What did the *teacher* do?

What roles or activities were reported? Did the teacher lead development? Was the teaching described thoroughly enough to guide others?

The teacher makes GBLT distinct from GBLL, and though many reports stress that 'the role of the instructor is crucial and computer simulation games in no way provide a substitute for ESL practitioners' (Miller and Hegelheimer 2006: 323), the problem remains that 'what [instruction] should look like … is still unclear and will require a great deal more research and practice' (Filsecker and Bündgens-Kosten 2012: 64). GBLT can benefit from explorations of teacher 'roles' in game-based teaching in other fields (e.g. Molin 2017).

I considered categorizing teaching from 'passive to active' or from 'traditional to progressive' or from 'irrelevant to crucial'. I finally categorized teaching by reports of activity in various stages of GBLT (i.e. choices, design, before, during and after the game).

6.2. Did the paper report any *choices* that the teacher made before the lesson?

Did the teacher choose goals, choose a game or choose to connect the lesson to students' needs? Did the teacher want to make a difference? Did the teacher intend to interact with students?

7. Did the paper report any *design work* that the teacher did before the lesson?

Did the teacher make a game, make a website or instructions, create a lecture or make a worksheet?

8. Did the paper report any *teacher roles or interactions before gameplay*?

Did the teacher pre-teach language, give a lecture or orient the student to a specific aspect of work?

9. Did the paper report any *teacher roles or interactions during gameplay*?

Did the paper report teachers facilitating, participating, adjusting, reacting, asking questions, giving advice, helping, inspiring, administrating technology, organizing groups, observing, correcting, giving feedback, giving 'just-in-time' instruction, discussing work with students, drawing attention to game elements or social connections, evaluating students or modelling work? Did the paper report something the teacher did that changed students' learning trajectories?

10. Did the paper report any *teacher roles or interactions after gameplay*?

In addition to the above, did the teacher facilitate a discussion or debriefing? Did the debriefing include a plan for future actions?

11. Were *teaching materials* shared (to help other teachers)?

Did the report share lesson plans, teaching scripts or worksheets, not just research instruments (e.g. questionnaires or tests)?

12. Did the paper *offer practical advice* to teachers?

Did the authors try to bridge theory-research-data and practice and advise teachers on classroom implementation?

13. Was the project *continued* (not a one-off)?

Were continued explorations mentioned? Did the authors continue exploring GBLT or was the report research-focused, exploratory and moved on from?

In terms of research:

14. What *learning outcomes* are shown?

Did students develop? Did students transfer something to other contexts? I downplayed papers on affect; many of these do not link enjoyment and transformation.

GBLT, all things considered

I categorized twenty-nine reports by these fourteen categories. In Table 12.1, ◯ indicates that the element featured prominently in the report, △ indicates that the element was somewhat present and x indicates that the element was not present.

Because hypothetical, GBLL and gamification papers were excluded from this investigation; the papers reviewed do report actual practices of teachers (and teacher-researchers) using various games to teach language. However, none of the papers reported all of the GBLT criteria prominently. The papers prominently reported details about the projects' context (24/29) and structure (18/29), teacher (and teacher-researcher) choices (22/29), material design (22/29), instruction before gameplay (18/29) and learning outcomes (16/29) much more prominently than teacher roles or interaction during (6/29) or after gameplay (3/29), or shared materials (3/29), or advice to teachers (8/29), or continued explorations of GBLT (5/29).

In terms of *language teaching and learning theory (criteria 1)*, many papers referenced specific theories. GBLT literature shows a dominance of communicative (presentation production and practice (PPP), communicative language teaching (CLT), total physical response (TPR), task-based language teaching (TBLT)) theories related to language teaching and learning. There were only a few instances of literacy and sociocultural theories and approaches.

In terms of *other ideologies or purposes (criteria 2)*, most projects aimed to develop students' vocabulary skills, speaking skills or motivation for language learning. Many papers mentioned games' technological affordances and the popularity of games as a rationale for GBLT. A few papers focused on pragmatics or text genres. A few papers included connections between language and culture, but some treated culture as content. Few projects tried to connect games and classwork to students' lives, other academic work or society.

In terms of the *context (criteria 3)*, the majority of projects were conducted in classrooms (either the authors' or a collaborating teacher's) or campus computer labs. Just a few projects involved a physical community off-campus, or an online community.

In terms of the *structure (criteria 4)*, several projects were conducted in regular classes. Others were controlled classroom experiments that compared a traditional class to a game-based class, or groups inside a class that either used traditional materials or a game.

In terms of *integration (criteria 5)*, some projects do report connecting games to a course or curriculum textbook or learning objectives. Some projects report using games to help students prepare for proficiency examinations. Some projects report choosing web browser games or board games because

Table 12.1 Features of GBLT in the research literature

		Theory	Practice			
		1	2	3	4	5
		Approach	Other	Context	Structure	Integration
CLT with traditional games	Uberman (1998)	○	X	○	△	○
	Nguyen and Khuat (2003)	○	X	○	○	X
	Rama et al. (2007)	○	○	○	△	○
	Tuan (2012)	○	○	○	△	X
	Chou (2014)	○	X	○	○	○
CLT with digital games	Coleman (2002)	X	X	○	○	○
	Miller and Hegelheimer (2006)	○	X	△	△	X
	Ranalli (2008)	○	X	△	△	X
	Yip and Kwan (2006)	X	X	△	△	X
	Bryant (2007)	○	X	○	○	○
	Neville, Shelton and McInnis (2009)	○	X	○	△	X
	Sykes (2009)	○	X	○	○	○
	Suh, Kim and Kim (2010)	X	X	○	△	X
	Holden and Sykes (2011)	○	○	○	○	○
	Reinhardt and Zander (2011)	○	○	○	○	○
	York (2014)	X	○	○	○	○
	Hitosugi et al. (2014)	○	△	○	○	○
	Reinders and Wattana (2014)	△	X	○	○	○
	Butler (2015)	○	X	○	○	○
	Shintaku (2016)	X	△	△	△	○
	Shirazi, Ahmadi and Mehrdad (2016)	○	X	○	△	X
	Zhou (2016)	X	○	○	○	○
	Franciosi (2017)	○	○	○	○	△
	Vasileiadou and Makrina (2017)	X	○	○	○	△
	Janebi, Enayat and Haghighatpasand (2019)	X	X	△	△	X
CLT in beta	York (in press)	○	○	○	○	○
	Bregni (2017)	X	○	○	○	○
New pedagogies in beta	Rasmussen (2017)	○	X	○	○	○
	Warner, Richardson and Lange (2019)	○	○	○	○	○
Out of the 29 reports, how many prominently featured (○) the criteria?		19	11	24	18	18

| | | | | | Research | | | |
| Teacher roles and actions | | | | | 11 | 12 | 13 | 14 |
6 Choices	7 Design	8 Before	9 During	10 After	Materials shared	Advice for teachers	Continued	Learning outcomes
○	○	○	X	X	X	△	X	○
△	△	○	X	X	X	△	X	X
○	X	X	X	X	X	○	X	○
○	X	X	X	X	X	X	X	○
○	○	○	○	X	X	X	X	○
○	○	○	△	○	△	X	X	X
○	○	△	△	X	X	△	X	○
○	○	X	X	X	X	X	X	○
X	○	△	△	X	X	△	X	○
○	○	○	○	X	X	○	X	X
○	○	○	X	○	X	○	△	△
○	○	○	X	X	○	X	△	○
△	○	X	X	X	X	X	X	○
○	○	○	X	X	X	X	X	△
○	○	○	○	X	X	△	○	△
○	○	X	X	X	○	○	X	X
○	○	○	X	X	X	X	X	○
○	○	X	X	X	X	X	X	X
X	○	○	△	X	△	X	○	X
○	○	△	△	X	△	○	△	○
X	X	○	X	○	X	X	X	○
X	X	○	X	X	X	△	X	○
○	○	○	X	△	X	X	X	○
○	X	○	X	X	X	X	X	○
X	○	○	X	X	X	X	X	○
○	△	○	X	△	△	○	○	X
○	○	○	○	△	△	○	○	△
○	○	△	○	△	○	○	X	X
○	○	X	○	△	△	X	○	△
22	22	18	6	3	3	8	5	16

of technological or financial constraints. A few projects were explicit about connecting games to other activities, exercises or projects. However, many projects did not report, and did not seem to be connected to any classroom or curriculum goals or materials or activities. Many projects seem deliberately designed to be controlled experiments about what students could learn from games in a classroom context (and are borderline GBLL projects). Very few projects refer to gameplay or related work being graded or assessed, and reasons for, or for not, grading (whether related to ethics or purpose) are not common.

In terms of *teacher choices (criteria 6)*, many papers report teachers (or teacher-researchers) choosing a specific game based on gameplay or technological affordances or students' linguistic needs. Some papers report choosing to include worksheets alongside gameplay. A few papers reported choosing to debrief students following gameplay. A few teachers chose to let students choose games themselves. A few papers chose to connect games to social participation or social issues. Only a few papers report the teacher choosing to guide or nurture students. It was surprising, especially for the papers with sociocultural learning theory foundations, how little teacher mediation was reported as a choice or priority.

In terms of *design work (criteria 7)*, some papers report the creation or modification of a game. A few papers report the teacher making language lists. Some papers report creating instructions or websites that were used in game and traditional instruction comparisons. Many papers report the creation of supplemental materials to be used alongside games – including vocabulary, grammar, listening, speaking exercises and essay tasks.

In terms of *teacher roles or interactions before gameplay (criteria 8)*, some papers reported teachers teaching vocabulary and modelling target language. Some papers reported teachers explaining the rules of the game. Some papers reported teachers (perhaps researchers) instructing students to complete the materials that they had designed. A few papers reported teachers directing students' attention to specific aspects of a game. A few papers reported direct conceptual instruction about language.

In terms of *teacher roles or interactions during gameplay (criteria 9)*, very few were reported. Some papers were explicit about research designs necessitating zero teacher interaction. Some papers reported teachers monitoring or guiding students, but no specific details were given. A few reported directing students' attention to language during the game, or correcting students' language during play. One reported the teacher pausing the game and asking students questions. A few reported the teacher playing games with students.

In terms of *teacher roles or interactions after gameplay (criteria 10)*, most papers reported giving tests or questionnaires for research purposes, not for formative assessment. The few reports of debriefing were not described in any detail. It was surprising that authors described the theoretical importance of debriefing, but did not report on their post-game continued mediation of students' learning.

In terms of *teaching materials (criteria 11)*, very few were shared. Some worksheets, some related linguistic information and some technical information were shared as appendices or hyperlinks.

In terms of *practical advice (criteria 12)*, most papers did not devote significant space to this. Discussions tended to focus on implications for research or design. Many papers closed by suggesting that teachers consider using games and that teachers should choose appropriate games. A few papers suggest that teachers act as facilitators or monitors around games without detailed advice.

In terms of *project continuation (criteria 13)*, most were not. A few papers mentioned continued exploration, and some authors' websites showed evidence of continuing work. One theme that has continued in the literature is that of research on supplemental material mediation around games.

In terms of *learning outcomes (criteria 14)*, many of the papers reported improvement in terms of vocabulary or speaking skills. A few reported improved reading and writing test scores. Only a few papers reported student improvement in terms of speech acts, discourse or transferred learning outside the classroom.

GBLT is vaporware

'Announcing 'GBLT!' ... again!'

> Vaporware: 'a product, typically computer hardware or software, that is announced to the general public but is never actually manufactured nor officially cancelled'. (Wikipedia n.d.)

Many GBLT (and GBLL) papers begin with statistics demonstrating the popularity of games, prior research and teaching interest in games (often in other subjects) and the lack of GBLT research. Each 'announces' (like a PR rep announcing a new game) the concept of GBLT, and excites researchers to notice or invest in the potential of the technology. The research literature (especially that on digital GBLT and GBLL) seems to ride the coat-tails of gaming technologies and gamer cultures. In GBLT literature, the 1980s shows a surge in computer game research; the 1990s and early 2000s focused on console games, then

MMOs. I found papers on trendy modern board games (York 2019) and VR and AR (Sykes 2018). A constant refrain in GBLT is the announcement of the potential of a new technology to afford different and better language teaching and learning.

> Hype cycle: 'There is a repetitive cycle of technology in education that goes through hype, investment, poor integration, and lack of educational outcomes. The cycle keeps spinning only because each new technology reinitiates the cycle.' (Toyama 2011)

GBLT follows the typical trend of a hype cycle. GBLT researcher-teachers seem to become interested in games, run one or two technology-focused projects and then stop. Then the field, through other GBLT researchers, moves on to another game and the cycle continues. We jump from game to game or platform to platform rather than prefacing work with discussions of pedagogy or practicality. Without focused research investigating how to concretely integrate games into the constraints of a typical classroom, the 'field' will continue to hype popular games, make hypothetical arguments about the potential of the media and run a few studies (most likely on short-term vocabulary improvement) before the field, through new blood, moves on to the next technology and similar announcements of potential. GBLT seems to continue its trend away from pedagogical investigations (Cornillie, Thorne and Desmet 2012) and seems grounded in behaviourist or cognitivist paradigms rather than progressive and transformative approaches (Filsecker and Bündgens-Kosten 2012; Thomas 2012).

'Will GBLT ever come out? ... it's been delayed? Again?'

GBLT 'products' connecting a theoretical backbone, detailed practical implementation and research results do not exist. GBLT is not currently 'on the market'. Conceptual models, hypothetical lesson plans, collections of games and controlled lab or classroom experiments do not deliver on the touted potential of games to transform or contribute to language education. There is too much theoretical and technological speculation and not enough evidence of how teachers connect games and pedagogy to learning outcomes. GBLT literature is an echo chamber of theory and speculation, smoke and mirrors rather than substance.

> Game design document: 'The purpose of a game design document is to unambiguously describe the game's selling points, target audience, gameplay, art, level design, story, characters, UI, assets, etc.' (Wikipedia n.d.)

Theory crafting and pedagogical think pieces inspire, and experiments create knowledge, but without classroom implementation, these papers resemble 'design documents' rather than finished products. We need pedagogically oriented work that demonstrates that what brilliant thinkers have speculated about can be done. Ideas must be playtested in classrooms.

> Playtest: 'The process by which a game designer tests a new game for bugs and design flaws before bringing it to market. Playtests … are very common with computer games [and] board games [and] have become an established part of the quality control process.' (Wikipedia n.d.)

GBLT has few solid playtests – reports of teachers in classrooms using games to foster learning outcomes. GBLT ideas abound; we need to playtest these ideas. Only continued, deliberate, practical projects (some may be in alpha or beta stages and must be supported) can see GBLT finally released.

> Praxis: 'an integrated approach to engaging theory with research and teaching practices … a dialogic back-and-forth between action and reflection grounded in reasoning and experience'. (Reinhardt 2018: 2)

GBLT reports do not demonstrate praxis; theory and research feature prominently and pedagogy is always an afterthought. GBLT seems caught in never-ending waves of hype cycles around technology, refusing to focus on the pedagogy that might rebalance the field. This cycle needs to be broken. Many papers begin by categorizing GBLT as in early stages. Are writers critiquing the field for its lack of development? Or are they justifying continued exploratory, experimental and descriptive studies? We need to go deeper to move the field to more productive stages of pedagogy and technology integration.

> Normalization: 'the state in which the technology is so embedded in our practice that it ceases to be regarded as either a miracle cure-all or something to be feared'. (Chambers and Bax 2006)

GBLT does not seem to be something in a teacher's 'toolbox' used consistently for a specific purpose. Peterson (2013: 56–8) illustrates papers' focus on game features, hypothesized benefits and theoretical justification. GBLT is not a body of empirical, practical tests of pedagogy. GBLT seems to be about 'potential' rather than practicality or pragmatism. GBLT papers do not seem to be for teachers, or teaching-focused researchers. The audience for most of the GBLT literature seems to be researchers or designers. Many papers cite and pay lip service to the problem that specific pedagogical guidance is not available and should be a focus of continuing research, but this does not happen. Many of the pedagogical suggestions in these papers are vague. Most papers discuss and conclude more in terms of continued game feature research and material mediation research than on teacher roles and different mediation in actual classroom contexts. Are language teachers right to mostly ignore games, and just continue to use them, from time to time, as time fillers or speaking practice? Without a normalized GBLT product 'on the market', why should teachers take GBLT seriously?

Can GBLT go gold?

To go gold: 'the game has been completed and is now in the final stage before release'. (JeebusJones 2015)

Can GBLT avoid staying vaporware? Can it go gold? Will GBLT become normalized in classrooms and in the literature, whether in single studies, or across the ever-growing field? Can games become a well-understood and practical and effective tool in the teacher's toolbox along with other relatively easily implementable tasks?

Crunch time: 'the point at which the team is thought to be failing to achieve milestones needed to launch a game on schedule'. (Wikipedia, n.d.)

For GBLT to go gold, we need to go into 'crunch time'. We can pressure ourselves with a 'release date' and development schedule for a GBLT product – a detailed example of effective pedagogy- and technology-integrated teaching and learning. Without exerting effort, technology hype and potential benefit vaporware will continue. Pressure would make us wrestle with deep questions: What roles do teachers play in learning? Does our research reform education or society? Why are we teaching language? What are our biases and blind spots? How do we grade gameplay? Pressure would make us deal with difficult pedagogical constraints instead of 'easier' motivational or technological affordances. Let's address teachers not knowing about games, the difficulty of L2 gameplay, the lack of pedagogical materials, the difficulty of managing large classes and games not matching curricular and student goals.

We need to research teacher mediation in classrooms. Miller and Hegelheimer (2006) and Ranalli (2008) conducted important studies that helped push the field away from 'games only' explorations and towards mediation with games – in their cases, supplemental worksheets and materials. But, too many technology-focused projects take the teacher 'out' and there is little to no mediation other than choosing games and creating worksheets. GBLT seems to reduce language to vocabulary and teaching to choosing games and distributing worksheets. These are important elements of GBLT, but without continued teacher mediation before, during and after gameplay, GBLT really does start to resemble a field searching for a magic bullet (since teachers don't seem important in affecting the learning). In order to normalize GBLT, it's time to put the teacher back 'in' and explore how instructors, students, games and materials interact. Let's stop looking for a magic bullet. Let's share more practices and materials. Let's roll up our sleeves and get involved in the learning process around games.

We need projects that are conceptualized, conducted and shared to focus on normalizing, integrating, using praxis and producing something other than vaporware. We need studies that are radical in terms of their pedagogical (not technological or theoretical) base.

> Iterative design: 'a design methodology based on a cyclic process of prototyping, testing, analyzing, and refining a product or process. Based on the results of testing the most recent iteration of a design, changes and refinements are made. This process is intended to ultimately improve the quality and functionality of a design.' (Wikipedia n.d.)

Let's iterate more. It's hard to deal with classroom constraints, unfamiliar teacher and student roles and the complex interactions between games and learning. Although supplemental material mediation is a continuing research topic in the literature, many great GBLT projects were not continued. Novelty effects may be a serious issue for our field to consider. It's hard to know if projects stopped because of lack of funding, ended partnerships or new research interests. Many authors cite the popularity and motivational elements of games. Why aren't more researchers motivated to continue researching games? Since researching teaching practices long term is so difficult, let's start small by putting just a few of our many teaching ideas into practice. Then, let's investigate what works well, cut the things that don't and *continue* to refine and share and scale projects until GBLT is normalized.

I'm committed to continuing to integrate games with pedagogy in my context. Are there other like-minded 'tinkerers?' If you are interested in GBLT, please get in touch with me. I'd love to learn more from other game-based language teachers, and doing hard work with other praxis-passionate teacher-researchers.

Going gold is hard (no one likes grinding)

I realize researching and teaching with games is difficult; I don't blame researchers for moving on to other topics, and I really do want to help teacher-researchers in the middle of planning or researching their teaching. I hope readers understand I am trying to push the field to focus on teaching, and that I struggle to improve my teaching and research. When I started, I hyped technological affordances (deHaan 2005a). I also observed gamers and didn't mediate (deHaan 2005b, 2013a). I conducted experimental studies without mediation (deHaan and Kono 2010; deHaan, Reed and Kuwada 2010). These are all GBLT vaporware. Thankfully, after meeting dedicated teachers and teacher-researchers, I am trying to practice pedagogy-first GBLT. I am using the Pedagogy of Multiliteracies (New London Group 1996) for its connection of the why, what and how of language and literacy teaching to games and my context (deHaan 2011, 2013b, 2019). I try to help my students develop personally, academically and socially, not just linguistically. My 'Game Terakoya' project is challenging to teach and report, but:

1. In my first playtest (deHaan 2019), one student played games, analysed online reviews, explored academic concepts and wrote and shared her own review on a fan site. I was able to mediate very closely because of the one-on-one extracurricular context.

2. In my classes, mediation is more difficult, of course. Students have played the wargame 'Diplomacy' and satirical board games about the environment, social structure and international relations. Students investigated the realities behind the games, the fans of the games, the language in the games, then remixed the games and shared their work (#gameterakoya on Twitter). I carefully mediate their work via worksheets and discussions.

These are not 'one-off' projects, but continued testing and tweaking of a pedagogy-first approach with games. I gladly share my resources and welcome critique: https://sites.google.com/site/gamelabshizuoka/home/gameterakoya_seminar_2019.

Looking for an indie-friendly publisher?

Journals that focus on the integration of language teaching and learning and downplayed technologies, especially games, are rare. It can be difficult to publish detailed descriptions of teaching practice, and praxis-oriented GBLT research will go unnoticed if it can't get published. The articles that I reviewed in this chapter might have wanted to include more details about teaching and mediation and materials if the authors had had more space or flexibility. To create a place for non-vaporware GBLT articles and teaching reports, James York and I recently started an open-access, open peer-reviewed journal named *Ludic Language Pedagogy* (LLP). Its home is: https://www.llpjournal.org/. We want to confront all of GBLT's troublesome topics, constraints, biases and critiques head on. We conceptualized the journal as a place for concentrated praxis – one place for the field to share ideas, research and practice. We will publish 'traditional' research articles on this subject. We especially want 'walk-throughs' of playtests of GBLT in classrooms. The online-only format allows us to publish longer articles that detail teaching practices. LLP will host a 'compendium' of materials that teachers and researchers can share. We want reports of ideas tried in classrooms. We want first-person narratives and descriptions of the successes and failures and lessons learned. Let's playtest and iterate together. We will encourage conversations between different perspectives and approaches. The journal is open peer-reviewed so that teachers and researchers can talk directly to each other. We will be recording regular podcasts with contributors to give listeners an additional look into the background and intentions of authors and the field. We will be active on social media about GBLT research and teaching. We are very happy to chat with anyone about a project they have run, are running or plan on running, to see if LLP might be a place to submit it. We are very open to suggestions that make LLP a great place to publish non-vaporware teaching and research projects.

Should we shut GBLT down?

> Postmortem documentation: 'a process, usually performed at the conclusion of
> a project, to determine and analyze elements of the project that were successful
> or unsuccessful'. (Wikipedia n.d.)

If other GBLT teacher-researchers are not committed to a shared vision, working together, addressing biases, tampering hype, pushing reforms and overcoming classroom constraints, then it is probably time for us to pull the plug on GBLT. If we can't rally together during crunch time, then it's time to shut down our studio(s). It might be time to write a post-mortem on our several-decades-long failed project. We can leave a collective reflective piece and then go our separate ways. We can collect the lessons we've learned, and the mistakes that we have made. We can be clear about why we have not and cannot work together on praxis-focused GBLT teaching research. We can put a pin in things, and perhaps leave it to other people to take up much later down the road. We can collect a (short) list of research-based best practices for using games, which, based on the literature reviewed in this paper, could start (and perhaps end) with:

1. Communication games in CLT classrooms let students practice communication skills.
2. Vocabulary games (played either in class or for homework) help students learn more vocabulary.
3. Worksheets+games is a more effective approach than games alone.
4. Games as 'time fillers' every once in a while make students feel good about learning language.

To be continued?

It's time for an inter-studio meeting. Who's bringing the croissants?

Acknowledgement

James York, Peter Hourdequin, Aaron Chia Yuan Hung and D. M. Jones were invaluable play testers on an early version of this paper.

References

Bregni, S. (2017), 'The Italian Digital Classroom: Italian Culture and Literature through Digital Tools and Social Media', *NEMLA Italian Studies XXXIX* Special Issue: 42–71.

Bryant, T. (2007), 'Games as an Ideal Learning Environment', *Transformations* 1 (2): 1–8.

Butler, Y. G. (2015), 'The Use of Computer Games as Foreign Language Learning Tasks for Digital Natives', *System* 54: 91–102.

Chambers, A., and S. Bax (2006), 'Making CALL Work: Towards Normalisation', *System* 34 (4): 465–79.

Chou, M. H. (2014), 'Assessing English Vocabulary and Enhancing Young English as a Foreign Language (EFL) Learners' Motivation through Games, Songs, and Stories', *Education 3–13* 42 (3): 284–97.

Coleman, D. W. (2002), 'On Foot in SIMCITY: Using SIMCOPTER as the Basis for an ESL Writing Assignment', *Simulation & Gaming* 33 (2): 217–30.

Cornillie, F., S. L. Thorne and P. Desmet (2012), 'Digital Games for Language Learning: From Hype to Insight?', *ReCALL* 24 (3): 243–56.

deHaan, J. (2005a), 'Language Learning through Video Games: A Theoretical Framework, an Analysis of Game Genres and Questions for Future Research', in S. Schaffer and M. Price (eds), *Interactive Convergence: Critical Issues in Multimedia*, vol. 10, 229–39, Oxford: Interdisciplinary Press.

deHaan, J. (2005b), 'Acquisition of Japanese as a Foreign Language through a Baseball Video Game', *Foreign Language Annals* 38 (2): 278–82.

deHaan, J. (2011), 'Teaching and Learning English through Digital Game Projects', *Digital Culture & Education* 3 (1): 46–55.

deHaan, J., ed. (2013a), *Video Games and Second Language Acquisition: 6 Case Studies*, Chicago: Common Ground Press.

deHaan, J., ed. (2013b), *Game Camp: Out-of-School Language and Literacy Development*, Chicago: Common Ground Press.

deHaan, J. (2019), 'Teaching Language and Literacy with Games: What? How? Why?', *Ludic Language Pedagogy* 1: 1–57.

deHaan, J., and F. Kono (2010), 'The Effect of Interactivity with Warioware Minigames on Second Language Vocabulary Learning', *Journal of Digital Games Research* 4 (2): 47–59.

deHaan, J., W. M. Reed and K. Kuwada (2010), 'The Effect of Interactivity with a Music Video Game on Second Language Vocabulary Recall', *Language Learning and Technology* 14 (2): 74–94.

Filsecker, M., and J. Bündgens-Kosten (2012), 'Behaviorism, Constructivism, and Communities of Practice: How Pedagogic Theories Help Us Understand Game-Based Language Learning', in H. Reinders (ed.), *Digital Games in Language Learning and Teaching*, 50–69, Cham: Palgrave Macmillan.

Franciosi, S. J. (2017), 'The Effect of Computer Game-Based Learning on FL Vocabulary Transferability', *Journal of Educational Technology & Society* 20 (1): 123–33.

Hitosugi, C. I., M. Schmidt and K. Hayashi (2014), 'Digital Game-Based Learning (DGBL) in the L2 Classroom: The Impact of the UN's Off-the-Shelf Videogame, Food Force, on Learner Affect and Vocabulary Retention', *CALICO Journal* 31 (1): 19–39.

Holden, C. L., and J. M. Sykes (2011), 'Leveraging Mobile Games for Place-Based Language Learning', *International Journal of Game-Based Learning (IJGBL)* 1 (2): 1–18.

Janebi Enayat, M., and M. Haghighatpasand (2019), 'Exploiting Adventure Video Games for Second Language Vocabulary Recall: A Mixed-Methods Study', *Innovation in Language Learning and Teaching* 13 (1): 61–75.

JeebusJones (2015, October 24), 'What Does It Mean When a Game "Goes Gold"? [Msg 1]', Message posted to https://www.reddit.com/r/OutOfTheLoop/comments/3py9fm/what_does_it_mean_when_a_game_goes_gold/ (accessed 22 March 2019).

Mark Rasmussen – MA TESOL: An Academic Profile and Informal Writings on Language, Culture and Teaching (2017, September 10), 'Making Functional

Grammar Explicit: Game Design-Enhanced TBLT Lesson Plans for "Firewatch" [Blog post]', Retrieved from https://markrass.wordpress.com/2017/09/10/making-functional-grammar-explicit-game-design-enhanced-tblt-lesson-plans-for-firewatch/ (accessed 13 April 2019).

Miller, M., and V. Hegelheimer (2006), 'The SIMs Meet ESL: Incorporating Authentic Computer Simulation Games into the Language Classroom', *Interactive Technology and Smart Education* 3 (4): 311–28.

Molin, G. (2017), 'The Role of the Teacher in Game-Based Learning: A Review and Outlook', in M. Ma and A. Oikonomou (eds), *Serious Games and Edutainment Applications: Volume II*, 649–74, Cham: Springer International.

Neville, D. O., B. E. Shelton and B. McInnis (2009), 'Cybertext Redux: Using Digital Game-Based Learning to Teach L2 Vocabulary, Reading, and Culture', *Computer Assisted Language Learning* 22 (5): 409–24.

New London Group (1996), 'A Pedagogy of Multiliteracies: Designing Social Futures', *Harvard Educational Review* 66: 60–93.

Nguyen Huyen, N. T. T., and K. T. T. Nga (2003), 'Learning Vocabulary through Games', *Asian EFL Journal* 5 (4): 90–105.

Peterson, M. (2013), *Computer Games and Language Learning*, New York: Palgrave Macmillan.

Rama, J., C. C. Ying, K. R. Lee and A. Y. L. Luei (2007), 'Using Games in English Language Learning', Retrieved 1 December 2011 from http://conference.nie.edu.sg/2007/paper/papers/STU543.pdf.

Ranalli, J. (2008), 'Learning English with the Sims: Exploiting Authentic Computer Simulation Games for L2 Learning', *Computer Assisted Language Learning* 21 (5): 441–55.

Reinders, H., and S. Wattana (2014), 'Can I Say Something? The Effects of Digital Game Play on Willingness to Communicate', *Language Learning & Technology* 18 (2): 101–23.

Reinhardt, J. (2018), *Gameful Second and Foreign Language Teaching and Learning: Theory, Research, and Practice*, Basingstoke: Palgrave Macmillan.

Reinhardt, J., C. Warner and K. Lange (2014), 'Digital Games as Practices and Texts: New Literacies and Genres in an L2 German Classroom', in J. P. Guikema and L. Williams (eds), *Digital Literacies in Foreign and Second Language Education*, 159–90, San Marcos, TX: CALICO Book Series.

Reinhardt, J., and V. Zander (2011), 'Social Networking in an Intensive English Program Classroom: A Language Socialization Perspective', *CALICO Journal* 28 (2): 326–44.

Shintaku, K. (2016), 'The Interplay of Game Design and Pedagogical Mediation in Game-Mediated Japanese Learning', *International Journal of Computer-Assisted Language Learning and Teaching (IJCALLT)* 6 (4): 36–55.

Shirazi, M., S. D. Ahmadi and A. G. Mehrdad (2016), 'The Effect of Using Video Games on EFL Learners' Acquisition of Speech Acts of Apology and Request', *Theory and Practice in Language Studies* 6 (5): 1019–26.

Squire, K. (2006), 'From Content to Context: Videogames as Designed Experience', *Educational Researcher* 35 (8): 19–29.

Suh, S., S. W. Kim and N. J. Kim (2010), 'Effectiveness of MMORPG-Based Instruction in Elementary English Education in Korea', *Journal of Computer Assisted Learning* 26 (5): 370–8.

Sykes, J. (2009), 'Learner Requests in Spanish: Examining the Potential of Multiuser Virtual Environments for L2 Pragmatic Acquisition', in L. Lomika and G. Lord (eds), *The Second Generation: Online Collaboration and Social Networking in CALL*, 199–234, San Marcos, TX: CALICO Monograph.

Sykes, J. E., J. Reinhardt, J. E. Liskin-Gasparro and M. Lacorte (2013), *Language at Play: Digital Games in Second and Foreign Language Teaching and Learning*, New York: Pearson.

Sykes, J. M. (2018), 'Digital Games and Language Teaching and Learning', *Foreign Language Annals* 51: 219–24.

Thanyawatpokin, B., and J. York (2021), 'Issues in the Current State of Teaching Languages with Games', in M. Peterson, M. Thomas and K. Yamazaki (eds), *Digital Games and Language Learning: Theory, Development and Implementation*, 239–56, Cham: Palgrave Macmillan.

Thomas, M. (2012), 'Contextualizing Digital Game-Based Language Learning: Transformational Paradigm Shift or Business as Usual?', in H. Reinders (ed.), *Digital Games in Language Learning and Teaching*, 11–31, Cham: Palgrave Macmillan.

Thorne, S. L., and J. Reinhardt (2008), 'Bridging Activities, New Media Literacies, and Advanced Foreign Language Proficiency', *Calico Journal* 25 (3): 558–72.

Toyama, K. (2011), 'There Are No Technology Shortcuts to Good Education', *Educational Technology Debate*, 8. Available online: http://edutechdebate.org/ict-in-schools/there-are-no-technology-shortcuts-to-good-education/ (accessed 24 March 2019).

Tuan, L. T. (2012), 'Vocabulary Recollection through Games', *Theory and Practice in Language Studies* 2 (2): 257–64.

Uberman, A. (1998), 'The Use of Games for Vocabulary Presentation and Revision', *English Teaching Forum* 36 (1): 20–7.

Vasileiadou, I., and Z. Makrina (2017), 'Using Online Computer Games in the ELT Classroom: A Case Study', *English Language Teaching* 10 (12): 134–50.

Warner, C., D. Richardson and K. Lange (2019), 'Realizing Multiple Literacies through Game-Enhanced Pedagogies: Designing Learning across Discourse Levels', *Journal of Gaming & Virtual Worlds* 11 (1): 9–28.

Wikipedia (n.d.), 'Crunch Time', retrieved 10 September 2019 from https://en.wikipedia.org/wiki/Video_game_developer#%22Crunch_time%22.

Wikipedia (n.d.), 'Game Design Document', retrieved 10 September 2019 from https://en.wikipedia.org/wiki/Game_design_document.

Wikipedia (n.d.), 'Iterative Design', retrieved 10 September 2019 from https://en.wikipedia.org/wiki/Iterative_design.

Wikipedia (n.d.), 'Playtest', retrieved 10 September 2019 from https://en.wikipedia.org/wiki/Playtest.

Wikipedia (n.d.), 'Postmortem Documentation', Retrieved 10 September 2019 from https://en.wikipedia.org/wiki/Postmortem_documentation.

Wikipedia (n.d.), 'Vaporware', retrieved 10 September 2019 from https://en.wikipedia.org/wiki/Vaporware.

Yip, F. W., and A. C. Kwan (2006), 'Online Vocabulary Games as a Tool for Teaching and Learning English Vocabulary', *Educational Media International* 43 (3): 233–49.

York, J. (2014), 'Minecraft and Language Learning', in C. Gallagher (ed.), *An Educator's Guide to Using Minecraft in the Classroom: Ideas, Inspiration, and Student Projects for Teachers*, 179–96, San Francisco, CA: Peachpit Press.

York, J. (2019), 'Promoting Spoken Interaction and Student Engagement with Board Games in a Language Teaching Context', in M. Farber (ed.), *Global Perspectives on Gameful and Playful Teaching and Learning*, 1–26, Hershey, PA: IGI Global.

Zhou, Y. (2016), 'Digital Vocabulary Competition as Motivator for Learning in CFL Classrooms', *Journal of Technology and Chinese Language Teaching* 7 (2): 1–22.

Index